] mps

How the Democrat Party is Using Hitler's Playbook to Make America Socialist.

By Dumitru Sandru
Artwork by Dumitru Sandru

Chivileri Publishing

ISBN: 978-1-942612-19-3
101421

I dedicate this book to the memory of a wise and great man, my good friend Wolfram Herbert Klawitter.

Table of Contents

THIS BOOK IS PROHIBITED FOR ADVERTISEMENT ON AMAZON

Introduction.

If we lose our freedom here, there is no place to escape to. This is the last stand on Earth.
Ronald Reagan

Communism-Socialism Credo:
If you're not with us, you are against us. Then you'll be reeducated or eliminated.

It was the second night of our attempt to cross the socialist border to freedom. My friend and I survived the previous evening, nearly being caught by a horse-mounted border patrol, followed by a thunderstorm in the wheat fields of the border area. After hiding all day in a bush, we approached the border cautiously in the evening, hunched down to minimize our silhouettes because even in the dark, the border patrol could detect us.

Tall watchtowers demarcated the border, which could be visible for miles during the day, or even early evening against the dusky skies. Those towers gave me the impression of being inside a NAZI concentration camp. We were not, only in a country resembling a concentration camp. We were attempting to escape from the Socialist Republic of Romania, the communist "heaven" of the proletariat. Life was "heaven" under Socialism. My friend and I were about to risk death to escape from Hell. The Socialist State did everything possible to keep its people inside, captives, and prevent us from leaving the country, just like slaves on a plantation.

The towers were unguarded at night, but armed border patrols guarded the grounds with dogs, ready to shoot anyone trying to escape. My friend and I were very cautious, listening for any unusual sounds, spying on any cigarette ambers from the patrols smoking. We walked slowly and carefully to avoid stepping on tripwires that would shoot up flares and expose us. I was tense and numb with fear, but there was no going back. We were about to cross our "Rubicon." I have rather died than keep living in a country that was the equivalent of a slave plantation, and I was one of the millions of socialist slaves.

The following is an excerpt from my book "Escape from Communism" describing what happened that evening:

Suddenly, on our left, a green flare popped up into the sky. It became as bright as daylight, and we could see our shadows and everything around us. We flattened to the ground and froze. The flare was close by, almost on top of us, it seemed. We did not dare move or breath, hoping that it was not intended for us and that we were not spotted.

We lay as flat as pancakes on our stomachs in a field with nowhere to hide. We were sitting ducks. Another green flare popped farther on our left. After the pop and while the flare was still illuminating the fields, we heard a lot of commotion from that side. People yelling, dogs barking, more people yelling and screaming. Something was happening not far from us.

And then the chilling ra-ta-ta-ta-ta burst of a Kalashnikov. Oh my God! The border patrols were shooting. Who were they shooting at? We heard more yelling, orders given, shouts and screams, dogs barking again. We heard one more single pop, maybe a flare; I couldn't say since I had my eyes closed. Then all was quiet.

After a while I saw a red flare erupt in the sky, watching it from the corner of my eye, my head buried under my arms. There was major trouble; we could hear shouts coming from farther away on our left side. We tried to lie as flat as we could. The commotion from the border patrols started again. They were no farther than two hundred yards from our location. In the open field, that distance felt like two hundred feet. I did not dare raise my head and glance in the direction of trouble, I just listened with my nose buried in the grass, arms around my head. We stayed put, praying that we would not be spotted or sniffed out by the dogs. And the gunshots - what happened? Did they shoot someone? I was beginning to feel nauseated.

I, at least, was scared shitless. Were we going to be discovered next? Should we run to get away from this hot spot? Even if I could have tried to run, my legs were so weak and trembling that I couldn't even get up. Fear kept us paralyzed. It took a while but the commotion died down. From time to time we could hear voices, laughter, and shouts. Dogs were barking again, but this time it seemed that the patrols were playing with their dogs. We hoped that they would not come our way.

We stayed there for perhaps another hour, until everything was completely quiet.

I was born and educated under Socialism for the first 18 years of my life, and my existence would have been that of a State slave. I had to be obedient to the Socialist State and the Communist Party controlling the country. The Socialist State would determine my life, not my parents or me. They managed where I would be educated, how much education I would receive, where I would work and live, and even where I could travel. The State was in control of the Radio, Media, Cinema, and TV, broadcasting only "wholesome socialist" information. Listening to foreign, free, radio stations was punishable by imprisonment. The State's Secret Police strictly enforced the political oppression against freedom using fear, intimidation, arrests, beatings, and incarcerations. The State police, Securitate, could eavesdrop on any telephone conversation, as all phone lines were opened to them. Not only when the phone was in use but at all times, as the receiver was an open microphone to listen what people talked in their home. They expected everyone to spy and report on everyone else.

If your lips spell treason,
You'll end up in prison.

Romania was a prosperous country once, but Communism-Socialism reduced it to a Third World country as it does with any country it controls. Under the Socialist State, the State employed us; we shopped for food and all other necessities at the State shops, with prices determined by the State, not competition. We got medical treatment from State hospitals and ride on State provided transportation. Everything was in short supply, including toilet paper, and long lines around the block were the norm everywhere. Five abreast, the people waited patiently for hours to buy any goods when they were available, in cold, or hot weather, rain or shine or snow. A grim, oppressed life shortened the life expectancy of the people, and most families had only one child. As a result, Romania's population stagnated.

So, who cares what happened in a distant land, a long time ago? Unfortunately, history repeats itself, and Socialism, or neo-Socialism, is about to become a reality in the United States of America. As someone who experienced the atrocities of Communism-Socialism, it is my responsibility to inform interested people what Hell is awaiting us. We must fight and stop Socialism if we love freedom and a happy life.

I arrived in the Land of the Free in the spring of 1972. What a difference between the time when freedom thrived in this land and today when the neo-Marxism-Socialism, Critical Theory, and Critical Race Theory strangles freedom. I am bewildered by what is happening, right in front of our very own eyes, and how we allow the anarchists and neo-socialists to take over our country and become Socialist under the pretense of Democracy.

We had shortages during the 2020 pandemic because of the Chinese Covid-19 virus, including toilet paper just the way it was under Socialism. The Marxist-Leftists, Universities, Hollywood, Mainstream Socialist Media, Digital Communist Platforms, even the Business Corporations, and Congress enforce political oppression against the American people and freedom of speech.

One striking similarity between Socialist Romania and today's America is the discrepancy between what we hear and see on the Mainstream Socialist Media and the reality in our lives. The Socialist propaganda back in Romania told us how good we had it, while the reality was abysmal misery. Today the Mainstream Socialist Media tells us how awful life is in America, about Systemic Racism, rampant poverty, injustice, and the need for "transformation." Is this your reality? Not my reality. I see a great country with possibilities available for all who want to get educated and work hard to prosper. In my daily life, at work, in society, I see no racism. But we're told about Systemic Racism. Equality is racist, and must be replaced by Equity, which is reversed discrimination. The White people are White Supremacists. I don't see any Nazi-like storm troopers harassing the population. Instead I see the mayhem and destruction caused by Black Lives Matter and Antifa, and threats that if we do not meet their demands, they'll burn down the country. Yes, our country is in chaos, but all for the wrong reasons.

Another similar aspect today to that of socialist life I experienced is the censorship and punishment of dissenters. Censorship caused by the Mainstream Socialist Media, MSM, and Digital Communist Platforms, DCP - Facebook, Twitter, and Amazon Advertising, etc., specifically, and the shaming and even firing of people who step out of line. After the Capitol Riot, the FBI can arrest anyone on suspicion of being a domestic terrorist. Political arrests in the United States? Yes, just as it was under Socialism.

The military and police protected the Socialist Governments against the people that they claimed to serve. All Socialists countries were police States. Our Democratic Government was "protected" by over 30,000 national guards, and a 10-foot fence with barbed wire enclosed the Capitol. We seem to be a dictatorship masquerading as democracy achieved through fraudulent elections.

Welcome to Socialism, folks! If the current situation continues, the worse is rapidly approaching.

I believe that Freedom Trumps Socialism, but in the meantime, as the momentum is with the Marxist-Leftists, we experience what Socialist-Communist Hell is all about. I hope this book will enlighten those who do not understand that the Marxist-Leninist ideology is the most monstrous political system devised by humanity. Marxism is the ideology of antagonism and hatred.

This book will address the crimes committed against freedom by the Marxist-Socialists in the past, the perils awaiting us, and how to fix them before it's too late. There are ways to overcome the Communist-Socialist enslavement and bring back freedom to our land. It's all up to us, not the deranged, fanatic neo-Marxists.

America, the Bastion of Liberty and Freedom, is about to be no more if the Democrat Socialist Party will prevail. The Marxist-Socialists do not believe in democracy and freedom. Only in total control of people's lives, the government, and the economy.

The following words available online, https://www.reformer.com/opinion/letters/letter-patience-and-tolerance-almost-gone/article_d31d9aa9-fbc8-5779-a1e8-f4a92345d5c9.html says it all. I'm surprised that the Digital Communist Platforms (Google. Twitter, Facebook, etc.) did not erase it. I present it here along with my thoughts contained between brackets [---]

I was never an evil monster until you decided I was

I never cared if you were "gay" [LGBTQ] until you started shoving it in my face, and the faces of my children [or started teaching my children about such things, or populate all entertainment with them]

I never cared what color you were until you started blaming my race for your problems

I never cared about your political affiliation until you condemned me for mine

I never cared where you were born until you wanted to erase my history and blame my ancestors for your current problems

I never cared if you were well off or poor, until you said they discriminated against you, when I was promoted because I worked harder [get educated and continued to improve]

I never cared if your beliefs differed from mine until you said my beliefs were wrong

[I was not a racist until you told me I was]

[I was not a misogynist until you told me I was]

[I never care what you said until you stop me from saying what I want]

[I never cared what you think about guns until you try to take my guns]

[I never cared what you know about history until you try to change the history of my country]

NOW I CARE! [Because I'm Mad as Hell and Can't Take it Anymore]

My patience and tolerance are gone.

I'm not alone in feeling this way, there are millions of us who do......and we have had enough!

[It's time to fight like hell against the Socialism evil.]

Does the above resonate with you? If it does, and it should, that's why we have problems in our country. Even the Woke Zombies would agree with these statements if they could listen and reason again. But, if we believe in freedom, how could the deteriorations in our liberties we see today happened? That's the subject of this book.

It used to be: Live and Let Live

And as a Conservative-Libertarian, I'm all for it. Everyone should live the life they want without discriminating against and without being forced to believe in others' reality, except what's legal and moral.

But now it is: *Live the Way We Tell You*
I left a country that stood for:
The Government Rules
The Government gives people their rights
God does not exist.

I arrived in free America that stood for:
In God we trust
God created the people with certain unalienable rights
The Government serves the people.

Today America stands for:
The Government provides
We serve the Government
God is irrelevant.

The speed and completeness of the Neo Marxism-Socialism and Critical Race Theory, CRT, ideologies conquest of the United States of America happened only twice in our recent history, during the Italian Fascist take over the government in Italy in 1922, and the National-Socialist election in Germany in the 1933. Fascism and National-Socialism are Socialist ideologies based on Marxism.

What is more incredible is that the American Democrat Party, infiltrated by the neo-Marxism and Critical Race Theory, CRT, uses Hitler's playbook for the political takeover of our democratic country.

I'm observing in horror as the United States of America becomes a country just as described in "Atlas Shrugged" by Ayn Rand and "1984" by George Orwell.

Only two types of countries become Socialist: The poor and ignorant or the prosperous and oblivious.

Folks we are in a war between the Good, Freedom, patriotism, life, liberty and the pursuit of happiness versus Evil, Marxism-Socialism, antagonism, hatred, misery and poverty. We are at the eleventh o'clock hour. What will our fate be?

One thing I cannot help you with, and this is no joke, folks, is how to manage the FEAR that Socialism will put in your soul. Fear that you never experienced before. Worse than what you think the NAZI did.

Book 1. Ideologies, Politics, and Wealth

Ideologies are a set of beliefs by which an individual or group or society guides itself. Ideology would be just philosophy if we ignore politics and economics. Politics is the organization and management of societies to reconcile the ideologies and economics in our lives.

Chapter 1. Political Ideologies

This is a political book, and it is as controversial as discussing religion. But with religion, there is one consensus among all different beliefs; they all agree in Heaven and Hell, after we die, of course. With politics, Heaven and Hell are here and now, and Hell is any totalitarian ideology. I lived under both political systems, Socialism and Free Market Democracy. In my experience, Hell is Socialism. Heaven on Earth does not exist, regardless of ideologies or political systems. Still, heaven gets as close as possible when we live in Freedom, Democracy and Capitalism.

The following diagram depicts of the political ideologies:

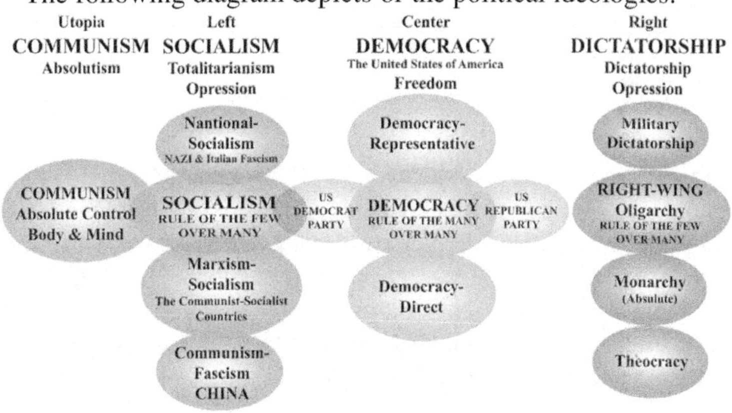

Except for Ancient Greece, early Roman democracy and a few other civilizations, the world always lived under dictatorship. We established democracy in America in 1776. In 1789 democracy was attempted in France through revolution and bloodshed, but eventually, it failed a few years later, and since then, France had five republics. In the 19th century, new ideologies emerged. In the 20th century, they put those ideologies into practice as Marxism-

Socialism and Fascism/National-Socialism. The Socialist political ideologies caused 200 million deaths and great poverty in the world. The ultimate goal of Marxism-Leninism is Communism, explained later. In that political system, if it ever succeeds, absolutism will reign. The State will have complete control over your Body and Mind, as in the book "1984" by George Orwell. Big Brother will watch us 24/7.

We divide the political spectrum as the Left, Center, and the Right. The political systems of the Left and the Right represent the Rule-of-Few-Over-Many. How could the Left and the Right be similar? Both the Right and the Left rule as Totalitarianism or Dictatorship, but not the same culprits are in charge. In the case of Socialism, the elite of the Communist Party rules autocratically without being elected or responsible to the people. In the words of Lenin or Trotsky, this rule is the dictatorship of the proletariat. On the Right, the Oligarchy rules autocratically without being elected by the people. The Oligarchy is the establishment, monarchy, imperialists, military, or religious clergy. Two similar systems of oppression and exploitation, operated by two dissimilar actors. The Left declares they rule for the benefit and in the name of the working people. The Right says they rule in the name of God, monarchy, and nation. In the case of military dictatorships, they govern in the name of God and the preservation of the country.

Only the Center represents the Rule-of-Many-Over-Many, and that is Democracy. The people decide who should rule over them for a limited period. The elected rulers are from the people at large, as members of the parties of different political ideologies from the Left to the Right. Only in Democracy you have Freedom, because Democracy cannot exist without Freedom. Only in Democracy you have a Free-Market Capitalist economy open to all people to prosper.

Who designated the notion of Left and Right? Aside from the fact that the Democrats sit on the left in Congress, as you view the Speaker and the Republicans on the right, who made this arrangement? It dates back to France, in the 18th century, where the members in the National Assembly were divided by political allegiances. The supporters of the Ancien Régime, the old regime of

France, the monarchy, Church and Nobility, the Oligarchy, sat on the Right while the merchants and bourgeois representatives, on the Left. Therefore, the Liberals on the Left and Conservatives on the Right came into existence. Liberals pursued Liberty. The Conservatives wanted to maintain the status quo.

However, these terms are relative. When I lived in Communist-Socialist Romania, I was a Liberal because I was seeking freedom and abolishing the Communist Party Regime. The Communists were the Conservatives making sure that they stayed in power by any means necessary, including imprisoning and executions.

Marxism-Socialism, the Left, claims to be for all people to prosper equally, while holding back anyone from getting rich at the expense of the others. The Right, the Oligarchy, cares only about themselves and their caste. The Right has been the dominant political system from the time that people organized themselves into tribes. In due course, humanity has become enlightened and demanded equality. The problem ever since is what kind of equality and how to achieve it.

In the United States, we had a Leftish wing and a Rightish wing until a few decades ago. The members of both parties formed the Center with moderate political views. As a result, we never had extreme political ideologies in Congress. It doesn't mean that we didn't or don't have other radical parties. Still, they never impressed the American people and gain power. But today, we witness the extreme Left take over the Democrat Party, making it a de facto Democrat Socialist Party.

The Right, the Conservatives, the Republicans want to maintain the principles on which this country was founded: Freedom of speech and assembly, Political freedom, freedom of religion, free-market (no intervention by the government in the economy), the right to personal property and the sanctity of the family all based on the Constitution and God. Our Declaration of Independence captures the following principles:

> *We hold these truths to be self-evident, that all men are created equal, that they are endowed by their Creator with certain unalienable Rights, that among these are Life, Liberty and the pursuit of Happiness.*

(The word Property was included in the original Constitution, but it was removed from the final version.)

Equality for all, freedom to pursue one's ideals and happiness in life. It is up to each of us to fulfill those principles for our own benefit, and the State cannot dictate what we do and how we live our lives. The Republicans used to be the party of the industrialist and the rich, but no longer. This party has shifted to the Center, representing the working people of all races. In contrast, the Democrat Party has become the party of fringe minorities, illegal aliens, new digital-billionaires, Hollywood, Corporate Bureaucrats, and Intellectual Elites.

The Leftists, Liberals, or Progressives believe that the Constitution does not apply anymore in our modern life and want to change it according to the current political beliefs and fads. In other words, a "revisable Constitution." Under the "new Constitution," individual freedom is subject to society's rules. To enforce them, the State must be in charge. Thus, the Government becomes our master instead of the other way around.

We might consider the Bible too old, let's revise the Bible based on what we believe in today's morals. But basic human behavior has not changed since we became human.

> *The Conservatives believe in as little government as possible and individual freedom is supreme, while the Liberals believe that the big government is the solution and the individual should do as the State dictates.*

What remains of Marxism-Socialism are the countries of North Korea, Laos, Cuba, and Venezuela. The Cubans are fed up with socialism; the government issues coupons for food, gasoline, or medicine, which have finally taken a toll on the Cubans and they are revolting. The Socialists were almost finished when the Soviet Union collapsed and stopped supporting them, and now Venezuela, their new benefactor, is socialist and cannot support itself but support Cuba as well. Socialism always fails, but until then, the people live in Hell.

China is an exception; it used to be a Communist-Socialist country, but it evolved into a Communist-Fascist country. Vietnam seems to follow China's example.

What may strike you as absurd is that NAZI and Fascism are on the Left. NAZI, the National Socialist German Workers Party, was a Socialist ideology. If you cannot get your head wrapped around the fact that Hitler was a Socialist, here is his speech from 1927, at Clou restaurant center in Berlin, as noted in the book "Adolf Hitler" by John Toland:

> We are socialists, we are enemies of today's capitalistic economic system for the exploitation of the economically weak, with its unfair salaries, with its unseemly evaluation of a human being according to wealth and property instead of responsibility and performance, and we are determined to destroy this system under all conditions. [48: pg. 224-225]

How shocking! Does this sound like Nazism or Fascism to you? Or maybe something like socialist Bernie Sanders or Alexandria Ocasio Cortez would say? But Hitler said it. Hitler insisted that National-Socialism was the true Socialism, and the Marxists stole that name from them. In his own words, he considered himself a socialist and anti-capitalist, just like Marxism-Socialism advocates. Hitler and the NAZI-Socialists created a classless, egalitarian society and followed most Marxist rules, and therefore it belongs on the Left side of the political spectrum. What's even more surprising is that the Fascists and National-Socialist parties in those times were populist parties.

Then who told us that the Nazi-Socialism were Fascists? No other than Joseph Stalin, the mass murderer of the USSR. He decreed that any political ideology that does not follow the Marxism-Leninism ideology of Moscow, and be under the control of Moscow is Fascist and of the Right. From the Wikipedia:

> At its 6th Congress in July 1928, Stalin informed delegates that the main threat to socialism came not from the Right but from non-Marxist socialists and social democrats, whom he called "social fascists"; Stalin recognized that in many countries, the social democrats were the Marxist-Leninists' main rivals for working-class support.

The National-Socialism/Fascist parties were competition for the Bolsheviks. Benito Mussolini was a Marxist-Socialist before forming the Italian Fascist Party. Fascist derives from fascia, meaning unity—the united people working together under the leadership of the State for the betterment of all.

In 1922, Mussolini and his Italian Fascist Party started the March on Rome and took over the Italian government in a bloodless coup d'état. As a result, Italy became a Fascist state. That action was a problem for the Marxist-Leninists. Fascism was another Leftist ideology that could grab political power in a bloodless fashion, not as the Bolsheviks did, through revolution and bloodshed. That was not allowed, and Stalin ensured that Fascism (National-Socialism) was not a Leftist ideology but of the Right, and the Leftist media obeyed.

Fascism and National Socialism are Leftist ideologies, just like Marxism.

The Leftists go hysterical over the fact that Marxism-Socialism and National-Socialism are ideological brothers. Mussolini was a Marxist-Socialist before becoming a fascist. Hitler studied Marxism and applied it in the NAZI ideology, and said:

> I have learned a great deal from Marxism. I admit that without hesitation. ... I've learned from their methods. [15: p126]

To be sure, there are differences between Marxism-Socialism and National-Socialism. Those are:

- Marxism is Internationalism-Globalism. National-Socialism, as the name implies, is nationalistic. It benefits one country's people, not the entire world. They don't intend to solve the problems of the world.
- Marxism is the ideology of Personal-Wealth-Abolition. No individual can profit from another individual or keep the wealth. Therefore, everyone will be equal economically, equally poor, that is. The entire economy will become State-owned. Instead of the capitalists exploiting the working people, the government bureaucrats will do that. National-Socialism does not eliminate personal wealth and profit. The capitalists can own and profit from their wealth. But then, how would the less fortunate people prosper under National-Socialism if capitalism continues? The Fascists control the Capitalists, and they have to improve the people's standard of living. Similar to Crony-capitalism. In addition, where Marxism confiscates the wealth of the country's wealthy citizens, National-Socialism confiscates the wealth of

another nation for the benefit of its citizens. That's why Hitler invaded the Soviet Union. The USSR was Hitler's planned source of wealth. China derives its source of wealth from the United States of America, that's why is fascist.

One word you do not see in the above diagram is Nationalism. It has a bad connotation nowadays because of the NAZI, National-Socialism. When American patriots display the American flag, showing that they are nationalists, they are called fascists, meaning of the Right. However, the Communist-Socialist countries were ultranationalists as well, and they were not called fascist countries.

We associate Nationalism, mistakenly, with racism. That is false. I am a nationalist and a patriot, making me love my nation and country (Patria) regardless of the mixture of races in the United States of America. I am not an American white-nationalist. That would make me a racist. I am an American Nationalist, period.

Adolf Hitler and the NAZI-Socialist party were racist, without argument. But that doesn't mean Nationalism is racism. Benito Mussolini was a nationalist, but his fascist party was not racist. Many Jews were part of his Fascist party and government, and there was no retaliation against them. Only after Mussolini became dependent on Hitler for his political life, he capitulated and extradited the Italian Jews to the extermination camps. President Macron of France wants to distance himself from Nationalism and be called Patriotism on account of the NAZI-Socialism. In my opinion, he and others like him are full of *merde*. (Pardon my French)

Nationalism is not divided by the Right and the Left political allegiances, and it crosses all spectrum of political beliefs. Remember what happened after nine-eleven? Our Nationalism rose among all the political views in America.

However, to institute Globalism –Internationalism– by the Leftists, Nationalism as a word and belief must be eliminated. Nations just like individuals do not count under the Global Socialism.

But how about Spain, under Franc Franco, weren't they fascists? No, they were Falangists, a Right-wing ideology representing the oligarchy, the controlling Families, the Military, and the Religious establishment. Do we have such classes of people in America? I don't think we have oligarchies, military dictatorship, or Religious establishments. We have controlling Families, or better said, we had them, but these families have grown and are of different ideologies. Some of the old Families are on the Left as much as they are on the Right. And the digital billionaires are all on the Left, not surprisingly.

Then who are the Fascists the Left so often accuses? If you are *white, heterosexual, Christian, middle-Class and a patriot* like me: You and I are called *Fascists*.

Do you feel you are a fascist? Do you think you are a Leftist? If not, whoever tries to insult you with the name fascist, remind them you are not a Leftist/Socialist.

You and I, the patriots, are the problem for the Left. We prevent them from changing our country from a Democracy to a Totalitarian-Socialists tyranny. Today the Left views the white men like the Jews of Nazi-Germany.

And then there are the Proud Boys. Their motto is "I'm a proud Western chauvinist, I refuse to apologize for creating the modern world." According to Wikipedia:

> The Proud Boys is a far-right, neo-fascist, and male-only white nationalist political organization that promotes and engages in political violence in the United States and Canada.

Being a white supremacist or racist does not automatically designate belonging to the Right. Just by calling a white person a racist, and there is plenty of black racism against the whites among the Socialists.

The Proud Boys *seem* to be a Right-wing organization. Still, if they truly believe and follow the National-Socialist agenda, they belong to the Left ideology, just like Hitler. Of course, the Proud Boys might protest loudly being called Leftists. But, here is the litmus test. Are the Proud Boys rich kids fighting to maintain their wealth, class, prestige, and privileges? Of course, not, and what they want is socialism for the white people, like themselves. So, they are Leftists.

And as far as Proud Boys being white-supremacists, their chairman is Henry "Enrique" Tarrio, a Black man. He took part in the "Unite the Right" rally in 2017 in Charlottesville, protesting the removal of Confederate statues.

So much for White-Supremacy.

Chapter 2. Liberty, Equality, Equity, Systemic Racism

Allegedly, Lenin said:

> It is true that liberty is precious; so precious that it must be carefully rationed.
>
> No amount of political freedom will satisfy the hungry masses.

Liberty and freedom can lead people astray. Look what happened to us. Marxism-Socialism is free to destroy our liberty.

The people must be protected and nourished on the "wholesome" diet of Socialist slavery, and everyone will have to do as dictated. If you don't comply, the punishment is severe.

Luckily Lenin is not in charge, and we still have Liberty and Freedom. At least for the moment.

Liberty came as a demand of the French Revolution of 1789 and their motto was:

> *Liberté, égalité, fraternité*
>
> or
>
> Liberty, Brotherhood, Equality

Back then, the people wanted Social Equality, which they hoped would become economic equality. The nobility and clergy were the top class, and if one did not belong to it, they excluded one from certain positions and privileges. For example, one could not become an officer in the military unless he was of noble descent.

Our Constitution states that we are all equal under the law regardless of sex or race or religious orientation or political affiliations, country of origin, or social class. And that's why America prospered. Anyone can advance in life based on one's abilities. However, for many centuries the black race was enslaved and excluded from equality under the law, but the Civil Rights Act of 1964 and Voting Rights Act of 1965 corrected that wrong.

Although we recognize equality under the law among ourselves, many factors make us unequal. Nature and Nurture determine who we are, and consequently, it differentiates how successful we are or not in our lives.

Nature gives us our sexual differences, mental and physical capabilities. Some of us are born intelligent, others not so much. Some are born good-looking, others are average, some are tall and slim, others are stocky and fat, and so on. Let's not forget ability in sciences, literature, sports, acting, dance, and other creative capabilities. Nature is the way we're born, and very little can be done to change that fact.

Nurture is our upbringing. Family and immediate people around us and country/culture have an immense impact on each one of us. Nature takes us so far, but nurture can break most barriers. For example, suppose you're born as a white person in the Western World from an educated and wealthy family. In that case, you'll have an enormous advantage over a kid in Somalia, herding goats. Not because the kid is black, but Somalia is a politically dysfunctional country, and poverty is the reality of life. His nurturing would not differ from that of a kid 10,000 years ago. However, the same kid raised in a family of doctors in the USA would have a completely different life, including becoming a doctor.

Thomas Sowell in his book "Discrimination and Disparities" mentions about what difference it makes in what family you are born:

> Children of parents with professional occupations have been found to hear an average 2,100 words per hour, while children from working-class families hear 1,200 words per hour, and children from families on welfare hear 600 words per hour. [32: Pg9]

Are the educated more talkative? No, the more you know, the more you understand, and the more you can express verbally what you see or hear, and your child benefits. And that is not the only benefit of a child's upbringing. Thomas Sowell says:

> Of the 29 original astronauts in the Apollo program... 22 were the first born or an only child. [32: Pg8]

The order of one's birth in a family affects nurturing as well. Firstborns have more chances of success. So, as there are so many variables that can make a person more successful than others that equality is hard-pressed to keep everyone equal. Even with Natural abilities, there is no guarantee for success if that child was not taught to be industrious, disciplined, take the initiative, and reasonable risks in life. This is the reason not all of us are Nobel Laureates, doctors, or Olympians, even if we were the firstborn.

Equality is not limited to classes but to race and nationality. In my home town, Timisoara, besides Romanians there were Hungarians, Germans, Serbs, Jews, Gypsies, and even a sprinkling of Turks – from the time my town was a fortress occupied by the Turks. Was there animosity among the different ethnic groups? Of course, there was, but at the ground level, where people knew each other, the feeling of hatred disappeared, especially when you are neighbors, co-workers, or classmates.

Equality among races is a demand more predominant in a country like the USA, which has all the world's races. Yes, white people discriminated against all other races in the past. Western technology gave the West Europeans the means by which they could colonize other territories populated by non-white races. By being slaves and considered property, the Blacks were not viewed as humans, and slavery would not have happened if the blacks were considered otherwise. Those were the beliefs during those times. We all come from a common ancestor in Africa. Originally there was an "Eve" who gave birth to our modern genus of Homo. In our modern society, race inequality cannot exist. I'll expand on this subject in the chapter "The Black Plight."

Based on our nurture —not nature— inequality is the natural order of things. The most significant inequality of all is wealth. I'm not disputing that we cannot improve the situation by helping the less nurtured to succeed by teaching them how to work, but not by feeding them. The Marxists want to reallocate wealth from the haves to the have-nots. You either have the freedom to acquire wealth, keep it, or be taken away from you and given to the "less fortunate." However, when part of your work is taken and given to someone else, that is slavery. What is even worse is the neo-Marxists theory of economic equality is weaponized now by *Equity*.

Equity, so much talked about by the Leftists; what is it? Unlike equality, where you are free to do the best depending on your abilities, equity promotes the least endowed at the expense of the God gifted and well nurtured. Imagine several athletes on a track running the 100-meter dash. Physical ability varies among them based on their nature. Nurture influences each based on how much each one trains. But each one's capabilities are known, and the best will always win. That's equality, each can compete, but the outcome will be unequal.

But that's not fair, say the equity advocates. To even things out, we must give the less capable an advantage, such as starting from a different position in a track race. The most talented lineup at the starting line and the least talented start closer to the finish line. Is this fair? This is taking the freedom of all athletes to compete equally and giving an advantage to the less able to make it equitable. It would mean in a hundred-meter race, the black athletes will start at the starting line, and the whites would start down the track closer to the finish line. Equity would not be fair to black athletes.

If you don't see a problem with that philosophy, imagine that we do piecemeal work, get paid based on each's productivity. You are a good producer and get paid well. I work by your side, and produce less. I get paid less as well. Equity entitles me to be paid more for each unit I produce such that I get paid the same as you. Equity came from the Critical Race Theory, which champions equity as a solution to discrimination, while equality is discriminating. And if we apply equity to even things out because you are white and I am another race, let's say, what will you think? Is it fair to you?

I read an article where a Cuban restaurant was located in a city that had 20% of its population black. The Black Lives Matter spoke loudly against this restaurant because the restaurant did not employ any blacks, and demanded that 20% of the restaurant employees must be black. That's a simple request, right? Unless you're the owner, trying to make ends meet. You need hard working employees, regardless of race. If he can hire black employees and everything works out, good for everyone. But what if the black workers don't work as hard as the others? Fire them, and risk law suits? Or keep them, and hire additional employees to fill in for the less performers? The restaurant's bottom line will be affected and he may not be able to compete and go out of business. Equity destroys entrepreneurship.

The hiring of black people is a big dilemma for small businesses. If black employees don't perform, and they're fired, the employers may get sued for discrimination. Even competent black employees are the last in line to be hired because of this threat.

Equity is nothing else but naked Communism based on Karl Marx's "*From each according to his abilities, to each according to his needs*." Thus, if you are unable or unwilling to produce, your needs will be satisfied at the expense of other hard-working folks.

Equity addresses one's needs, not one's production based on hard work, skills, and/or education. Is that fair? Is that liberty, freedom?

Equity and Freedom are incompatible.

Marxism is an ideology of class struggle, a philosophy of antagonism and hatred. It does not intend to raise everyone's standard of living but take from those who can produce more and give it to the ones that lags. In essence lower the standard of living for everyone to the lowest denominator. The world today differs from how it was in the 19th century. The proletariat had always aspired to become the bourgeois. Not all the proletariat had become bourgeois, but many have become middle class, living comfortable lives. The middle class benefited and benefits from capitalism, as long as politicians don't get involved. Because of competition, the capitalists had to develop better technologies, which improved productivity and the compensation for the proletariat. Marxism theory has proven disastrous when applied in practice, destroying and rendering destitute entire cultures and hundreds of millions of people.

Marxism is an ideological cancer.

Unfortunately, the ideologues, the people with learned theoretical knowledge and zero practical experience, don't get it, continuing to push for utopia and humanity's ruin. The Marxists cannot sell their old ideology and evolved into neo-Marxism using the Critical Race Theory as an amendment to Marxism. Today the racial struggle replaced the class struggle. Never mind that the racial situation has improved since the mid-twentieth century, just like class struggle improved since the 19th century. If you tell a big lie loud and often, the people without actual life experience will believe the lies. Propaganda and reality in most people's life are not in synch, but they give credence to the propaganda, if it is more frequently and louder shouted at us. People like my daughter, college-educated, not working around black people or interfacing with black people, believe the indoctrination she received in college about Systemic Racism. They used guilt for what happened in the past to the black people.

Equity, and Systemic Racism, makes Marxism marketable again. In the United States, we are one nation made of distinct races, and one race, the black race, lags all the others. The Government passed the Civil Rights Act and the War on Poverty laws to eliminate the discrimination against blacks and bring prosperity upon them. One thing is to pass anti-discrimination laws to eliminate racism and ensure Equality for all, and another is to pass Welfare programs to establish equity and expect improvement in the black society's life. However, as sure as the sun rises in the East, the Welfare program did not bring economic prosperity, but has exasperated the economic inequality.

In our modern times, I thought that we have "diversity and inclusion," but not according to the neo-Marxists. According to them, if the population is half female and half male, all the professional positions should be half in half, regardless of each sex's professional preferences. The same should apply to races. If that's true, then the NFL and NBA should have 60% white players and 13% black players, not 90% black players. We want to watch the best for our entertainment, but for our military that defends our freedom, we want equity. Imagine what our enemies will do to our equitable troops. The strong will kill the weak.

To achieve "equity," "social justice," and "diversity and inclusion," Obama ordered FAA to hire non-white Air Traffic Controllers. So, they selected them on the color of their skin, not their skills, and put them through training to make them Air Traffic Controllers. Wonderful example! But wait. What happened to the other applicants of lighter skin color who had experience and knowledge of the aviation discipline and could learn a lot faster than those who didn't know that Air Traffic Controller jobs even existed? They did not hire the qualified. That is *discrimination.*

Obama did not stop at applying equity only to FAA, but many other departments in the government.

Joe Biden's administration is determined to abide by the Critical Race Theory. They awarded billions of dollars to small farmers to help them with the financial loss because of the pandemic. But this aid is only for small farmers of *color*. "Whites need not apply." How would you feel if you see "Blacks need not apply?" Racism? That's what the Biden Administration is all about.

If we insist on having freedom, we will have meritocracy and inequality, but that will be a better life for the majority.

If we insist on having "equity," "social justice," "diversity and inclusion," and "culturally responsive teaching," we will have mediocrity and poverty.

What do you think China is doing? Hint: The opposite of what we're doing.

Chapter 3. Socialism

> "*A government big enough to give you everything you want, is a government strong enough to take everything you have*." Thomas Jefferson

Thomas Jefferson was a genius and such a visionary. If a government can take care of you, it will have to be strong enough to take it from someone else, or even you, everything you have.

Socialism comes in many forms, such as Reactionary Socialism, Bourgeois Socialism, Democratic Socialism, National-Socialism, Fascism, or Marxism-Socialism, and they have one common cause:

> *Socialism tries to provide for the society through a unified dogma applicable to all citizens with no deviation, or reinterpretation, meaning that Socialism's*

rule is imposed on all individuals of that society without exception, for their supposed benefit.

At first glance, this seems to be wonderful; the entire population will benefit. What's not to like about Socialism? Nothing if you are destitute and have no desire to succeed in life, but if you have two pennies to your name or want to make more, you're not allowed to have any more money than the next guy. Marxism-Socialism can be achieved only by confiscating wealth from the rich to be redistributed to the poor. If you think that's right, you'll not cheer much after you read the chapter on the illusion of wealth.

- Marxism-Socialism is achieved only through the Government ownership of all the economy and land, and becoming the only employer.
- Marxism-Socialism is achieved through heavy taxation of the rich.
- Marxism-Socialism can be achieved only through one-party rule, either the Socialist or Communist Party.
- Marxism-Socialism must be followed with no deviation or reinterpretation. The State Secret Police will enforce strict compliance.

They invented political Correctness under Communism-Socialism.

Political Correctness is a tool of *Thought Control.*

Our entire language is re-engineered to control us. In the Real Estate sales terminology, the "master bedroom" is the "owner's suite" or "owner's bedroom." Master designates the man and must be discarded. Slaves had masters, and we don't want to insult anyone. I'm surprised that "owner" did not fall in disgrace; no one can own anything under Socialism. The "walk-in closet" is offensive to people in wheelchairs, and blind people cannot see "spectacular views," so let's not use those words. Overseer is unacceptable since we used it in slavery. Like Mark Twain's old books are removed from reading curriculum because it has the name "nigger" written in them. Most of the great writings are not taught anymore because White Men wrote them. Even Dr. Seuss's books are banned. In Congress, Nancy Pelosi wants to abolish the words father, mother, son, daughter, sister, brother because they show the sex of that person. They took the

LGBTQ bullshit lingo to new utopian highs. The examples have no end in stupidity and mob rule.

You can only express yourself by what is permissible, not to cause ambiguity and express clearly what the socialism dogma permits.

Under Socialism: *You Can Do Only What Is Permitted.*

If a particular action, thought, speech, writing or idea was not specifically codified as acceptable, most of the time by law, you better not do it if you value your little freedom. Individual freedom is subservient to the common cause of socialism or the collective. We experience this today. You're not allowed to say anything negative toward the Democrats, Socialism, Marxism, and all their minions. But it's OK to say anything negative toward the conservatives, white people, even threaten to kill white people.

Socialism and Freedom are Incompatible.
Personality is a Liability.

Therefore, freedom dies under socialism. You no longer can object; you must do as you're told. You will eat, drink, get clad, work, dwell, enjoy life as permitted, talk, read, watch only prescribed entertainments, write, be told how many kids to have, and even stay alive as prescribed by the socialized national health care system. No one can be better off than the next guy. You will be an ant or a bee in more ways than you can imagine.

You will not decide your life. A group of self-elected socialist elites will decide. They will live in splendor, not like the rest of the masses. As it happened during the pandemic, when everyone had to stay home, not be able to go to the gym, beauty parlor, or barbershop for a haircut, or dine out. But comrade Mayor de Blasio could go to the gym. But Nancy Pelosi and Chicago mayor Lori Lightfoot went to the hair salons. California Governor Gavin Newsom enjoyed fine dining with friends at the French Laundry restaurant, but not you at that restaurant or anywhere else. The elite will defund the police, but the powerful elites have special police detachments or personal bodyguards to protect them around the clock, with guns.

In the book "The Big Lie" by Dinesh D'Souza, he mentions a socialist that is persona non grata among the Marxists today. His name is Giovanni Gentile, an Italian Fascist–Socialist –from the beginning of the 20th century, and this is what Gentile professed:

> Society and the state – for Gentile, the two were one and the same. Gentile saw the centralized state as the necessary administrative arm of society. Moreover the state is, as it were, unaccountable to citizens. "The authority of the State is not subject to negotiation," he writes. It is entirely unconditioned. It could not depend on the people, in fact, the people depend on the State. Morality and religion…must be subordinated to the laws of the State." [20: pg53]

The State is the Master and Ruler. Under socialism fighting the City Hall is a crime. The question is, who is this State-god with unquestioned power over us? The Socialist Government, of course. And who are the members of this Socialist Government? Socialist elites govern over us without consequences for their actions. They know better what's good for us than we do. All Socialist States followed the same rules as Gentile expressed above, the Socialist Government is god.

My older daughter, a science teacher, who I love very much, succumbed to the Dark Force of Socialism after knowing full well what Communism-Socialism is all about and how I risked my life getting out of that horrific place. I raised my daughter to be a conservative until she went to college. And then later, she took her master's degree online. In one year, she became *Woke+*. I didn't know what that was until my daughter became a BLM fanatic. I mentioned to her that Black Lives Matter has nothing to do with black lives, it is a Marxist-Socialist organization. I even gave her to read the BLM demands, and she found nothing wrong with their demands. Those are socialist demands I mentioned. She replied, "What's wrong with socialism?" Considering that she knows I risked my life to escape from Communism-Socialism, that was surprising. The academia brainwashed her. I asked her if she read "Escape from Communism", my story about how I risked my life to get out of hell. She did not. My daughter doesn't hate me, and that's not the reason she didn't read "Escape from Communism." In her mind, it's forbidden to read anything that would be contradictory to what she "learned." My books "Escape from Communism," "Hitler was a Socialist," and "Freedom Trumps Socialism" would make her doubt Socialism, and doubt is not allowed.

This is what socialism does to one, it instills fear of learning anything that is contrary to Marxism. For them there is only one truth, Marxism. They believe fanatically in the Marxist ideology, a godless religion. So, I concluded I took for granted that people understood how horrible socialism is. I was mistaken.

But not only my daughter succumbed to the woke zombies, my dear sister, who I brought, along with my parents, to America and who lived for 15 years under Communism-Socialism, to have a better life has turned to the Dark Force of Socialism. She's graduated from UCLA, works in Hollywood, and the allure of socialism has made her forget how hard life used to be. Of course, she's watching programs like Daily Show with Jon Stewart or Real Time with Bill Maher, where republican-haters and socialist propaganda are administered in large doses that would alter anyone's mind. After repeatedly listening to the same lies, you believe them as truth. Or following the Bitchy Pundit spewing her poison and making my sister say that she hates capitalism. How quickly she forgot how awful it was under socialism and how comfortable her life is under capitalism. Fortunately, Romania is not a Communist-Socialist country anymore, and unfortunately, she cannot get a refresher course of the hell she left behind by visiting Romania.

Our schools tell the students that socialism is a better alternative to capitalism without any comparative facts. Since life is good under capitalism, it is easy to think and even believe that socialism will be even better.

Most people get their knowledge via media, TV, and movies. From the many films made, everyone knows how horrible the NAZI-Socialists were. But there are very few movies that depict the atrocities committed by Communism-Socialism. Some movies I would suggest seeing are: "Bitter Harvest" movie about the Ukraine famine caused by Stalin, "The Death of Stalin" a dark comedy about Stalin's death, and "Milada" the film about a woman who survived

NAZI prison, just to be hung by the communists in Czechoslovakia after the war.

What is so alluring about Marxism-Socialism? Socialism is based on taking from the haves and giving it to have nots and forbids the possibility that there will ever be haves. What's wrong with that? Let's remember the Ant and the Cricket story:

> The Ant works hard all summer to gather provisions for the winter. The Cricket plays all summer long and saves nothing for the winter. When winter comes, the Cricket cannot find any food to eat. So, he goes to the Ant and asks her for food. What should the Ant do? Feed the Cricket, or tell him to hit the road Cricket-Jack! In a Free-Market economy, everyone is responsible for themselves. Under socialism the haves, the Ant, is responsible for the have nots, the Cricket. Therefore, if socialism takes over, the state will confiscate all the Ant's provisions and distribute them to the needy Crickets. Dispirited, the Ant packs up and immigrates to America, hoping that she'll never see socialism again. What happens under socialism with no ants and a bunch of loafing crickets? Famine ensues.

That's why socialism brings poverty; it oppresses the hard-working and rewards the lazy.

Mediocracy reigns supreme under Socialism.

In the Simple English Wikipedia, they define socialism:

> Socialism is an economic and political system. It is an economic theory of social organization. It believes that the means of making, moving, and trading wealth should be owned or controlled by the workers. This means the money made belongs to the people who make the things, instead of a group of private owners.

Clarification: The "controlled by the workers" means controlled by the dictatorship of the proletariat government, which is *the dictatorship of the elites*.

It sounds wonderful. No more capitalists, no more exploiters, no more bosses. Not really, someone owns the economy, and the State will become the new exploiter. Under these conditions, who will ever start any business, considering all their hard work will be shared by people who enjoy the cricket's life? Under Socialism, everyone works and divides the gains equally. Sounds equitable and straightforward, but it is catastrophic for the economy and all of us in practice. Who is the worker when everyone is an owner, a boss? Do committees manage the businesses? And if the economy slows down, who would be laid off? If the business fails because of poor management by *committee*, who will be financially responsible? There is a vast difference between a worker and a business owner. The worker worries about the business 8/5, 8 hours five days a week. The businessman worries about the business 24/7.

The answer of who will start a new business is simple, the State. Is Russia an industrial powerhouse today? No. But the USSR was an industrialized country. Not really. World War II gave the USSR a tremendous boost by obtaining Western/American technology and German engineers and factories. They were the first in space because they put to good use their German rocket engineers, unlike the United States that "parked" von Braun in Texas. However, WW II technology became obsolete, and the USSR could not steal enough technology to keep up with the capitalist countries and it collapsed. The difference between Socialist economy and Free-Market Capitalism cannot be any more blatant than East and West Germany. Or the two Koreas, North Korea is dirt poor, while South Korea is prosperous.

Bernie Sanders, Alexandria Ocasio Cortez, AOC, and the Marxist professors never ran a business in their lives, but they advise other naïve-fools how to run our economy. "Socialism doesn't work because of poor management," which is the excuse always given. Or blame the United States for economic embargoes.

Socialism is anti-achievers. Mediocrity is rewarded.

Socialist systems can exist only as a Totalitarian form of government. Dissension is not permitted, and suppression of freedom is mandatory. Why? Because Socialism always fails, and in a democratic country, the people will vote them out of power. That means all the elites, promising the moon and the stars, will be voted out, but only after they destroy the economy. But getting kicked out of power is not an alternative for them. So, the only protection they have to stay in control is the Totalitarian Police State.

However, there is a difference between Marxism-Socialism and Nationalism-Socialism, which is why the Marxists deny the "socialist" name to the nationalists. And that reason is private property and profit/wealth. Nationalism-Socialism and Marxism-Socialism intend well at first—economic equality for all. But they go about it in two different ways:

The Marxism-Socialism's strategy for equalizing wealth is to take from the nation's wealthy and give to the nation's poor. Redistribution of wealth.

Under Marxism-Socialism: Wealth and Profit are Forbidden.

The National-Socialism's strategy for equalizing wealth is different. The following are a few points from the 25-point program of the National Socialist German Workers Party:

- We want land and territory (colonies) to feed our people and to settle our surplus population. [Imperialism]
- Every citizen has a job. We think that the government's first job is to make sure every citizen has a job and enough to eat. [Right to a job]
- All citizens shall have equal rights and duties. [Elimination of social classes]
- The abolition of incomes unearned by work. The breaking of the slavery of interest. [Anti Capitalism and Financiers]
- We want all very big corporations to be owned by the government. [Nationalization]
- Big industrial companies should share their profits with the workers. [Redistribution of wealth]
- We want a healthy middle class. [Improve the standard of living]
- We want to change the way land is owned. [The land belongs to the government for redistribution]
- We want to change the system of schools and education, so that every hard-working German can have the chance of higher education. [Elimination of social classes]

- If poor parents cannot afford to pay, the government should pay for education. [Free education]
- We want to get rid of the old army and replace it with a people's army that would look after the ordinary people, not just the rich officer class [Elimination of social classes]

I put an explanation in [_] for each point, which is as socialist as it can get.

Under National Socialism: Wealth and Profit are Allowed, but not at the detriment of the hard-working.

Right there, the Marxists will say, National-Socialists are not socialists because they allow wealth and profit. Case closed.

Not so fast. Impoverishing the rich will enrich no one.

I'm not saying that National-Socialism is identical to Marxism-Socialism. But both of the political ideologies are Socialist because their doctrines are similar.

And about the National-Socialists allowing private businesses, the National-Socialist State controls the economy completely. Experts manage the economy, giving them the profit incentive. But they'll have to share the profits. The National-Socialist State dictates what and when stuff is produced. The industrialists will also enforce the State's edicts.

In the book "Hitler" by Joachim Fest, he wrote about what Hitler said when asked about nationalizing the economy:

> "Do you think I [Hitler] am so mad as to destroy the economy? The State would intervene only if the employers were not acting in the interests of the nation."
> Should they fail to meet the demands set for them, "it is not Germany that would be ruined, but at most a few managers," Hitler has hinted that as early as the autumn of 1936 in a memorandum concerning his economic program. [15]

If the capitalists don't produce as told, the NAZI-Socialist Gestapo will arrest the owners and managers for painful experiences.

Some argue that they don't want Soviet-Style Socialism, but the Scandinavian socialism, like Norway, Sweden, and others from that part of the world. I have news for them, Norway, Sweden, and the others are not Socialist countries. They experimented with it just as UK did until Margaret Thatcher became the Prime Minister and reversed to a Free-Market economy and prospered since. The

Scandinavian countries reversed course a long time ago after seeing what socialism was doing to their economies. The confusion about being socialist comes from the fact that their social benefits take care of the population from the cradle to the grave, a universal medical system, and other social perks. That is not socialism, those are societal programs for which the society volunteered through free elections to pay enormous income taxes to pay for these programs. Even the lesser paid people pay the high taxes. Yet, the free-Market economy thrives, and Capitalism provides the prosperity to support such programs in those countries.

For the Scandinavian countries, the social programs work well because of their culture of honesty, hard work, discipline, and respect for each other and the laws of the society. Those societies have *high-trust* among their people that each will do their part. In his book "Wealth, Poverty and Politics" Thomas Sowell describes an experiment performed in Western Europe regarding cultures. They left ten wallets in the streets from Sweden to Spain. Nine wallets were returned to the police station in Sweden. They returned fewer and fewer wallets as they observed the experiment going south. In Portugal, only one wallet was returned to the police station. But a tourist from Denmark returned it. That experiment reflects the different cultures in few European countries, and their societies behave according to their cultures. What is the culture of the United States population? We are a combination of the cultures of the world. Some people are respectful and hardworking, and others live on Welfare without working. Would a National Health plan work efficiently or be abused by people not paying into it and others scamming it? All I can say is that I don't believe it will work as well as in Sweden or Denmark. Many people will pay into the system just to get the same help as those who don't pay a dime. But, that's *Equity*.

A common mantra runs along Marxism-Socialism and National-Socialism, and those are "the right" and "we demand." Expressed in socialist lingo, they are:

- You have the right to a job
- You have the right to living wages
- You have the right to paid time off

- You have the right to recreation
- You have the right to housing
- You have the right to food and clean water
- You have the right to medical services
- You have the right to education

They sound nice and compassionate. By another name the rights are entitlements. However, if you don't see anything wrong and absurd about those rights, let me offer another right:

- You have the right to One Million Dollars.

Any reasonable person would think twice about the million dollars "right." But there is no difference between the right to a million dollars and the above-listed rights. Who will give us the million dollars? Would the banks open their vaults and give us the money? Where would they get their money from? Money doesn't grow on trees.

Let's take the "right to a job and living wages." Who will give you that? All those rights are dependent on being made available by someone else. The employer will offer job opportunities if they need additional workers at competitive salaries. In other words, the market, demand, and supply of workers dictate the job openings and wages. If there is no demand, there are no jobs.

In a Socialist State, the government will provide jobs and wages since it owns all the economy, which they confiscated from the capitalists. The capitalists don't hire if they don't need the labor. The socialists will provide you a job because you are in their keep and got to eat. But the employment is not based on productive needs, and eventually, the entire economy collapses from too many employees, not to mention unproductive employees. Under socialism, there is no relationship between productivity, jobs, and wages in people's minds. The government provides. As a result, the so-called living wages decrease. But everyone is employed. Worst yet, the quantity and quality of the goods decrease as well.

But certain rights surely must be provided by the government, like education and medical services. Yes, but only if the economy is productive and prosperous to create a surplus, which is taxed and offered back to the population for the benefit of everyone. An educated and healthy population will be more productive and a better life for all.

The only *right you have* is what *you can do* by being born free. That's why:

- You are born with certain unalienable Rights: *Freedom*.

Individual freedom allows all the other entitlements to be made possible. Without freedom, poverty and misery will be the result. Freedom can only be taken from you, not given to you by someone else, like the government. And when you're free, you can pursue life and happiness, but it's all up to your efforts, not someone's else.

Bottom line, why should you care if our government is Democratic or Socialist, if the economic life, supposedly, for most people will be the same? Who cares about freedom and the ability to vote for the government representatives?

If the economy would be prosperous, Socialism would exist today and would flourish. But it failed miserably all over the world. The degrading economy will cause the population to ask, "why don't we have as much as we used to have under Free-Market-Capitalism?" But, anyone who asks such a question will question socialism itself, and that is forbidden. The Secret Police will come knocking. That's when the people will understand the value of Freedom, and what they lost. You are prohibited to question the miserable life under socialism. When you cannot do anything about it will make you unhappy, desperate, and rebellious. Socialism can beat us down into submission for only so long. Humans were born free, and socialism cannot destroy that fact.

Under socialism, over-employing and paying everyone "living" wages reduces productivity, and inevitably the socialist country collapses economically. Moreover, lack of incentive causes workers and managers to slow down and stop innovating and increase production. There is nothing for them to gain if they take risks as the entrepreneurs in Free-Market economies do.

But according to the socialists, the most significant reason Socialism fails is that Free-Market economy countries undermine the progress of the Socialist countries. That's why Marxism-Leninism-Communism must take over the entire world and eliminate the temptations caused by the Free-Market economies with their "unjust," better living.

Chapter 4. The Socialism's Atrocities

Marxism is the ideology of hatred.

The following is an extract of a complete chapter from my book "Hitler Was A Socialist", describing how socialism has killed millions of people throughout the world:

The atrocities committed by Hitler and his party *would never have been committed by good socialists*. Really? Like the *good socialists* of the rest of the world? Let's see what history tells us about the *Good Socialists*:

- The good Communist-Socialist Mao Tse-tung killed one hundred million—100,000,000—of his people.
- The good Communist-Socialist Joseph Stalin, and his predecessors Lenin and Trotsky, killed fifty million—50,000,000—of his people.
- The good Communist-Socialist Pol Pot, killed only two million—2,000,000—Cambodian people out of a population of eight million in just four years.
- The good Communist-Socialist comrades from the rest of the world like Ho Shi Minh (one million deaths) in Viet Nam, Fidel Castro (unknown deaths) in Cuba, Kim dictators (two million deaths and counting) in North Korea, Nicolae Ceausescu and his predecessor Gheorghe Gheorghiu Dej, (three hundred thousand deaths) in Romania, or all other *good* Communist-Socialists in East Germany, Poland, Czechoslovakia, Hungary, Albania, and Bulgaria who killed more millions of their citizens. Let's not forget the millions killed by the Marxist-Socialist governments or guerillas in

Africa and Latin America. Altogether, the above-mentioned socialist states and their revolutionary killings could amount to more than twenty million—20,000,000—deaths.

Like all the other socialists, Hitler killed eleven million—11,000,000—people, half of them Jews and the other half political prisoners, the infirm, the racially unfit, and other ethnic groups like the gypsies.

The above morbid numbers represent Socialism and its "greatest" leaders.

Wait! Those killings were committed by Communists! Well, Communism is Marxism-Leninism. The parties in charge were Communist, but the countries were Socialist implementing the 10 Rules of the Communist Manifesto.

War casualties are not included in the above deaths. The figures shown above are taken from a variety of sources, such as *The Black Book of Communism: Crimes, Terror and Repression*, or the topic of "Mass killings under communist regimes" in Wikipedia, and other old resources that have vanished from the Internet. Not surprisingly considering Google's leftist agenda. The figures vary widely as many of these killings were never properly recorded or the information was destroyed. Some critics, no doubt Marxists-Socialists, argue that famine should not be counted in the total number of killings. Regardless, if the governments used famine as a weapon, which they did, or the government policies caused the famines as in the USSR, China, and Africa, the deaths were caused by Socialism. The Marxist-Socialists and their adherents in the online media try to lower the death figures to minimize their atrocities, just like the white supremacists and the Muslims deny the Holocaust ever happened. Who knows? One day we might find mass graves in China and Siberia revealing mind-boggling atrocities committed by the Communist-Socialists.

Don't excuse socialism and blame only the individual leaders. Socialism and any totalitarian political system are the breeding grounds for such evil people, who surface and metastasize into monsters without exception. And mass killers like Hitler, Stalin, and Mao would not have committed their atrocities without help from the entire political system.

Yes, but did Hitler, Mao, or Stalin line up that many people against a wall and shoot them, or gas them? Many of them *were* executed by shooting. Stalin, while transporting the condemned for execution, used exhaust gas from trucks to kill them, just like Hitler.

In the words of *The Black Book of Communism*, people were killed in many ways:

> The pattern includes execution by various means, such as firing squads, hanging, drowning, battering, and in certain cases gassing, poisoning, or "Car accidents"; destruction of population by starvation, through man-made famine, the withholding of food or both; deportation, through which death can occur in transit (either through physical exhaustion, or through confinement in an enclosed space), at one's place of residence, or through forced labor (exhaustion, illness, hunger, cold). [12: pg 4]

And this unimaginable killing was done over a span of many years, even decades. Hitler was in charge for twelve years. Mao's terror reign was twenty-six years. And Lenin-Stalin's terror reign lasted thirty-six years.

Only Pol Pot, of the Khmer Rouge, is in a class by himself. He deliberately murdered the Cambodian population over a period of four years. After his thugs rounded up the suspects; took them to detention centers, which in many cases were high school buildings; tortured them to confess their crimes and divulge the names of other associates, they were condemned to immediate execution. Every night the condemned were taken by truckloads to the "killing fields" for execution and burial in mass graves. Most were killed by hitting them on the head with a stick that had a nail protruding from it, after which they were pushed into a previously dug mass grave and buried, even if many of them were not yet dead. Mothers with young children were killed as well, but only after their children were swung by the feet to crush their skulls against the trunks of trees nearby. Imagine the horror at these sites, as Khmer Rouge Socialist propaganda music played from loudspeakers to mask the screams of the victims.

Bulldozers filled the mass graves covering the convulsing bodies, after which they dug fresh mass graves for the next night's massacre. In the meantime, Pol Pot's soldiers rounded up new suspects, and the process repeated day and night. I gathered this information personally at one of the killing fields when I visited Cambodia.

But only Hitler specifically killed the Jews, 5,500,000 of them, because of their ethnicity and religion. We should not put him in the same socialist basket as the Marxist-Socialists. True and appalling about killing the Jews, especially after seeing the pictures of the concentration camps, the corpses, or visiting the NAZI-Socialism industrial extermination camps. Unfortunately, we don't have pictures to document exterminations at Soviet gulags or Chinese concentration camps. The Soviets and the Chinese were not defeated in war and caught bloody handed, exposing their extermination camps and the millions of corpses they disposed of. Soviet camps have long disappeared, while the Chinese camps are thriving as the Chinese Communist Party will never run out of enemies to kill, real or imaginary.

Stalin starved to death up to 11,000,000 Ukrainians because they opposed him and because they were Ukrainians. In the purges of 1936–38, he also killed untold numbers of Soviet-Polish citizens because they were Polish. Do you think the Jews in the Soviet Union were treated humanely? Only in the pro-socialist movies. Under Stalin they were tolerated as a necessary nuisance.

The following is an excerpt from an article "Vladimir Lenin Was Part Jewish, Say Declassified KGB Files" suggesting what was in store for the Jews under Stalin:

> This fascinating morsel of information, gleaned from declassified KGB files, is not a minor detail in a country where anti-Semitism was a recognized state doctrine for decades. Starting in the 1930s, the Soviet regime—spurred on by its leader Joseph Stalin—launched a violent discriminatory campaign against Jewish citizens.
>
> A few years later, Stalin began to purge Jews from among the leaders of the revolution. Prior to his death in 1953, furthermore, he was preparing to send the whole Jewish population living in the Soviet Union to concentration camps in Siberia. [5]

That was the thank-you Stalin gave to the Jews after they had spied for him and had given him the American nuclear-bomb secrets.

After invading Poland in 1939, Stalin had 22,000 Polish military officers, police officers, and intelligentsia shot in the Katyn Forest, just because they were Polish, not to mention the ethnic cleansing

Stalin imposed in the newly acquired territories of Moldova, Bessarabia, the Baltic States and many other such regions. Millions of ethnic Romanians were removed from their homes in Bessarabia and Moldova and relocated to Siberia, after which the Romanian homes were repopulated by Russians. The process was called *Russification*. The Romanians sent to Siberia were lucky if they survived and were able to tell their horrific stories decades later. The same thing happened in Ukraine. Why do you think that there are so many Russians living in East Ukraine and that this region wants to secede from Ukraine and join Russia? The list goes on to include millions of others, like Cossacks, Chechens, Russian-Germans, Tatars, and probably just about any ethnic group in the Soviet Union. How many died during relocation or were killed by famine and harsh weather in Siberia? We may never know.

Why did the Socialists killed so many people and how would that be possible?

From *How Socialist was National Socialism?*:

> Professor Stackelberg also makes it plain in his work that he considers the Left to be the "progressive" end, and although he accepts that at the extreme ends of the spectrum there will be "*movements who will go to any lengths to achieve their utopian ideal…* [18]

Yes, be that the Marxist-Socialists, National-Socialists, or the Fascist-Socialists they will go to any lengths, including murdering hundreds of millions of people to achieve their Socialist ideal. But aren't those Socialists human beings? Yes, they are human. Fanatics. Marxism-Leninism-Communism-Socialism is a godless religion and a political belief all in one. God is not allowed under Socialism, because God is competition for the people's hearts and minds. Do you think a God-fearing person would commit the atrocities listed above? Not likely.

From what I read about Stalin, every night he and Beria, Stalin's secret police chief, were going over lists of undesirables, or deplorables, selecting who will be executed the following day, after which Stalin went to sleep without remorse. Perhaps happy that he eliminated another round of imagined enemies.

Continuing the theme of genocide, must it refer to just a racial or ethnic group? How about an entire *social class* of people? The bourgeois, the rich? It didn't matter if you built your wealth with your own hands, sacrificed, and lived frugally, as it happened to my maternal family; all it took to be executed or sent to the gulag was the fact that you possessed wealth.

The following was the thought among Bolsheviks at the end of 1918, expressed by one of their political police officers, Latvian M. Latsis, a member of Cheka, the Soviet secret police:

> We don't make war against any people in particular. *We are exterminating the bourgeoisie as a class.* In your investigation don't look for documents and pieces of evidence about what the defendant has done, whether in deed or in speaking or acting against Soviet authority. The first question you should ask him is what class he comes from, what are his roots, his education, his training, and his occupation. [12: pg 8] (Emphasis added.)

The class a person belonged to, determined the fate of that individual. Indeed, this is what the Bolshevik Red Terror, when people were executed for who they were not for what they did, was all about. Just like the Jews in Germany. That's why the Communist-Socialists killed so many millions of people. Based on Marxist-Leninist principles, it was extermination of an entire class of people.

And to make sure that the killing went on unabated, consider the following from *The Black Book of Communism*:

> From the end of the 1920s, the State Political Directorate (GPU, the new name for Cheka) introduced a quota method – each region and district had to arrest, deport, or shoot a certain percentage of people who were members of several "enemy" social classes. [12: pg 15]

The only other time in history when an entire class of people was killed was during the French Revolution when aristocrats and clergy were sent to the guillotine.

The crime of *genocide* has been expanded as a crime against humanity to include, as the French Criminal code states:

> *The deed of executing a concerted effort* that strives to destroy totally or partially a national, ethnic, racial or religious group, or a group that has been determined on the basis of any other *arbitrary criterion*. [12: pg 8] Emphasis added.

But who cares if the Communist-Socialists killed the filthy rich, the exploiters and thieves of the upper classes? Aren't the Jews portrayed in the same way? It makes no difference why you exterminate a class or race or people. They are all people.

But not all people are counted the same, as we are told in literature and movies, and the NAZI-Socialists are villainized more than the Communist-Socialists, who killed more people by far. There seems to be only so much hatred that the people can accept from any of those killers.

The Black Book of Communism says:

> For Nazism's unique status as "absolute evil" is now so entrenched that any comparison with it easily appears suspect.
>
> Of the several reasons for this assessment of Nazism, the most obvious is that the Western Democracies fought the World War II in a kind of global "popular front" against "fascism."
>
> The ultimate distinguishing characteristic of Nazism, of course, is the Holocaust, considered as the historically unique crime of seeking the extermination of an entire people, crime for which the term "genocide" was coined. . .. And therewith the Jewish people acquired the solemn obligation to keep the memory of its martyrs alive in the conscience of the world. [12: pg xii]

The Jews have done an outstanding job at keeping the genocide alive in our minds, and should continue to do so. But Hollywood is predominantly Jewish and Leftist and has accomplished two goals with the anti-NAZI movies: They remind us about the Holocaust, which must be remembered, but also cause us to ignore the atrocities against humanity that the Communist-Socialists have committed—and that is inexcusable.

From *The Black Book of Communism*:

> Hitler and Nazism are now a constant presence in Western print and on Western television, whereas Stalin [or Mao] and Communism materialize only sporadically. The status of ex-Communist carries with it no stigma, even when unaccompanied by any expression of regret; past contact with Nazism, however, no matter how marginal or remote, confers an indelible stain. [12: pg xiii]

In this book you'll learn that the Devil is the same, and its name is Socialism. We must remember the hundreds of millions of other people killed by Communist-Socialists along with NAZI-Socialists. Killing is killing. For every one Jew killed by Hitler, thirty-five other people—Russians, Ukrainians, Poles, Germans, Romanians, Hungarians, Bulgarians, Chinese, Vietnamese, Cubans, Africans, Nicaraguans, and Venezuelans among many others—were killed by the Communism-Socialism, *a thirty-five to one ratio.*

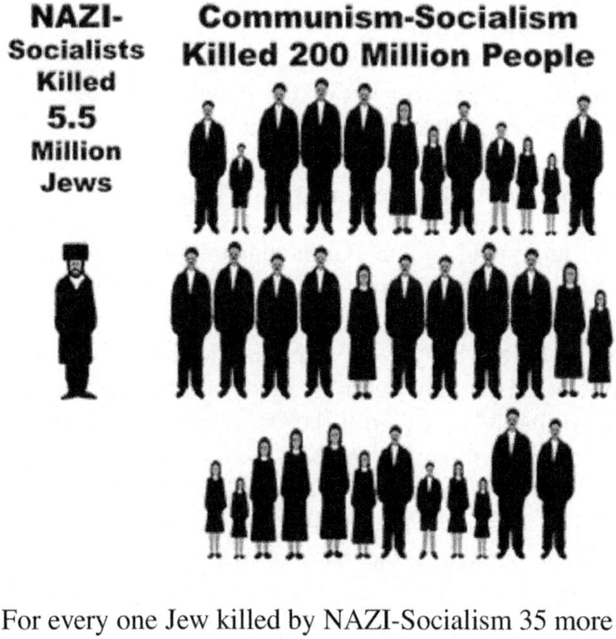

For every one Jew killed by NAZI-Socialism 35 more people of all ethnicities, ages, or sexes were killed by Communism-Socialism.

Who is mourning and remember these people? Where is the monument in their memory showing the atrocities committed by the Communism-Socialism? There is none.

You may wonder why I mentioned Africa as being included in the killings by Socialism.

This is what was said in *The Black Book of Communism*:

> One particular feature of Communist regimes—their systematic use of famine as a weapon.
>
> This policy was a recipe for creating famine on a massive scale. Remember in the period after 1918, only Communist countries experienced such famines, which led to the deaths of hundreds of thousands, and in some cases millions, of people. And again, in the 1980s, two African countries that claimed to be Marxist-Leninist, Ethiopia and Mozambique, were the only such countries to suffer these deadly famines. [12: pg 9]

Socialism in any form kills with impunity.

Chapter 5. Communism

> Communism is the doctrine of the condition of the liberation of the proletariat. Wikipedia.

Incredible! *Liberation* of the proletariat? How about enslavement? In this chapter you'll see what communism will do to all of us.

You'll hear and read about Communism or Socialism, or Communism-Socialism as I refer to it, and may wonder what is the difference between Socialism and Communism?

It all started in 1848 with "The Communist Manifesto," which is the "bible" for Socialism, although it's called "communist." Fredrich Engels explained that Marx called it the "Communist Manifesto" to distinguish it among all the other socialist fads at the time in the 19th century. In 1917, when the Russian revolution took place, Lenin applied socialism forming the USSR. The new ideology was Marxism-Leninism, which is the base of the Communist Parties throughout the world.

However, despite calling the former Communist countries "communist," only their parties were/are called communist. No country in the world had/has the name "Communist" in their country's name. Most of them call themselves "The Socialist Republic of..." "The Democratic Republic of...", "The People's Republic of...." and not to forget "The Union of Soviet Socialist Republics (USSR)." The granddaddy of all, the USSR, didn't contain the name communist in the country's name.

A brief explanation between the two ideologies is:

Marxism-Socialism: Everyone is kept economically equal by preventing anyone from owning any wealth that will create more wealth, or exploiting another human for profit. The ownership of the economy belongs to the State. The entire population will be employed and *paid salaries in the form of money*. Money exists under Socialism, and it is as important as under capitalism to obtain the necessities of life, even buy an apartment, house or car. Becoming richer than anyone else is not allowed, although some people earn more because of their skills and education and are better off. The State will grant the people all their rights to serve the State.

Communism: Marxism-Socialism is the mother of Communism. The Communism will be similar to Socialism, except there will be *No Money*.

The Rules for Communist Utopia are:

1. *Dissolution of all political parties. Communist ideology will rule. The State leaders will be selected from among the Elites.*
2. *Abolition of military. Peace keepers will enforce the people's behavior. (This will be a supper-police State.)*
3. *Everyone must contribute. (That means work.)*
4. *No ownership of anything. No possessions. No money. Each will be a custodian of stuff awarded to them by the State.*
5. *All children will be reared by the State in government institutions. They will be groomed based on their natural abilities to serve the society.*
6. *Elimination of all religions or any other beliefs.*
7. *Indoctrinate all people in new philosophies and moral standards as prescribed by the Communist philosophy.*
8. *Abolish the nuclear family. Abolish marriage.*
9. *Population control and Eugenics will create the new Global human.*
10. *The Communist State is the master and god.*

If some of the above points sound similar to the song "Imagine" by John Lennon, you're not wrong.

Under Communism you own nothing.

Communism is based on Karl Marx's pronouncement:
From each according to his abilities, to each according to his needs.

Because there is no private property, everyone will work diligently according to their ability. The people will get what they need from stores/distribution centers for "free" or as long as the supplies are available. Dwellings will be allocated as needed. Mass transit transportation only, and private, personal automobiles will not exist. Recreational holidays and vacations will be awarded based on availability.

—For personal transportation, cars, the neo-communists point out that cars with AI will be available on call when needed and the cars will be used more efficiently, 24/7, and not rusting in garages as they do now. You own nothing and will be happier. Wrong! Personal cars represent personal freedom, to go wherever and whenever you want. But personal freedom is not allowed under communism—.

Everyone works according to their capability, and everyone can live according to their needs, provided that there will be enough for all; otherwise, goods will be rationed, (like in Cuba in 2020.) If you think that sounds wonderful, let's imagine how the Communist world would function.

Everything available for our survival derives from *labor*, purposeful work, as explained in the book "The Wealth of Nations" by Adam Smith. The fruits and vegetables don't extract themselves from the ground and cook themselves for us to eat them. Pigs don't barbeque themselves and serve the pork ribs to our table. Someone needs to work to make them available for us. If the population doesn't work, we all starve.

However, most work is not pleasant; it can be physically exhausting, psychologically stressful. Everyone who is employed knows the unpleasant aspect of work. Very few people enjoy their work, and have the privilege to work doing something they want.

We work for survival and/or enjoyment of life –the pursuit of happiness. If survival is assured under Communism, why would a person study for 18 years to become a doctor? Because being a doctor is rewarding? For some, maybe, for others, they can earn more money, but there is no pay for one's work under Communism. Why study/work so hard if there is no personal economic gain in it? Does a person who cleans toilets and sewers enjoys his work? Or the person who has to repair a broken water pipe in the middle of the winter, at night, works with pleasure? Not all jobs are equal or easy or pleasant.

There is a difference between being an accountant in a lovely modern building or a drafty barrack working for a state-owned agricultural company. There is a big difference between digging a trench or working in an office. How about being a teacher working in the city, with all its cosmopolitan amenities, or being a teacher working in a snowbound, three months of the year, mountain village, without indoor plumbing or heating, and muddy roads when it rains. Work is work, but work is not equal in its effort, rewards, and quality of living. Under Communism, everyone must work, but without pay. *You must work according to your ability*.

What if you don't work? Under Socialism if you didn't work, you didn't earn money and starved, and you could not get "free" medical care either. That's how *free* the health care system was under Socialism. What would happen under Communism? You work based on your ability. But if you don't have any "ability," you are still entitled to fulfill your needs, like the American Welfare system; you are entitled to eat but not obligated to work. Is there any surprise that people on welfare don't work when there is no pressure from starving? After the Chinese Covid-19 Pandemic ended, some people didn't return to work because they made more money from government help than if they worked.

The same analogy to the quality of work applies to the quality of your needs. I like fillet mignon and lobster, and an excellent cabernet. Billions of people would like the same thing. I like to live in a beach house in California. So are billions of people. And I like long, luxurious cruises in cabins with a balcony. And so many others. The problem is that the supply for our needs varies in quality and quantity. Whatever is abundant will be available for all. Then what will happen with the distribution of scarce items? The Free Market system regulates the demand based on one's earning ability and prices. I eat fillet mignon and lobster and drink a nice Cabernet twice a year, maybe. I don't live in a beach house, but 70 miles inland, where I can afford to own my home. And when I go on cruises, I search for specials and stay in an inside cabin, the most inexpensive, if possible.

To solve this predicament, communism will either have to ration the best and scarce, use a lottery system, or do away with extravagant items and foods. Because there is no money, the population will have only what society produces, as planned and ordered by the State. If the economy grows only cabbage, then the people will eat only cabbage. Having a closet full of clothes and shoes will be part of the past. Too many varieties and styles will cause hoarding, shortages, and envy. The people will wear what they are allotted. The food will not come in a large variety, and meat may disappear altogether as being too expensive to supply for everyone.

There were many jokes I remember from socialism: "Under Communism there is no money and everyone goes to the market and there is a mound of potatoes, from which you get as much as you need for dinner." One comrade says, "But I don't like potatoes," the answer was, "Don't worry, comrade, you will, you will." There will be no other choices.

Another humorous example I heard is about a hotel restaurant in Moscow after the Revolution. A customer asked for a bottle of specific vintage wine. The waiter said, "Sorry, comrade, red or white wine?" the customer was surprised, knowing that the restaurant had a well-stocked wine cellar. As it turned out, they covered all the labels of all the bottles of wine with labels of Red or White wines. Quality was irrelevant, bourgeois fanciness. If you're a wine drinker, you'll have a choice of red or white wines only, if they will produce wine at all. Yes, wines will be produced along with other cheap alcoholic beverages. Alcohol was the Socialism's choice of mind-numbing substance. There was never a shortage of alcohol in Socialist Romania, if you didn't mind that some of the alcohol could get you blind.

For housing, they will allot it to everyone based on need. Since there will be no nuclear families a one-bedroom apartment in a multistory building may be given to a couple. Single people will be housed in dormitories or bedrooms in multi-bedroom houses, if there are not enough apartments. Clothes will be of the type of uniforms, perhaps unisex.

Under Communism, everyone must contribute to the welfare of society to assure everyone's survival. It will be a drab, grey life. Drabber and greyer than Socialism.

But wait, how do I know that's the way it will be? I lived under Socialism, where money existed, and life was miserable. Under Communism, conformity will be the rule. You may wonder why not equality? Equality is freedom, not allowed.

But there is more.

Drastic measures must be taken to achieve Communism. Originally Lenin and others envisioned that Socialism will be a transitional phase. Karl Marx was sure that eventually, humanity would evolve into Communism. But since we didn't become full socialists how would we evolve to communism? That was a dilemma the Marxists could not unravel. It was not until the 1920s that Marxist minds at Frankfurt School in Germany discovered the impediments to why socialism doesn't take roots worldwide and prevent communism evolution. The barriers are us, the people. Yes, *you and I are the problem*, the obstructions to achieve utopia. No matter how poor an individual is, each will aspire to a better life and become a bourgeois if possible. Greed is the problem —everyone for themselves.

A complete sociological transformation of the population must be undertaken. People behave the way they do because of scarcities, cultures, religions, greed, and family teachings. All of those "human unacceptable behaviors" need to be eliminated, and the only way to stop them is for the State to take over everyone's life. The State will need to *re-image* the human character. I couldn't resist using the word re-image, as in re-image the police trumpeted on CNN and MSNBC.

The transformation will start at infancy for every person. (That's one demand from Black Lives Matter, by the way.) Yes, under communism, people will be allowed to procreate, but after the babies are born, they'll take them to State Institutions to raise them to adulthood. Parents cannot see their children again because parents can be a "bad influence" on their children. Only trained Communist caretakers will know what's best for future generations. Religion and family affiliation will not exist. The Communist society is everyone's parent, brother, sister, leader, and god.

They will educate the children on communist principles and values. A standard communist curriculum applied worldwide. Excellence, not equity, will rule in all aspects of life. To have more, to eat more, to have better clothes or housing than another is forbidden. As the children mature, a committee will analyze each individual and channel each into the education and later profession for which they have the best aptitude. The one who has no talent will clean the latrines or the sewers. The education and future work each will perform fully complies with "*From each according to his abilities.*"

Equity will be a thing of the past, a good tool to implement Socialism, but useless under Communism. Although Communism will try to control Nature, they'll be in full control of Nurture. Since all children will be raised per Communist standards there will be no racial discrimination, and therefore the best individual will obtain the best jobs per their abilities and skills. Surprise, surprise, competition will be back, just as China is applying it today.

You may wonder what happens to the cunning and the shrewd? They will be part of the elite, the government. How about the lazy who pretends to be not good at anything? Or the criminal element? In spite of "*From each according to his abilities*" not working or pretending to be a totally useless person will not be an excuse. To partake in the communist society, one must provide your fair share to the community. What will they do with such people? The State has absolute control over the young people since birth and those determined unredeemable special correctional departments will resolve those issues. If nothing works, a special committee will recommend euthanasia. You read right, euthanasia. There will be no such thing as life sentence in prison. But that's Nazism. Yes, and Nazism is Socialism, and under Communism-Socialism the individual is irrelevant.

They will put the criminal element to work in the most brutal conditions to rehabilitate them. Communism cannot afford to support unproductive people, nor the mentally or physically imperfect. Eugenics is much easier to undertake with modern medical sciences. Any genetically deficient fetus will be aborted. Suppose a specific strain of genes is desirable. In that case, those humans will be allowed to reproduce in more significant numbers. At the same time, the not-so-desirable, the deplorables, will be sterilized.

They will monitor continuously the population, every person will have an implant tracking their location and even what they say and listen to, via the implant. Anonymity will not exist.

The communist economy will have a low productivity, no matter how much they will indoctrinate the children in the communist culture. Therefore, they will adjust the entire global population to balance the Earth's resources and the population's demands. Having hungry and deprived people will lead to uprising and destruction of the communist world, that's why population control, genetic control, along with everything else needed, will be the rule to make a perfect Communist World.

Science will take over Nature.

But wait, technology, Artificial Intelligence, AI, and robotics could help the world's productivity. Yes, it could if the advancement in technology will continue. Socialism will inherit good automation machines from the Free-Market economies, and it will be passed on to Communism, if stagnation and obsolescence will not take place. Innovations and inventions happen when a need, a consumer demand, a pain point arises, and inventors find answers for them to *prosper*. Under Socialism-Communism, anything innovated or invented belongs to society, not the inventor. But lack of incentive is not the highest obstacle in the Communist world. The risk of failure is immense, and for anyone to take the initiative, a committee must approve it. If they authorize something that fails, they'll be held accountable. No one wants to jeopardize their position in the communist society and the few privileges allowed with their jobs.

For Communism, the Holy Grail is mind control. The Digital Communist Platforms, Facebook, Twitter, YouTube, Amazon-Alexa, and the rest of the spying devices we use today. Brain implants will reveal each one's thoughts. They will perfect the technologies used by China for face recognition. Like in George Orwell's "1984" Big Brother will see you when you are on your computer or even watch TV. In my book "The Pregnant Pope" every citizen will pass through a scanner identifying down to the molecule and DNA each person, all in the name of societal security.

Communism, anyone?

Chapter 6. Democracy

Democracies have been described by other people as follows:

> *Just because you do not take an interest in politics doesn't mean politics won't take an interest in you.* Pericles

> *One of the penalties for refusing to participate in politics is that you end up being governed by your inferiors.* Plato

> *If a nation expects to be ignorant and free, in a state of civilization, it expects what never was and never will be.* Thomas Jefferson

> *Democracy is beautiful in theory; in practice it is a fallacy. You in America will see that some day.* Benito Mussolini

> *...the longer a man possesses an object the more readily he grows tired of it. He craves something new: therefore one needs two parties. One in the office, the other in opposition. When the one has played itself out, then the opposition party comes in power... As everyone knows, this system is given some such name as "Self-Government of the People."* Adolf Hitler Mein Kampf

> *We [USSR] allow other parties to exist. However, the fundamental principle that distinguishes us from the West is as follows: one party rules, and all others are in jail! [12: pg 7]* Mikhail Tomsky from The Black Book of Communism

Or killed.

Democracy is the worst-best political system or compromise humanity could come up with, but it is better than dictatorship although it represents more closely humans' *wiring*. Yes, most of us want to follow a leader and not make many decisions. The more ignorant a population is, the more it is inclined to accept dictatorship. We can say the same thing about the Free Market economy; it is the best-worst economic system, although the most effective and efficient system. Democracy doesn't please everyone all the time. But then, can you please all humanity about everything, every time? In times of prosperity and when there is little divisiveness among the people, democracy works. The tenet of the winning majority does not imprison the minority, the party that lost. Democracy works best when the political situation is grey, nothing particularly infuriating about either side of an issue. But when it becomes black and white (nothing to do with race,) democracy has a hard time.

Democracy is the Rule-of-Many-Over-Many, and occasionally throughout our history it was used as a governing form by more enlightened civilizations, but eventually, it disintegrated in Dictatorship/Monarchy/Tyranny —the Rule-of-Few-Over-Many. Democracy is the most demanding system of government to maintain. It requires a well-educated, engaged, freedom-loving, and voluntarily taking part in the republic's affairs. It also requires law and order. In a time of distress, economic or political, the people will revert to the basic needs, food, shelter, safety. (As per Maslow's Hierarchy of Needs.) In those dire times, expedient, short-term solutions need to be implemented. Democracy cannot function on an empty stomach or fear of doom. When Vesuvius explodes, there is no time to gather and decide democratically what to do. The order is given: *run for your life*.

Under the democratic political system, logic and reason are paramount. A king may decide with no logic, and as long as he doesn't screw up royally, he keeps his head and his throne. In a democracy, every member of the ruling body must show (theoretically) why taking one action over another is better. But democracy succeeds only as long as the population supports it, which means voluntary involvement by many and an informed electorate. Considering how many people know little about politics, economics, and social issues, when they vote for a candidate or party, they could make as bad of a decision as an ill-advised king.

Democracy sounds good, power to the people. The people cannot be wrong. Maybe. Adolf Hitler and the NAZI-Socialist party were elected democratically. If enough people believe in an ideology, a party, or leader, what's stopping dictatorship or monarchy or religion from taking over. The vociferous majority dictates, and if the majority decides to sell their soul to the devil, Satan will rule.

To prevent the demise of democracy, our founding fathers created an elaborate form of government based on three branches of government with equal powers so that no one branch can take over and establish tyranny. All democracies depend on the will of the people, but to prevent the will of the people from self-destruction, the Constitution is necessary. What's a Constitution? In the simplest terms, it is a Policy Manual, a guide, on how the government does its job.

Our Constitution is a wonderful document that specifies the organization of our government; three branches: Legislative, Executive, and Judicial. What power each has, election rules, for how long the elected serve, and each branch's responsibilities. The relationship among states and the Federal Government and their responsibilities. It addresses what kind of democracy we have —a Constitutional Federal Republic. Meaning the laws of the land are based on the Constitution; we are a Federation of States, forming a Republic —the United States of America.

It even specifies how the President will be elected through the Electoral College so that the more populous states will not dictate the outcome in their favor, at the expense of the smaller states. Much debate and arguments exist about this method of selecting the President. It all has to do with the representation of each State of the Union. In other words, the state or states with most people would always decide who the president is. California has 40 million people, while Alaska has 0.7 million (731 thousands.) Alaska's vote is insignificant, it has 1.8 % of California's population. It might as well not vote. California has as much population as the lowest 23 ½ states combined. If we add the illegals, who vote, California has as much population as 25 states. Considering that California is a Socialist State it would have a great influence on what party the President will represent.

Of course, the Constitution can be revised, or even discarded with two-thirds of the votes in Congress. Or completely ignored. Therefore, the Constitution is not absolute; it is revisable. That can be good or bad.

How bad? Take a look at the Gödel's loophole:

> In summary, Gödel's loophole is that the amendment procedures set forth in Article V apply to the constitutional statements in Article V themselves. In addition, not only may Article V itself be amended, but also it may be amended in an upward or downward direction. Lastly, the Gödelian problem of self-amendment or anti-entrenchment is unsolvable.
>
> [Ref. https://brianmlucey.wordpress.com/2016/11/17/godels-loophole-turning-the-usa-into-a-dictatorship-constitutionally/]

By changing the Constitution, any part or whole, the revision may contribute to the end of Democracy and the Rise of Tyranny. Yet, this is what the Leftists and the Democrat Socialist Party are attempting to do to secure permanent political power and revise or eliminate the Constitution.

Is democracy a fallacy? Was Mussolini predicting what's happening today? Or as Hitler said: *Two-party system like ours, one in power, the other waiting its turn when people will tire of the one in power*. Are the people voting for hard choices or easy ones, for which we'll pay later dearly? Are we the people really in power, or minority interests govern us? (Minority doesn't mean race.)

In reality we are governed by minorities. An interest group, a minority, is the one that proposes an action plan, and if they are good at selling us their "plan" they win. There are many such interest minorities competing for our votes. There is this theory of the 3% minority which influences how we're governed. Supposedly it takes only three percent of the population to impose their will on the rest of us, for the better or, the worse. Is that bad? Let's examine the human's mental stance, which fall into three categories:

1. The Naïve, the vast majority (90%)
2. The Idealists, a large number (9%)
3. The Shrewd, a minority (1%)

All of us fall into one of those categories one time or another during our lives. I've been in all three, but depending on the subject of discussion, I, like the rest of us, fall in the Naïve category. Not all leaders are shrewd; some are idealists. But if they don't wise up, the shrewd will replace them. Many of us are passive participants, the naïve, while the idealists fire us up and the shrewd lead us. In the end, the type of people who will be the leaders are always shrewd. However, being a passive participant is better than being an ignorant participant. The ignorant participants are led by the nose most easily by lying demagogues. Those voters are the ones most cherished by the Democrat Socialist Party and corralled to vote. When the voting laws are passed to prevent fraud —preventing ballot harvesting— the Democrat Socialist Party screams "Voter Suppression."

In a democracy, every citizen has the right to vote. Some countries make voting mandatory for everyone. That may be democracy, but that's not freedom. A citizen should have the right, not the obligation, to vote, although inferior people may lead us if we don't vote. Many people vote with no ownership interest. They have nothing to lose based on how they vote, while other people suffer the consequences of their voting by carrying the burden, most of the time financially.

Democracy is more vulnerable when a country is in a crisis or poverty has crippled that country. Desperate people do desperate things, including voting for the demagogue promising everything for everyone. With current influx of illegal immigrants, mostly poor people, the poverty will escalate in the United States, and those people used to be taken care by the government will vote in the future for socialism.

Democracy requires freedom, and the Bill of Rights specifies which of our freedoms the Government cannot take away. This implies, you may do anything you want as long as it is not *illegal*.

The US Constitution is becoming more and more like a Communist-Socialist Constitution that restricts or defines our liberty more narrowly. The more amendments, the more laws are passed, the more we become a Socialist country where we can do only what's allowed and not have the freedom to do anything we want as long as it is not illegal. This is a subtle difference, but with an enormous impact on our country, society, and each of us.

Chapter 7. Free Market-Capitalism

Since the publication of "The Communist Manifesto" in 1848, capitalism has got a bad rap. The capitalists were the bourgeoisie, the rich, the exploiters of the masses. However, through their entrepreneurial spirit, the capitalists had built things that didn't exist before, improved the life of all humans, and provided employment. Free market facilitated these opportunities, and the hardest and brightest of them blazed new trails. Capitalism is human nature, reflecting how God made us.

Capitalism, at its core, is all about profit. The capitalists kept the financial gain by producing a better mousetrap, better quality, a cheaper product. The Capitalists must compete among themselves, the survival of the fittest, the smartest, and the quickest. Unfortunately, we are not all equal by nature or nurture. Everyone has unique abilities, some more than others. Capitalism provides unequal benefits. The one who produces the most gets the most.

Capitalism nurtures the achievers.
Socialism nurtures the mediocrities.

The Capitalists understand best the complexity of their undertaking. An enterprise takes raw material, and by applying labor, it creates usable products, which they sell to make a profit. If they don't make a profit, they go out of business. If they make a profit, they can continue and grow to make more products and bigger profits. The Capitalists understand the difference between the two resources, material and labor. One can kick the material, it won't object, or go anywhere unless stolen. Or burn down. Material is property, and it doesn't go on strike.

Labor is people. They are not property. You don't kick the people and not expect a reaction. People will move away where the pay is better. Therefore, the Capitalists treat the people as a unique resource, a human resource. The wages he pays are based on the market, the demand and supply. A short supply of labor may raise the wages, and the products will be too expensive to sell, then the Capitalist won't make a profit, therefore no hiring. Everything happening in Free-Market Capitalism is a balancing act of many variables, and the reward is the profit.

Capitalism made America. Cornelius Vanderbilt's foresight was to see that railroads were the future, the much better, faster, and cheaper way of transporting goods across the country. John Rockefeller saw the opportunity to refine the crude for oil lamps, supplant whale oil, or candles for illumination. By building a bridge over Mississippi, Andrew Carnegie recognized the better quality of steel over iron, and the steel age began. The bridges were built longer and buildings taller, and the skyscrapers were born. Among many other inventions, Thomas Edison made electricity a viable source of lighting by perfecting the light bulb. George Westinghouse with Nicola Tesla introduced the more efficient AC electricity. And of course, Henry Ford improved the gasoline-powered automobile and produced it affordable for the masses.

The dirtiest word for capitalists is competition. To out-compete their competition, the capitalists must improve their products and make them cheaper. This drive to stay ahead is what made possible the progress of our civilization. And the consumers got better quality and lower cost products as a result.

Under socialism, the State owns all enterprises, a super monopoly. The companies don't have to compete; they produce what the central planning committee ordered. The socialist state monopoly eliminates competition and the need to invent, as a result economic stagnation will follow. Furthermore, the socialist economy does not rely on *profit* but on *need.*

The following is an example from the Soviet Union. It is cold in that country in the winter, and the people need overcoats. The central planning committee ordered the production of overcoats by weight. The manufacturer used the heaviest material to make them and even exceeded their quota. Under socialism, they always exceed the quota. The lucky Russians, who managed to buy overcoats, were happy; they were warm. But there were not enough of them to go around; the people were disgruntled. The central planning committee corrected the problem and ordered one million overcoats for the following year. The manufacturer used thinner material to make them and exceeded their quota. Now, there were plenty of coats for everyone, but the people were cold. And the people were disgruntled.

Socialism and disgruntlement go hand in hand.

A simple thing like *profit* would have fixed the problem by calibrating optimum quality for the optimum price as Capitalism would have done.

The reward for a well-run business is more profit and increased market share, therefore more wealth. In our economy, it is customary to see specific industry segments dominated by a few large companies, not monopolies since they are illegal, but large companies that eliminate competition from small businesses. Large companies can bankrupt small businesses by underpricing certain products, and they can afford the loss as long as they gain in the market share. Because of the increasing size of the companies and more and more people becoming employees, entrepreneurship within the population also decreases. Everyone becomes an employee.

New entrepreneurship happens more often when new technologies emerge and the dominant businesses don't understand them or are too slow to react. Examples are personal computers and software for operating them, Apple and Microsoft, and all the other industries that spun out from the Internet, such as Amazon, Google, Facebook, YouTube, Twitter, and others. These computing businesses, like IBM, were established, but the new entrepreneurs used a new technology, the Internet. The unusual situation that arose from the Internet applications is that all those companies became monopolies, and they stay as monopolies by buying out any new enterprise that competes with them or brings to the market a better product.

We passed the monopoly laws to protect the consumers from high prices, stimulate competition and progress. The Digital Communist

Platforms companies' products are free. It cannot get any better than that for the consumers. But DCP are a different type of business model. By using Google, Facebook, YouTube, Twitter, and other platforms, *WE* are the products. Information gathered from each user can be sorted and sold to producers of goods to market their products to us. And, of course, being monopolies and dominated by the new generations of workers who the Marxist-Socialist Academia brainwashed, they can influence our political beliefs and affect the elections, as they did in 2020, and perhaps even earlier.

The inventions and innovations brought to us since the industrial revolution were possible only under capitalism. Under socialism, new ideas were rare, and only through industrial espionage as the USSR practiced were they able to keep up with the Western economies. China has perfected the art of Intellectual Capital theft and challenges the USA as the economic superpower.

Curiously, the increase in the size of the businesses and employment has made it easier for the Federal and State governments to intrude on the businesses' affairs. Through laws and regulations, the government controls the companies. Because the employees are people, the government has an interest in the people, the employees. All the employees, including the management, have been bureaucratized. The government's laws and regulations dictate the companies who to hire, how to hire, what they cannot do after hiring, dictates what kind of at-work educational (brainwashing) seminars to conduct, and other influences that increase the cost of doing business. Unfortunately, if unchecked, capitalism will always take actions that become predatory, and some government control and monitoring might be needed, but what we have today approaches socialism and fascism. Why fascism? When the businesses carry out government initiatives that's fascism.

Capitalism has destroyed the feudal system and has brought up humanity to prosperity. With all the alleged detriments, capitalism has provided employment and a better standard of living. I heard many people blaming capitalism for all the ills of the world. Ask them:

Freedom Trumps Socialism

> *If you don't like capitalism give up your iPhones, flat panel TV, car, airplane travel, electricity, AC and every modern gadget that makes your life so comfortable.*

Would they?.

Capitalism is the *goose that lays the golden eggs*, and when it is caged as Socialism does, the goose gives fewer eggs. The goose needs *freedom to roam.*

Winston Churchill said in the House of Commons, on 22 October 1945:

> The inherent vice of capitalism is the unequal sharing of blessings.
>
> The inherent virtue of Socialism is the equal sharing of miseries.

He also said in Perth, Scotland, 28 May 1948:

> Socialism is the philosophy of failure, the creed of ignorance, and the gospel of envy.

The wealth situation is affected by the political philosophy of the State.

Capitalism believes in the right to produce and the right to keep the profits.

Socialism believes in the right to consume without the right to profits.

The above says it all. To consume, we need to produce. But if you cannot produce and keep the profits, there is nothing to consume. So, the Socialist State takes over and produces shabby quality and low quantities because of lack of competition. But if they allow competition, the enterprises may have to fire employees. But everyone has the right to a job. Do you see the continuous loop of idiocy?

Bottom line, if you want better and cheaper goods, services, and products, a better life, only the Free-Market Capitalism, will provide it. Forbidden Free-Market is what broke Socialism, and it will never change.

Chapter 8. Wealth Created by the Three Ideologies

Political ideologies are what they are, but it is the economy that counts, how much wealth is there and who has it. If we would live in a "perfect Communist world," where there is "plenty" for everyone, we wouldn't have any of these discussions or, worse, not allowed to have these discussions. But a perfect Communist world is Utopia; it cannot exist today without humans being "reprogrammed." Furthermore, even if the communist world would exist, certain goods would not be available because of the expense to produce and satisfy the demand. Therefore, it will be a value limit above which many products would not be available, as they were previously under the free market.

The following table describes what and cannot expect from these political ideologies.

Left	**Center**	**Right**
Few Rule Many	*Many Rule Many*	*Few Rule Many*
NO Freedom of Expression	Freedom of Expression	NO Freedom of Expression
NO Political Freedom	Political Freedom	NO Political Freedom
NO Elections/Fraudulent	Free Elections	NO Elections/Fraudulent
NO Personal Capital	Capital accessible to all	Capital in the hands of few
Income Equality = Poverty	Income Inequality	Income Inequality

As you see above only, the Left has Income Equality. And they do if we ignore a lower standard of living. The State keeps everyone *equally poor*, not by intention but by default. The State cannot provide everyone with Mercedes cars to drive, let alone Trabants as they did in East Germany. No one profits and becomes more affluent than the next guy. The Center and Right have Income Inequality. *That is the problem* screams the Left. As for the Center, the people have the freedom to take whatever actions are necessary to better themselves or stay poor. It is up to the individual —not the State—, for each to prosper or not. On the Right, the people have no freedom to prosper; the wealth is in the hands of the few rich to the detriment of everyone. The Right keeps the people poor by allowing opportunities only to the oligarchy, while the Left keeps everyone poor by blocking the opportunities to everyone.

The following graph illustrates the distribution of wealth in each of the three political ideologies:

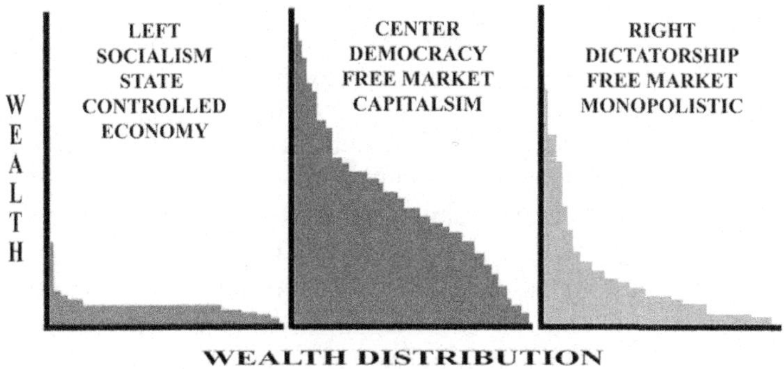

There is a striking difference among the three political systems. Socialism is the least prosperous, followed by the Right. Only in Democracy —Free Market— prosperity can happen.

Socialism.

This economic system does not allow private ownership of wealth-producing assets. The government, through Central Planning, handles all economic decisions. In theory, it sounds perfect. Instead of having thousands of individuals making microeconomic decisions, one group of "experts" decide on the most efficient and effective way to run the economy. But, there are problems with this approach. Socialism champions mediocracy; the bureaucrats will decide what to produce, not industrial experts selected through competition. If erroneous, and they often are, big decisions can cause Big Economic Disasters, which is the cause for millions to die from famine or malnutrition under socialism.

For example, Trofim Lysenko, a Russian scientist whose bogus ideas about agriculture caused massive crop failures in the Soviet

Union and starvation. Instead of trying his methods on a small scale at first, as would a business do, the central planning committee ordered the entire Soviet agriculture to follow his ideas, and disaster ensued. Some other well-doer in the Soviet Union decided to plow the fields deeper. The fertile soil on the steppes is thin, and when it's plowed deeper, the fertile soil is buried and the poor soil brought to the top. The Soviet harvest for the following summer was abysmal. Imported grains from the US saved them. In China, they planted the grains much denser. After all, the more seeds per unit of area, the larger the harvest. Yet the farmers never did that. The plants grew denser, a perfect environment for the plants to rot from fungus. Famine followed, and people died by the millions.

Collectivization is another reason for diminished agricultural production. Collectivization sounds good in theory; combine thousands of small farms in large collectives, and the farming can be mechanized, becoming more efficient. That part worked; what it didn't work was human nature. Nothing is dearer to a peasant than to own his plot of land. The Communist-Socialist State confiscated everyone's land, allegedly becoming common property for the betterment of all. Instead of the peasant working his land, he became an employee of the collective/state. There is a big difference in how much effort a peasant puts on his land and that of an employee working for the collective. (The principle of slave versus free man; who works harder?)

Vietnam applied the Communist-Socialist methods of agriculture. The main food staple is rice. Before unification, South Vietnam was self-sufficient in food production, but after unification and collectivization forced on the South the country starved. The peasants were employees now and worked as socialist employees. The government had to deploy go-to-work teams to bang on people's doors and bring them to the fields to work. It was not until they wised up and abandoned the collective method, after which their life improved. Although the land belongs to the state, they allotted each family five acres of rice field to work and keep the profit. Those greedy peasants! No. Just human nature. Today Vietnam is the third-largest exporter of rice. Capitalism always works.

There can be countless examples of why Socialism doesn't work, but that would fill an entire library. The bottom line is that the economy becomes inefficient because of central planning and the reluctance of workers to work harder without rewards. What's in it for them? They'll get paid the same if they work hard or not. How do you feel at your employment place if you see some co-workers loafing while getting the same pay and salary increases as you do? Are you going to work harder? You might, but you won't. We are humans, not robots. Now imagine the entire workforce of a country working at a slower pace. The people's labor brings prosperity to a country, but without incentives, laziness, and slow work is the result. And lower standard of living.

In the old Communist-Socialist Romania, there was a saying:

They [the government] pretend to pay us, we pretend to work.

Without an incentive to work harder, people will not work harder. In Communist China, in the early years, they paid everyone the same, in full compliance with Communist principles. They paid doctors and engineers the same as the manual laborers. The reasoning was work is work, and everyone's needs are the same and paid the same. What's the incentive to go for higher education and the hard work to get a degree if the next guy sweeps the streets with no worries as a doctor or engineer would have if the patients die or the bridge collapses. It didn't take long for the Communist Party to wake up and realize that work is not the same, higher knowledge is precious, and must be compensated accordingly.

All socialist economies and, therefore, their people become poorer until it reaches the point of economic collapse, as was the case of the USSR and the rest of the communist bloc in 1989.

Many thousands of individuals, if they're given the freedom to prosper, will work harder, wiser, and make faster decisions than a central planning committee.

Under capitalism there will be failures, but small failures, and the economy over all is not affected. And that's why Capitalist-Democracies prosper, while Socialism ends up in ruins.

The bottom line is that Socialism destroys the culture of work. Going from Free Market to Socialism is easy. Going from Socialism, after it collapses, to capitalism is hard. It takes more than one generation to reverse that trend, re-learn the ethic of work, and forget that the government is not the provider but the exploiter.

When I visited Romania after the Communist-Socialism ended, I observed what happens when you go from Socialism to a Free-Market economy. The hard-working people departed from Romania to the West for better wages. Romania is a mineral and land-rich country; it has plenty of potential for entrepreneurial folks to prosper. But they didn't. It is difficult to change from the Socialist culture of work doing as little as possible and being taken care of by the State to that of taking care of yourself by yourself. It takes time to understand personal freedom and independence from the State.

Are there wealthy people under socialism? Sure, those are the elites in the government. They live the good life with all the luxuries and benefits of the upper-middle class in democracies. Following the elites are the Intelligentsia, the managers, and other people of importance. Following them is the vast majority of the people earning relatively the same. These are the socialist middle classes, who live under the level of the so-called "poor working class" in democracies. Finally, are there poor people? Socialism does not change human nature. Some people, no matter how much they're helped, will not prosper. Laziness is a mental problem, and I don't think that will ever be resolved. Does the government support the poor with a welfare program?

There are no welfare programs under Marxism-Socialism. Everyone must work. Only the Capitalist countries can afford Welfare programs.

Communist-Socialist countries were not the most destitute countries in the world. The Third World countries are more impoverished. Then why don't we bring socialism to those countries to elevate them? Some third world countries attempted socialism and it failed in famine. The first thing to consider is that the former European Communist-Socialist countries were democratic and prosperous before socialism. Marxism-Socialism brought down their standard of living. Third World countries were colonies in the past, good or bad as it may have been, and their culture, despite colonialism, did not change from their old ways and adapt to the modern age. In many cases socialism took over the former colonies, and the first thing they did was chase the "Goose that laid the golden eggs" away. Those were mostly the white entrepreneurs. Socialism and Nationalism destroyed those former colonies. They still struggle today because they are unable to apply Free-Market Capitalism without encumbrance from government corruption.

Right Wing.

Are you surprised that the Right-Wing is doing better economically than Socialism? Right-Wing economies maintain Free-Market capitalism, but as monopolistic capitalism, restricting the people, especially the smart, dynamic, and entrepreneurs, from succeeding on their own.

Let's compare Spain's GDP, a Right-Wing country under Franco, with the USSR and China, Communist-Socialist countries, and the USA for the year 1974.

Country	GDP Value $	GDP per Capita
Spain -Right Wing	97,274,000,000	$ 2,750
USSR -Socialist	614,000,000,000	$ 2,455
China -Socialist	144,182,000,000	$160
USA -Democracy	1,545,200,000,000	$ 7,226

The USSR's economy was 6.3 times larger than Spain's. But USSR had a population of 250 million people or seven times that of Spain. Relative to the population, Spain's Right-Wing economy was 12% more prosperous than the USSR, although USSR is 34 times larger than Spain without the mineral resources of the USSR. And for China, with a population of 900 million at the time, or 26 times of Spain, the Chinese economy was only 48% larger than of smaller Spain. Thus, even the Right-Wing government is better off than the largest Communist-Socialist China and the USSR.

Needless to say, the US is the most prosperous because of freedom and democracy.

Democracy-Free Market.

How do the same countries compare today? The political landscape has changed. Spain is a Democratic country. The USSR is Russia now, a dictatorship disguised as a democracy under Putin. In contrast,

China has evolved from Communism-Socialism into Communism-Fascism. A country with Communist government, and a quasi-capitalist economy.

Country	GDP Value $	GDP per Capita
Spain -Democracy/Monarchy	1,663,000,000,000	$ 29,961
Russia –Dictatorship	4,390,000,000,000	$ 11,585
China - Communist-Fascist	14,140,000,000,000	$8,254
United States -Democracy	21,430,000,000,000	$ 55,809

Here we are, 46 years later, with changes in political and economic systems, the results are so different. Spain has a smaller GDP than Russia's, but the GDP per capita is 2.6 times larger than Russia's. China's economy has improved tremendously once it switched to a Fascist-Free Market economy. The question is, why Russia didn't prosper accordingly? As I said above, it is difficult to go from Socialism to Capitalism. Still, in Russia's case, they went from Socialism to Dictatorship, and most of Russia's economy is based on exports of minerals and gas, not manufacturing like China.

The previous graphs show that Free-Market Democracies are the most prosperous economies. The biggest positive of Free-Market economies is the growth of the middle-class. Even the Communist-Socialist countries have poor people, and poverty will not be eliminated no matter what system of government there is. As a matter of fact, in the United States, after the War on Poverty initiative, poverty has still not been eliminated. However, the Free-Market Democracies have the most benevolent welfare system approaching the Utopian Communism.

Free-Market Capitalism represents the survival of the fittest. Eat or be eaten. The fastest, strongest, smartest, hardest worker wins. The winner keeps all the winnings. When people are free to keep the fruits of their labor they work harder. But the losers can try again as long as one does not keep oneself down and cry for being a victim. In spite of the inequalities, the prosperity of capitalism brings up all the people's standard of living. Unfortunately, the Free Market Capitalism is not sympathetic to victims, although the Leftist politicians remedied that with the War on Poverty that caused more damage than it did good.

Chapter 9. The Illusion of Wealth

What is wealth? A good-paying job, cash in your pocket, money in the bank, gold, equities, Bonds, Real Estate, luxury items, or anything perceived as value? Wealth or lack of it can provide a good life or an impoverished life for one. Under Utopian Communism there is no need for wealth; you have a good life without having or worrying about possessions. That's what they say, without any proof. You own nothing, and they say, you'll be happier. The Romanian people, under Socialism, were not happy by owning very little to nothing. In the real world, wealth matters.

If you are not sure what wealth is, I recommend two excellent books to read about that subject, "The Wealth of Nations" by Adam Smith, and "Wealth, Poverty and Politics" by Thomas Sowell. The source of wealth comes from only one endeavor: *Labor*.

Wealth can be *created* or *transferred*. For example, a house builder creates wealth, an actual tangible outcome; a dwelling has been produced from his work. A house is a capital or wealth. A Real Estate Broker/agent who sold the house is not creating any wealth. She transfers wealth from the builder/seller to herself for services, labor rendered in selling the house. Don't look at transferring wealth as something bad. Most times, it is necessary because of how the economy works most efficiently. However, creating wealth and transferring wealth have a bad side as well. The maker of illegal narcotics is a creator of wealth, which destroys lives. Or the stock speculators who manipulate the markets for their enrichment at others' expense, that's a bad transfer of wealth. Lawyers and lawsuits are a transfer of wealth. Theft is an evil transfer of wealth or by the nationalization of one's property by Socialism. And war is transfer of wealth as well.

Taxes are the biggest transferor of wealth by the State. Taxes transfer people's and enterprises' wealth to the State coffers. The purpose is for the common good, such as building the country's infrastructure or protecting the country from foreign invaders.

Enforcing the country's laws is good, just as safeguarding the consumers from the private enterprises' questionable actions. For a society to prosper, educated people are necessary, and therefore education is free, financed through taxes. The salaries of the State apparatus, the bureaucrats, must be paid by taxes as well. And that's where the State should limit spending people's money. Big government is bad for the nation's wealth.

Unfortunately, that's not what is happening, as our Socialist State uses taxation to redistribute wealth, provide for our retirement and medical care, provide for the poor at home and other countries. All these are social programs, changing the character of our nation from Free-Market Capitalism to Statist-Socialist country. Yes, I realize that if the State doesn't help the poor and the elderly, no one will, and they'd end up in the streets as beggars. Except we can do it the smart way and not the socialist way as we do today.

All wealth that exists in the human society was created by work, physical or mental work. Even animals work when they gather food. A bison moves from pasture to pasture, or a lion hunts other animals to eat. That is work. Once satisfied, the animals rest or sleep.

And so are we, the humans. We work to provide for ourselves and ours. But modern humans have higher intelligence, and we don't live from hand to mouth like animals or like the gathering, hunting, primitive humans. A bison does not look at a pasture as wealth, just a source of food. A modern human looks at the same plot of land as wealth, based on what that plot of land could produce through labor. Is an apple tree wealth if it grows in the wild? It is not until a man climbs the tree to gather the apples. The same thing is with all the minerals in the ground. It has potential value, but only through work to extract the minerals and process them becomes wealth. So, wealth can have potential value or actual value.

Wealth has another characteristic; it depends on demand and supply. These terms are the principles of economics, which deal with wealth. Imagine you are stranded on a deserted island, and you find a pirate's chest full of gold coins. Is that wealth? If you cannot eat it or somehow prosper from it, it is worthless. There is no human nearby to exchange the gold for other goods, there is no demand for it, therefore it has no value in that place and time.

In another case, you are in 17th century Spain with that chest of gold. You are wealthy; the gold coins can buy you a castle and all the staff to tend to you. But the next day, a caravel arrives from the New World loaded with more gold, one hundred times more gold than you have. The caravel's gold could be placed in a basement for safekeeping, acting only as potential wealth, or they quickly put the gold into circulation, into commerce. That castle you planned to buy costs many more times than the price before the caravel arrived. The supply of gold increased, and it devalued your chest of gold. That's demand and supply. Large supply lowers the prices. High demand increases the prices. That's the illusion of wealth, it's never static.

I simplified the above examples to explain what wealth is. Now let's look at what happened to Dow Jones Industrial Average (DJIA) valuation from September 2008 to March 2009.

	DJIA	Percent Difference
September 2008	11433	100%
March 2009	6469	56%

In a span of six months, the value of the stock market dropped - 44%. Everyone's 401k became 201k. Where did that wealth go? This is the illusion of wealth, based on valuation, based on demand and supply. Wealth, at a macroscale, like a barrel of gold coins, does not have the same value for all times; it fluctuates in value. The same thing happened with Real Estate after 2008. In Southern California, the residential house price by the spring of 2008 went through the roof. In the spring of 2009, you couldn't give that house away for free, especially if it had a mortgage that was more than the appraised value.

The Stock Market is one gauge by which the value of a country's economy is measured, and it can go up and down caused by demand and supply. It also reflects how in aggregate all the enterprises are performing. Let's look at one enterprise, in particular, Facebook, and how its value would change if a specific law would pass. The founder of Facebook, Mark Zuckerberg, is worth $106 billion at the time of this writing. What if Congress decrees that Facebook cannot use its customer information for selling ads? Since Facebook's business is selling advertisements, that law will put Facebook out of business, and Mark Zuckerberg from a billionaire, becomes a pauper. His wealth vanishes.

Let's say, that the "glorious days" of Socialism have descended upon America, and the Socialist government of the United States nationalizes the entire economy. Since there will be no competition among the state-owned monopoly, there will be no need for advertisement. How much is Facebook, Google, and all other advertisement companies worth then? Nothing, and there is nothing to redistribute to the "less fortunate." I wonder if Mark Zuckerberg, Larry Page, Sergey Brin, founders of Google, Jack Dorsey of Twitter, and others have considered this possibility as they try so hard to push our country into socialism? But maybe they are part of the *elites* and have alternative plans.

Under socialism there will be no profit derived from the enterprises, and there will be no Stock Market. The so-called wealth represented by the Stock Market will disappear instantly. After a socialist nationalization, your 401k will become 0k. The only valuable things left will be the hard assets, the tangibles, such as buildings, factories, infrastructures, computers and software, land, and other such things. These assets have potential value. If this capital is put to work through people's labor to produce goods that people need, some wealth will be generated. However, the socialist wealth will be minute compared with the wealth under the Free-Market Capitalism economy. What wealth is left there for redistribution? Not much.

What's left is the jobs servicing the hard assets and a lot of unemployment. In the United States, 34% of the economy employs people in Finance, Insurance, Real Estate, Professional and Business Services, and so on. These sectors will vanish. But under socialism each has a right to a job; the State must employ those people. What kind of jobs? They'll be employed throughout the economy if the companies need them or not. What will that do for the rest of us? The economy will devalue by at least 34%, or our buying power goes down by 34%, because of inflation.

That's why Socialism means *Poverty and Misery.*

Is the Capitalist economy a house of cards with imagined wealth? No, we all live in it and make a living under the Capitalism system.

We can accumulate wealth and transfer it to our children. The Capitalist economy is based on specific rules, which work very well, with occasional self-corrections. Wealth is valuation, just like beauty is in the eyes of the beholder.

Chapter 10. The Writing Was on the Wall

Marxism-Socialism has always been an expansionary political system, not different from religions. At least the religious are selling God. Socialists sell Hell. When I was growing in Communist-Socialist Romania, there was not a moment without hearing *Proletariat of the World Unite* and *Communism will triumph in the world.* It makes sense, a united cause will succeed, and if the world as a whole is Socialist, no one can compare the abundance generated by the non-existent capitalism.

Moscow's Marxists-Leninists government conducted an aggressive campaign of expanding their ideology. It succeeded after World War II in the occupied countries of Central Europe, China, Mongolia, Korea, Vietnam, Cambodia, Cuba, Grenada, Angola, Congo, Ethiopia, Mozambique, Somalia, South Yemen, and for a short period in Chile.

To undermine the United States, one crucial document was issued by the Communist-Socialists listing *"The 45 Communist Goals" published in 1963.* You may disbelief what they planed back then and how much has been accomplished. Therefore, I included only applicable goals applicable today.

3. Develop the illusion that total disarmament [by] the United States would be a demonstration of moral strength.

Jimmy Carter and Barrack Obama tried but failed. But Communist China would like this very much to be implemented.

11. Promote the U.N. as the only hope for mankind. If its charter is rewritten, demand that it be set up as a one-world government with its own independent armed forces.

This is Globalization. The Communist-Socialists would easily control such a government.

12. Resist any attempt to outlaw the Communist Party.

The communist and socialist parties were not outlawed in the US, but some ex-communist countries outlawed this evil ideology after what they suffered under that tyrannical system. For example, Germany has outlawed National-Socialism, and Hungary the Communist party.

13. Do away with all loyalty oaths.

They are partially accomplished. Millionaire athletes protest the American flag and anthem by taking a knee. How shameful it was for the true patriots when the American Women Soccer team took a knee when our anthem was played at the Olympics. Patriotism is under attack in our country.

15. Capture one or both of the political parties in the United States.

Accomplished. The Marxists-Leninists have captured the Democrat Party.

16. Use technical decisions of the courts to weaken basic American institutions by claiming their activities violate civil rights.

Accomplished. ACLU has become an arm of the Marxist cause to abuse our freedoms and, in conjunction with liberal judges have weakened our constitution.

17. Get control of the schools. Use them as transmission belts for socialism and current Communist propaganda. Soften the curriculum. Get control of teachers' associations. Put the party line in textbooks.

Accomplished beyond the wildest dream of Communism-Socialism.

18. Gain control of all student newspapers.

Accomplished beyond the wildest dream of Communism-Socialism.

19. Use student riots to foment public protests against programs or organizations which are under Communist attack.

Accomplished beyond the wildest dream of Communism-Socialism. Black Lives Matter has become a tool for the Marxist-Leninists.

20. Infiltrate the press. Get control of book-review assignments, editorial writing, policymaking positions.

Accomplished beyond the wildest dream of Communism-Socialism.

21. Gain control of key positions in radio, TV, and motion pictures.

Accomplished beyond the wildest dream of Communism-Socialism.

22. Continue discrediting American culture by degrading all forms of artistic expression. An American Communist cell was told to "eliminate all good sculpture from parks and buildings, substitute shapeless, awkward and meaningless forms."

Done and then some more by tearing down statues of past heroes.

23. Control art critics and directors of art museums. "Our plan is to promote ugliness, repulsive, meaningless art."

Done, in addition, there is *Rap* music denigrating society, rule of law and women.

24. Eliminate all laws governing obscenity by calling them "censorship" and a violation of free speech and free press.

Done.

25. Break down cultural standards of morality by promoting pornography and obscenity in books, magazines, motion pictures, radio, and TV.

Done.

26. Present homosexuality, degeneracy and promiscuity as "normal, natural, healthy."

Accomplished beyond the wildest dream of Communism-Socialism. What will happen after LGBTQ is normalized in America? Polygamy of different combinations of sexes will be next.

27. Infiltrate the churches and replace revealed religion with "social" religion. Discredit the Bible and emphasize the need for intellectual maturity which does not need a "religious crutch."

Done.

28. Eliminate prayer or any phase of religious expression in the schools on the ground that it violates the principle of "separation of church and state."

Accomplished beyond the wildest dream of Communism-Socialism.

29. Discredit the American Constitution by calling it inadequate, old-fashioned, out of step with modern needs, a hindrance to cooperation between nations on a worldwide basis.

Ongoing work, but making progress.

30. Discredit the American Founding Fathers. Present them as selfish aristocrats who had no concern for the "common man."

Accomplished beyond the wildest dream of Communism-Socialism. They discredit the founding fathers for being slave owners. Tear down their statues too. High Schools in San Francisco took down names like George Washington or Thomas Jefferson and others like them.

31. Belittle all forms of American culture and discourage the teaching of American history on the ground that it was only a minor part of the "big picture." Give more emphasis to Russian history since the Communists took over.

Done. The Chicago school system is opposed to teaching history at all.

32. Support any socialist movement to give centralized control over any part of the culture–education, social agencies, welfare programs, mental health clinics, etc.

Done. Marxism has infiltrated the education unions.

33. Eliminate all laws or procedures which interfere with the operation of the Communist apparatus.

Done.

34. Eliminate the House Committee on Un-American Activities.

Done, and then some.

35. Discredit and eventually dismantle the FBI.

Why dismantle when you can infiltrate it. FBI will be our future Political Secret Police.

36. Infiltrate and gain control of more unions.

Partially successful. The worker's unions have nothing to gain from socialism, and they were reluctant to join, but not for long.

37. Infiltrate and gain control of big business.

It's going well with the influx of newly indoctrinated college graduates. The Social Media —Communist Digital Platforms— is all Communist now. Big Businesses are donating to BLM.

38. Transfer some of the powers of arrest from the police to social agencies. Treat all behavioral problems as psychiatric disorders which no one but psychiatrists can understand

Defund the Police.

39. Dominate the psychiatric profession and use mental health laws as a means of gaining coercive control over those who oppose Communist goals.

Not successful, but that will be next. The psychiatric institutions of the past were closed down, throwing the burden on the police to deal with the mentally ill.

40. Discredit the family as an institution. Encourage promiscuity and easy divorce.

Done, especially for the black society. This is part of the communist agenda.

41. Emphasize the need to raise children away from the negative influence of parents. Attribute prejudices, mental blocks, and retarding of children to suppressive influence of parents.

Done. Spank your child, and the social-Nazi workers will take away your child. This is also a demand by BLM, which is a Communist prerequisite.

42. Create the impression that violence and insurrection are legitimate aspects of the American tradition; that students and special-interest groups should rise up and use "united force" to solve economic, political or social problems.

Accomplished beyond the wildest dream of Communism-Socialism. Peaceful protesters were burning down buildings. Chris Cuomo at CNN considers arson and looting normal action for protestors.

44. Internationalize the Panama Canal.

Jimmy Carter gave it to Panama, which is about the same thing.

45. Repeal the Connally reservation so the United States cannot prevent the World Court from seizing jurisdiction [over domestic problems. Give the World Court jurisdiction] over nations and individuals alike.

Thankfully, not accomplished.

Out of the 34 viable goals I listed, 27 were accomplished or partly accomplished. Not bad, considering we did it by ourselves to ourselves and with little outside intervention. Do you feel distressed over how our democracy and freedom disappeared and disappears? The writing was on the "wall," but we all ignored it. Life is good in America, socialism could not happen here. But it is happening.

In an interview in 1984 with Yuri Bezmenov, a Russian journalist who defected to Canada, he outlined the four steps for Ideological Subversion to change a country's culture/political system/way of life.

1. *Demoralization.* Although Yuri Bezmenov used the word demoralization, he meant Indoctrination, which takes 15 to 20 years to affect one generation. Change the perspective of reality so that no one can make sense of what's right or wrong, a slow brainwashing

process. Although this interview took place in 1984, during Andropov premiership, he described to the letter what was going on in the USA then and now. The indoctrination started in the 1960s, and by now, we have three generations of people whose thinking is Marxist.

2. *Destabilization*. Once the new generation achieved adulthood and takes part in the economy, it will take 2 to 5 years to cause anarchy. The Economy, Foreign Relations, Defense will be affected. Not all the population has been brainwashed, and we still live in a democracy. Based on the people's mood and how they vote, the situation can deteriorate fast or slow. In my opinion, the end of Democracy begun in 2008, with the election of Barack Obama as the President of the United States. Because of his father, Obama hated Colonialism and considered the United States as an evil colonial power. As for the economy, we must remember what Obama said, those jobs are gone and won't return anymore, referring to all the jobs we lost to Mexico, and especially China. President Trump proved him wrong, and he reversed the destabilization started by Obama.

3. *Crisis*. It takes six weeks from the time it begins. The crisis is meant as the overthrow of the existing government and a new Socialist government taking over. Are we in crisis now? We have a pandemic that has changed our lifestyle. Some people live better on government support than when they were employed. Small businesses are going bankrupt and may never open their doors. Over time, new businesses will start again, but until then, recession or depression will prevail, and large protests in the streets make our situation even more desperate. The Democrats and the MSM do their best to make the situation worse, and made sure that on November 3, the Democrats won and took over the government. And it happened, the Democrat Socialist Party has complete power over our government. The conversion to socialism will speed up now since they have the power. The riot at the Capitol was not an insurrection, and we cannot consider it a crisis. However, the Democrat Socialist Party has made it into a crisis for their benefit, as you'll see later.

4. *Normalization*. The crisis will trigger a socio-political stabilization of some kind, making life seem normal. That's what the Democrat Socialist Party will try to do. But their Socialist intervention

in our lives and the economy won't lead to normalization unless enforced by the police and military.

Yuri Bezmenov, back in 1984, considered the US in a state of war. I say we are in a Cold Civil War today and was it going on since that time. Outsiders can see the problems we encounter more easily than we are, immersed in our daily, domestic lives.

Yuri Bezmenov proposed the following remedies to reverse the current trend:

- A national effort in the spirit of patriotism to reeducate people, although it will take a generation. Yes, I agree, but I'll discuss this subject later.
- Explain the danger of Socialism. Explaining alone won't work; showing what life was and would be under socialism could change indoctrinated minds.

Paul Harvey in an essay on radio in 1964 speculated how the Devil would destroy the United States:

> If I Were the Devil. If I were the Prince of Darkness I would want to engulf the whole earth in darkness.
>
> I'd have a third of its real estate and four-fifths of its population, but I would not be happy until I had seized the ripest apple on the tree.
>
> So I should set about however necessary, to take over the United States.
>
> I would begin with a campaign of whispers.
>
> With the wisdom of a serpent, I would whisper to you as I whispered to Eve, "Do as you please."
>
> To the young I would whisper "The Bible is a myth." I would convince them that "man created God," instead of the other way around. I would confide that "what is bad is good and what is good is square."
>
> In the ears of the young married I would whisper that work is debasing, that cocktail parties are good for you. I would caution them not to be "extreme" in religion, in patriotism, in moral conduct.
>
> And the old I would teach to pray — to say after me — "Our father which are in Washington."
>
> Then I'd get organized.
>
> I'd educate authors in how to make lurid literature exciting so that anything else would appear dull, uninteresting.
>
> I'd threaten TV with dirtier movies, and vice-versa.

I'd infiltrate unions and urge more loafing, less work. Idle hands usually work for me.

I'd peddle narcotics to whom I could, I'd sell alcohol to ladies and gentlemen of distinction, I'd tranquilize the rest with pills.

If I were the Devil, I would encourage schools to refine young intellects, but neglect to discipline emotions; let those run wild.

I'd designate an atheist to front for me before the highest courts and I'd get preachers to say, "She's right."

With flattery and promises of power I would get the courts to vote against God and in favor of pornography.

Thus, I would evict God from the courthouse, then from the schoolhouse, then from the Houses of Congress.

Then in his own churches I'd substitute psychology for religion and deify science.

If I were Satan I'd make the symbol of Easter an egg

And the symbol of Christmas a bottle.

If I were the Devil I'd take from those who have and give to those who wanted until I had killed the incentive of the ambitious. Then my police state would force everybody back to work.

Then I would separate families, putting children in uniform, women in coal mines and objectors in slave-labor camps.

If I were Satan I'd just keep doing what I'm doing and the whole world go to hell as sure as the Devil.

When Paul Harvey said the above, the Communist World covered "a third of its real estate and four-fifths of its population," but the apple was the United States of America. Therefore, to subvert the country of the free, they would eliminate God from the people's lives.

Ayn Rand, in her book "Atlas Shrugged," a fantasy, portrays how the United States succumbs to socialism, and the disaster that follows. Incredibly accurate for a fantasy book that was written 70 years ago, turning into a prophecy and showing how socialism takes over with the help of the elites. She had a keen sense back then of the issues we would face today, expressed in another book "Capitalism."

And so, it came to pass; we are becoming an atheist society, a Marxists-Socialist country with no fear of God, but with a Government of the Socialist fanatics.

Chapter 11. The United Socialists of America

The United States of America is the greatest country in the world, providing the best living conditions in the world's history, the freedom and dignity to succeed up to each one's ability. I am proof of that, along with other millions like me, who legally migrated here for freedom.

After I arrived in America, and I first read the Declaration of Independence, saying:

> *We hold these truths to be self-evident, that all men are created equal, that they are endowed by their creator with certain unalienable Rights, that among these are Life, Liberty and the Pursuit of Happiness.*

These are powerful words. I was elated and incredulous at the same time after I read them. This is what I thought all my life while living under the tyranny of Socialism. These exact words resonated with every fiber in my body and every thought in my brain. And here it was written as the foundation of freedom for all people to know that these words are universal for all people on Earth.

Were such words spelled out in any Communist-Socialist constitution? NO. In that political system, they dedicated the constitution to the Communist-Socialist ideology; the government was the grantor of rights, and the individual was just a tool of implementing Communism-Socialism all over the world. Obedience was enforced by law, and if you didn't comply, you ended up in the gulag, a concentration camp for hard labor or reeducation, and if you were part of the "basket of deplorables," torture, expulsion, many years or life in prison, or *execution*. Communism-Socialism murdered 200 million people worldwide to implement and enforce their ideology. And now Socialism is here in our country.

You may think socialism happened in the past. No way, we, Americans, would not allow that to happen. Are you sure? The following is a transcribe from Sean Hannity show on FOX News showing how it could happen here. Project Veritas, caught this on video what Michael Beller, principal counsel at PBS said:

> -Even if Biden wins, we go for all the Republican voters, the homeland Security will take their children away. And

> we'll put them [Trump supporters' children] into re-education camps.
>
> -What are you going to do if we [Biden] don't win? the reporter asked.
>
> -Go to the White House and throw Molotov cocktails. Americans are so f**king dumb. You know, most people are dumb. What's great is that Covid is spiking in all the red states, right now. So that's great. Because either these people won't come out to vote for Trump, you know the red states, or a lot of them [Trump supporters] are sick and dying.

Re-program the republican kids in re-education camps. Like China? Wanting death for the republicans? That's how the Socialists think. Eliminate the basket of deplorable.

You may think that this man is just one deranged Democrat-Socialist, but that's not the case. He was one of the higher-ups at PBS. Unfortunately, millions of them think that way and eventually implement their enslavement ideology when they come to power.

On Real Time with Bill Maher on HOB on Jan 15, 2021, Katie Couric said the following:

> How we're going to, literally almost deprogram people who had signed up to the cult of Trump.

Katie Couric has the right to free speech, but when she wants to deprogram people, she shows her Socialist beliefs to take the same actions as Hitler, Stalin, Mao, and the rest of the Communist-Socialists leaders have done. What are we? Beasts to be re-trained, re-programmed, re-educated, perhaps in concentration camps modeled after the Nazi, Soviet Union, or China. Free people have the right to have their own opinion and thoughts without the likes of Michael Beller, Katie Couric, Alexandria Ocasio-Cortez, and the rest of the Democrat Socialist Party to *re-program us*.

Worse yet, when it comes to racism against white people and shooting them. Dr. Aruna Khilanani, in a speech on April 6, 2021 at Yale School of Medicine, said:

> White people make my blood boil. I had fantasies of unloading a revolver into the head of any white person that got in my way, burying their body, and

> wiping my bloody hands as I walked away relatively guiltless with a bounce in my step, like I did the world a f***ing favor… White people are out of their minds and they have been for a long time. We are now in a phycological predicament, because white people feel that we are bullying them when we bring up race.

Got that, white people? You are to be exterminated the way Hitler and Stalin killed the Jews. So, who's Aruna Khilanani? She's of Hindu ancestry, born in the US, MD in psychiatry. She kept her job and has no worries. Imagine a white person saying that about any other ethnicity? But, racism against whites is allowed.

If the above words scared the crap out of you, you are not a Socialist. Only the Socialists are capable of such hateful speech.

Unfortunately, America is well underway to become a Socialist State. It began in 1964 with the War on Poverty. It was not Socialism that the Leftists intended to implement, but Communism. Only under Communism (they claim) people would receive support without working for it, and that's what the Welfare system is. And ever since, our country has slowly but surely shifted to become a Socialist country. The Marxists' job is not finished yet, but after the 2020 election, things will only speed up if we don't take action. When will we have full Socialism?

We will have socialism when poverty and misery will be equally distributed, and you'll be thrown in prison if you rebel politically. Watch what you say, or they may label you as a domestic terrorist. This is the beginning of political oppression. We're almost there, but you'll learn what is coming our way and how to prevent it by reading this book. We have nowhere to run.

Where is the proof that we are almost Socialist? The economy is in private hands, profit is allowed, the rich get richer, the poor get poorer, and we don't have a National Medical Program or Free Higher Education. Nor do we have a "right to a job." We are capitalists as hell.

We have minimum wages. That is Socialism. What's wrong with paying people minimum, livable wages? The State should not dictate economic rules to the Free-Market economy. Whatever the State touches, disaster follows. Minimum wages will create unemployment. That's a proven fact, as employers will resort to using technology to reduce the number of employees. Or export their jobs overseas. As a result, fewer entry-level jobs will be available for young people, which is necessary for them to gain experience and advance in life. Supermarkets and fast food outlets are working to eliminate the cashiers. Now we're self-scanning our items. Soon, a chip will be part of every price tag. When you walk through a scanner with your loaded cart, it automatically reads what you bought and charges your debit/credit card.

They can achieve income equality not by raising wages but by lowering the cost of goods. That is socialism as well. Today, many products are as cheap or even cheaper than they were in the 1980s by gutting our industry and giving it to China. But, just like minimum wages, this policy increases unemployment.

The Projects, the apartment buildings, the hive of unemployment, welfare, and crime is socialism. The government didn't have to pay people on welfare more to pay the rents, but constructing high-rise apartment buildings to house the low-income people, solved the problem. That's socialism.

You may or may not remember the school busing? To administer equal education for all, they bussed the black kids to white (more affluent) schools. Did the black kids or the white kids benefit? No. But it satisfied some demented Congress people's notion of equality. That's Socialism.

On the same line as the busing how about the Obama's "Affirmatively Furthering Fair Housing" (AFFH) rule, through which the federal government will enforce the building of low-income housing, or Projects in the suburbs. Somehow the suburbs have a wealth bug, which the low-income people could acquire. Will that bring equality or bring crime and misery to the suburbs? That is the meaning of misery and poverty equal distributed. That's Socialism.

How about the financial crisis of 2008? Low-interest rates and Bush's administration initiative to increase the homeownership of low-income people. Lend them money that they could not afford to pay back, and expect prosperity? After the collapse of the financial market, another Socialist undertaking took place, the bailout of the "Too-Big-To-Fail" financial institutions. Our Socialist government caused both the financial crisis and the bailout.

And of course, the Equal Employment Opportunity (EEO) signifies the ultimate control of the economy by a Socialist Government like ours. Under the disguise of eliminating discrimination, the government using the EEO and other rulings has taken control of the corporations. There is no need to confiscate the industry from private hands. Just regulate and control them to do the bid of our Socialist Government.

Our Educational System is socialist. The educated elite, hand in hand with the State, decides what's suitable for our kids and not the parents. The American Educational system is in full compliance with the Frankfurt Critical Theory. Change the society by teaching our kids socialism.

The Socialism initiative started in higher education in the 1960s. The US Academia has been overtaken by zealots, fanatic Marxists who believe in the utopian and completely discredited political system of Marxism. They brainwashed the new generations to believe that Socialism is wonderful, even though it destroyed the Soviet Socialist bloc, giving ample reasons what never to do again.

The Biden administration is dedicated to bring diversity in all aspects of our life through Equity, regardless of the qualifications of the individuals. Of course, that will increase mediocrity. But mediocrity is what socialism is all about.

The First Amendment of our Constitution states:

> *Congress shall make no law respecting an establishment of religion, or prohibiting the free exercise thereof; <u>or abridging the freedom of speech</u>, or of the press; or the right of the people peaceably to assemble, and to petition the Government for a redress of grievances.*

This is a monumental statement, prohibits the government, among many other things, from passing laws that would impair our freedom of speech, which is our God-given right.

Do we have freedom of speech today? Sure, we do; the government has not passed such laws. Yet. But it allows monopolies like Twitter, Instagram, YouTube, Facebook, Apple, Google, among many other DCP, to prevent Free Speech. The "Title 47 U.S. Code § 230 -

Protection for private blocking and screening of offensive material" is intended to protect DCP from being sued for what people post on their platforms. This law has empowered them to censor what we say, which is a de facto law against freedom of speech imposed by private companies. But the private companies can deny freedom of speech to anyone. Yes, but if they are monopolies, they might as well be the government. The Biden Administration is requesting the DCP to censure any information that is contradictory to Covid-10 and vaccination. And this is just the beginning.

Along the line of freedom of speech is the Politically Correct speech, which the Communists invented. If you say something that is considered politically incorrect in America today, you will be insulted, abused, doxed, or even fired from your job. God forbid if you say something against China if you are in sports or entertainment.

In a Socialist State there are political prisoners, and so we have them in America. In both cases, people who have written or made politically unacceptable movies found themselves in jail. I'm talking about Dinesh D'Souza.

Dinesh D'Souza is a conservative writer and filmmaker. He wrote and made such movies as: "Obama's America" an anti-Obama polemic based on his 2010 book "The Roots of Obama's Rage," "America: Imagine the World Without Her (2014)," "Hillary's America (2016)," "Death of a Nation (2018)," and "Trump Card (2020)." This man is a dangerous man to the Left cause. And he has a canny ability to show the truth and expose the Left and how they are destroying America.

In 2014, D'Souza was sentenced to eight months in a halfway house. The crime was one felony charge for making an illegal campaign contribution to a 2012 candidate. He donated more than allowed to a political candidate. Would he have been imprisoned if he didn't write the book "The Roots of Obama's Rage" in 2010? Of course not. Even if they had found out about his donation, he would have been given a slap on the wrist. But he offended Barack Obama, and his "wingman" General Attorney Eric Holder went after Dinesh. This was politically motivated incarceration. Dinesh was not silenced and continued exposing the Democrats and the Left. Fortunately, President Trump pardoned him.

If you think that's not enough to prove that our Justice Department is using Socialist Political retribution, let me remind you about how Roger Stone was arrested. An entire squad of FBI/SWAT agents came to Roger Stone's house to arrest him. The backyard was connected to a waterway, and they came by boat as well. By land and by sea, they came to arrest an old man in his underwear. The Justice Department tipped CNN —leaked information— to document his arrest. Heavily armed agents came to arrest an old man in boxer shorts and a t-shirt in the wee hours of the morning. Was that necessary? Was Roger Stone such a dangerous criminal to use that much force and manpower? Not at all. The FBI could have arrived at his house, arrested him, or even told him to surrender at the FBI office.

Similarly, Rudy Giuliani's office was raided by the FBI to collect evidence of alleged wrongdoing in his business dealings. But Rudy Giuliani was President Trump's attorney and whatever evidence they took is privileged. Attorney-client privileges don't count anymore in our Socialist-Gestapo system of justice.

So, why did they do it the Storm-Trooper way? **FEAR.** That's what our Justice Department and FBI want to instill in our minds: **FEAR.** That's the Socialist way to intimidate the population, to stop us from voicing our free opinion and make the population obedient to the Socialist State.

The adults in the Socialist countries received their indoctrination through papers, radio and TV. However, that was not the end of it. Weekly propaganda meetings were held to ensure that the workers were obedient. Our corporations are privately and publicly owned, and are not mandated to indoctrinate the employees in the government's edicts or socialist ideology. But they do, when they enforce vaccinations and Critical Race Theory seminars they enforce the will of the government. In my past employment I remember being called to attend instructional seminars regarding race jokes and sex abuses. But those were good. Well, I'm an adult and a free man, and because I'm employed by that corporation I was forced to attend "improvement" seminars. In other words, I'm not to be entrusted in my behavior, but reprogrammed by the Big Brother and the minion corporations. Of course, these seminars were complied with by the threat of lawsuits against the corporations if the employees' behavior was not corrected. This socialism is not the Marxist type, but the Fascist type of socialism, as the corporations aid the government's propaganda.

"Freedom Trumps Socialism" is not a Politically Correct book, aka Socialist Correct, because I want to reveal the truth through the eyes of someone who lived under the Communist-Socialist Hell. The time of niceties and politeness is over. We are on the precipice of our freedom's end and the beginning of a horrific life under Socialist slavery.

It didn't occur to me how much to the Left America shifted until after Barrack Obama was elected as the President of the United States of America. Although I didn't vote for him, I was proud of this country, *and not for the first time, like Michelle Obama*, a black man was elected to the highest office in the land. That election was evident proof that America is not racist, not that I saw much racism in my daily life, anyway. Barack Obama is a Marxist, which I found out after he was elected. But this is democracy. America is strong enough to have him as the President and hopefully not do too much damage.

In retrospect, I consider now 2008 as the year when democracy began to die in America. Fortunately, two years later, the American people voted the Republicans in the majority in Congress, counterbalancing the radical, leftist shift he was about to impose on America. But, unfortunately, the Republicans did not have the fortitude to take a more aggressive and constructive stance against Obama's policies and acted more like the "No" party, a feeble opposition party.

Sadly, we don't see what the reality is until years after it has already happened. For example, in 2012, the Republicans selected "boneless" Mitt Romney to run against Barack Obama. Although Romney had some success against the incumbent President at the beginning of the campaign, he became minced meat once the Dems figured out that Romney was a Remocrat (a Republican of Democrat conviction) and couldn't attract enough conservative votes. Also, Republicans like him are called RINO, Republican in Name Only.

The entire magnitude of the shift to the Left in our country became obvious after we elected Donald Trump for the President of the United States of America. The Leftist democrats had a conniption and dropped any pretenses of being "democrats" and declaring themselves Socialists, like Bernie Sanders, Elizabeth Warner, and Alexandria Ocasio Cortez. They thought they had forever sealed their dominance in the US government, starting with Barack Obama. But they were wrong; the Leftists didn't brainwash all Americans. After losing the election in 2016, the Marxists in the government showed their fangs. I'm talking about the attempt of a coup d'état by the FBI agents and the Justice Department to get rid of Donald Trump. The Russia hoax investigation followed, culminating with the Impeachment of the President over fabricated charges and another one in the last week of his Presidency.

Donald Trump was an aberration. For whatever reason he ran for the Presidency, he was the right man at the right time for freedom. Sure, he's rather rough when he deals with his opponents. Diplomacy and politeness are not his strength, at least in politics, and he thinks a lot of himself. But he stopped the Leftist tide. Temporarily, at least. Now the Democrat Socialists must act quickly before America awakes.

If he had not run for Presidency, Hillary Clinton would have been our President, and socialism would have marched on and take over the highest level of government and continued Obama's Marxist agenda.

In 2020 Donald Trump lost, the Socialists have full power until 2022. Then, unless they screw up royally, they'll be in control, and the United States of America will officially become the United Socialists of America. Biden is doing his best to bring Socialism in the government. Let's hope he'll fail.

Under the excuse of the riots at the Capitol, the Democrat Socialists controlling two branches of the government have free rein to undertake their Socialist initiatives. Republican congressional representatives must pass a litmus test of "purity," showing no Rightist blemish in what they say or write. Georgia Republican congressional representative Marjorie Taylor Greene was stripped of her committee seat for expressing politically incorrect thoughts. Freedom of speech does not exist even in Congress anymore.

According to Joe Biden, the white men are domestic terrorists, worse than Al-Qaeda and ISIS, while Antifa and BLM are heroes despite the mayhem they caused all summer of 2020.

The National Guard soldiers "protecting" the Lawmakers in the Capitol, assuring "democracy at gunpoint," must be vetted to make sure all those white soldiers are not white supremacists. President Biden's Secretary of Defense, Lloyd J. Austin III, —acting as a Communist Political Commissar— will conduct a white supremacist purge throughout the armed forces. Those heterosexual, Christian, white men of "faulty beliefs" must be kicked out or tagged as domestic terrorists.

Not even Hitler purged the German Wehrmacht, but Comrade Stalin did. By 1924 half a million military men were removed from the Red Army, and in the 1926-38 great-purge, he ordered tens of thousands of officers executed.

The new Democrat Socialist Party motto:

If you're not with us, you're against us.
And if you're against us, you will be reeducated or eliminated.

In the United Socialists of America today you better keep in mind this advice:

Beware of what you say,
Or your job may go away

Should we write a new Declaration of Independence, saying:

> *We hold these truths to be self-evident, that all humans are created equitable, that they are endowed by Nature and the Socialist Party with certain unalienable Rights, that among these are Duty, Obedience, and the Pursuit of Collective Happiness.*

Are we living under Socialism or Freedom?

Chapter 12. The Black Plight

I look to a day when people will not be judged by the color of their skin, but by the content of their character.

Martin Luther King, Jr.

How true it is. Dr. Martin Luther King wanted dignity and respect awarded to all people based on their character and not the color of their skin. Today, the Black activists want:

People of color get preferential treatment because of the color of their skin, but not by the content of their character.

This is racism against light color skin people, an ongoing work, with a complete effort of President Biden's administration to implement Critical Race Theory and Equity. If this comes to complete fruition, they will set the race relationships in America back decades.

The history of the Africans, the Black people, is a no ending of suffering. The Arabs enslaved them long before the white slave traders came to the West Africa's shores to buy black slave who were caught by their own brethren. Why so? Do the Blacks make docile slaves, or is it because once removed from Africa; a black person can be easily identified among lighter skin colors.

Whatever the reason, and there can be many more, over four centuries, they took 12 million slaves across the Atlantic to the plantations in South, Central, Caribbean, and North America. Great Britain abolished slavery in 1833. We abolished slavery in the US in 1865, while Brazil had slavery until 1888. But they did not abolish slavery in Africa until 1981 in Mauritania.

What is the incentive for a slave to work? Aside from getting food, shelter, and stay alive, not much else. They were not paid and lived to serve their masters. Lashing and beating were the common methods to force them to work. But as workers, were they productive? Alexis de Tocqueville observed the difference between two adjacent states, on the South that had slavery and, on the North, that didn't have slavery. The Northern State was far more productive than the

Southern States, although the two states shared the same quality of agricultural land.

It reminds me of how unproductive workers were in the former Communist-Socialist countries, where there was no incentive to work. Just like slavery, but without the beating, unless you rebelled.

Not all slave owners were white; there were black slave owners as well. However, all slave owners belonged to the Democrat Party, founded in 1829. In 1857, the Supreme Court ruled blacks were not citizens but property. Seven of the Justices who voted for this ruling were Democrats, while the two Republicans voted against it. It was not until they founded the Republican Party in 1854 as an anti-slavery party and later President Abraham Lincoln was elected that the slaves gained their freedom in 1863, at the cost of over 700 thousand White American men in the Civil War. Yes, there were black soldiers as well who fought for the Union.

Some of the following information came from "Racial Equality and Civil Rights Prager U" video, https://www.facebook.com/watch/?v=1708042499238599 :

After the emancipation, the black people were free, but they lived on the same plantation and had no money, not to mention that the only jobs they could have were from the same employer, the plantation. Union General William T. Sherman planned to give "forty acres and a mule" for each newly freed family as compensation for slavery. That happened in Georgia and South Carolina. But John Wilkes Booth, a Democrat, assassinated President Lincoln six days after the Confederate Army surrendered in 1865. Lincoln's VP, Andrew Johnson, a Democrat, became the new president, and he abandoned the plans for Reconstruction in the South, including any compensation for the freed slaves, and he was against integration.

The blacks were free, but they were at the mercy of the old owners in the South, which were members of the Democrat party. The Democrats opposed the abolition of slavery and started the Civil War. After the war, to prevent the blacks from gaining power, the Democrats formed the infamous Ku Klux Klan, imposed Segregation, and perpetrated lynching of the "trouble makers." In effect, the KKK was the equivalent of Hitler's Brown Shirts in white robes and was responsible for enforcing White Democrat Party rules against the black population through fear. The Democrats in the state legislations were the ones who imposed "Black Codes" like preventing the blacks from owning property and running businesses. After the Voting Rights Amendment was passed, the Democrats created Poll Taxes and Literacy tests to prevent the blacks from voting. The problem was that the blacks were voting Republican and that had to stop.

Jim Crow according to the Wikipedia:

> Jim Crow laws were state and local laws that enforced racial segregation in the Southern United States. These laws were enacted in the late 19th and early 20th centuries by white Southern Democrat-dominated state legislatures to disenfranchise and remove political and economic gains made by black people during the Reconstruction period. The Jim Crow laws were enforced until 1965.

After the emancipation, there was a short period of reconstruction, and the blacks as free men had the liberty to do what any other American could do. However, the Jim Crow laws affirmed by the Supreme Court decided the Blacks and Whites would be equal but segregated. Those set of laws kept the black society at a disadvantage, although nothing like the dependency the War on Poverty created later on.

The Democrat Party has quite a rap sheet on the crimes the committed against the blacks.

Yes, the blacks were free but with little civil and economic liberties. The Democrats were against the Amendments, 13th Abolish Slavery, 14th Citizenship for Blacks, and 15th Voting Rights. The first black citizens elected to Congress were Republicans. It was not until 1935 when the first black Democrat was elected to Congress. In the 1950s and 1964, the Democrats fought the Civil Rights Acts, filibustering in the Senate for 75 days against the bill. It was mostly the Republicans who supported the bill and Democrat President Lyndon Johnson, who shrewdly took all the glory for the Democrat Party.

And so, the black people were kept on the Democrat Plantation and kept voting for their master, the Democrat party. The War on Poverty championed by President Lyndon Johnson, with its welfare system, which destroyed the nuclear families, is afflicting the black society today, keeping them economically disadvantaged. The voucher program's opposition to school choice has kept the black kids from attending better schools, underperforming educationally. According to Shelby Steele or Thomas Sowell, the Liberal higher-education professors and administrations have done more damage to the black young by allowing them to attend universities way beyond their ability to perform and giving them phony academic credentials, which would not help them get employed. The business world knows the truth and is cautious to hire black "educated" people. The result is economic inequality.

The blacks seemed to be the preferred target by the Socialists in the past. The communists attempted to infiltrate America using the blacks but failed. According to "Color, Communism and Common Sense" by Manning Johnson, in the 1950s Moscow restarted a new effort of recruiting and indoctrinating black activists. They sent some of the more promising disciples to Moscow for higher studies. However, the Moscow communist initiative failed again since the blacks, the smart ones, soon realized they were just tools to create dissent among the population. Although the white communists were very friendly during their communist meetings, in public they did not socialize and pretended not to know their black comrades, as shown in the book by Manning Johnson:

> I was lured into the red movement by way of the American Negro Labor Congress, one of the many "front organizations" set up by the communists to trap the naïve, unwary, unsuspecting and idealistic Negro.
>
> Being a Negro top communist, I was placed on the National Negro Commission, an important sub-committee of the National Committee of the Communist Party. On this Commission, which was created on direct orders from Moscow to facilitate the subversion of the Negroes, I began to realize the full implications of how the Negro is used as a political dupe by the Kremlin hierarchy.
>
> These White communists wielded more power than the nominal Negro heads of the Commission. In a word, they are like White overseers. [16: pg 7-8]

Manning Johnson realized they were only tools of the Kremlin, and if one abandoned the cause, there were persecuted as deserters, including losing their job, being shunned from social circles, and denounced as *communists* by the communists. Typical methods employed by the Communist-Socialists in the past, present and future.

The only known outcome of that effort was the Black Panthers, which became a terrorist group. Today the blacks' most successful outcome of the Marxist movement is Black Lives Matter. Although BLM has blacks as "leaders," their handlers are white, rich Marxists, staying in the shadows. Without the millions of dollars supplied by the rich white, BLM would be just a Facebook platform.

Manning Thomas observed a fact about the black society that is so true today, as it was in the past. The white communists in the past and Marxists today have no intention of unfettering the black man or woman, and they want to keep the black society down and remove all the responsibilities from the blacks. The result for a black man is:

> (a) Feel sorry for himself;
> (b) blame other for his failures;
> (c) ignore the countless opportunities around him;
> (d) jealous of the progress of other racial and national groups;
> (e) expect the White man to do everything for him;
> (f) look for easy and quick solutions as a substitute for the harsh realities of competitive struggle to get ahead.
>
> The result is a persecution complex —a warped belief that the White man's prejudices, the White man's system, the White man's government is responsible for everything. [16: pg 44]

Independent minds, leaders, and achievers are not wanted. Black leaders like Jesse Jackson and Al Sharpton, among many others, including N.A.A.C.P. dubbed "The National Association for the Agitation of Colored People," keep the Black society down as victims on the Democrat plantation while enriching themselves. Unfortunately, there are not enough Bob Woodson(s) of the Woodson Center to inspire and uplift the black men and women to stop feeling like victims and stand on their own feet and be winners, self-reliable.

The movie "The Green Book" portrays a story about a black man, a piano prodigy, Donald Shirley, and his white chauffeur and bodyguard Tony "Lip" Vallelonga, taking piano concert tours through the South in 1962. Donald Shirley took this tour, playing for rich white people in the South to elevate the image of the black performer, especially playing classical music. The white driver/bodyguard was needed to protect Shirley from being harassed by the police and other elements in the South. They based the movie's name on a green guide book that was a hotel guide allowing black people to stay. Based on modern concepts, I found it disheartening, seeing the life in those times, during the Jim Crow laws, and disbelieving that life could be that way. But that was life back then, and we came a long way since.

A slight detail that wasn't explained in the movie reflects what Manning Thomas wrote in his book about the communist infiltration in the USA. Based on what they said in the film, Donald Shirley was a prodigy and studied music at the Moscow conservatory. How would a black young man from Florida end up studying in Moscow? That was part of the communist infiltration in America. Take a talented black musician, give him the finest education in Moscow, and send him back to the US to "provoke" the white society through his masterly playing of classical piano. Donald Shirley was accompanied by two string instrument players, who were Donald's communist handlers. The tour was to impress the White Southerners and present the supremacy of communism over racist America. This explanation is mine and was not part of the movie. Philanthropy does not exist under communism, only propaganda.

Unfortunately, today, by what I see on TV and the BLM polemic, most black people want to be judged by the color of their skin and not by their character. What is the Black society doing to better themselves? It is unfortunate that the Liberals and Lyndon Johnson have started the War on Poverty and have destroyed so many black families and their society.

This is what Don Lemon, CNN, said about Blacks when he cared about the Black society:

> More than 72% of African American community children are born out of wedlock. That means absent fathers. And the study shows that lack of a male role model is an express train right to prison. And the cycle continues. So please black folks as a I said, if this doesn't apply to you I'm not talking to you. Pay

> attention to and think about what has been presented in recent history as acceptable behavior. Pay close attention to the hip-hop and rap culture that many of you embrace, a culture that glorifies everything I mentioned, thug and reprehensible behavior. A culture that is making a lot of people rich, just not you and it's not going to.

He said this several years ago, before he "discovered" Systemic Racism and the fault of evil White Men, and in the process, he became Woke.

Is Don Lemon right or wrong? He is right. A society whose family structure has been changed by our Welfare System from paternal, nuclear families to single-mother households with multiple kids from multiple men has been a disaster for the black society.

Let's look at some statistics, not excuses.

The following median household income data as shown by American Community Survey 2018, https://en.wikipedia.org/wiki/List_of_ethnic_groups_in_the_United_States_by_household_income.

Race	Population	Median Household Income
Asians	22,137,269	$85,897
Whites	245,860,228	$65,777
Hispanic/Latinos	59,763,631	$51,404
Black	46,261,485	$41,911

The Asians are the most prosperous race, while the Blacks are least prosperous.

Let's look at family structure and how many families have single parents by race, percentage-wise. From:

https://www.actrochester.org/children-youth/single-parent-families-by-race-ethnicity

Race	Single Parent Percentage
Asians	20 %
Whites	34 %

Hispanic or Latinos	42 %
Black	66 %

The Asians have the least single-parent families. The blacks have the most single-parent families, at 66%, at least in this study, but it could be higher as Don Lemon said.

Let's see what is the employment statistics in 2018, https://www.bls.gov/opub/reports/race-and-ethnicity/2018/home.htm

Race	Unemployment Percentage
Asians	3.0 %
Whites	3.5 %
Hispanic or Latinos	4.7 %
Black	6.5 %

The Asians have the lowest unemployment rate, while the Blacks have the highest. The statistics were taken when the unemployment was the lowest in decades, under Donald Trump Administration.

Let's see what is the higher education situation among the four races in 2019, by enrollment and graduation, NCES Dept of Education and this site: https://www.bls.gov/opub/ted/2020/66-point-2-percent-of-2019-high-school-graduates-enrolled-in-college-in-october-2019.htm

Race	Enrollment %	Graduation %
Asians	89.9 %	74 %
Whites	66.9 %	64 %
Hispanic or Latinos	63.4 %	54 %
Black	50.7 %	40 %

Again, the Asians have the highest higher education enrollment and graduation, while the Blacks lowest. They discriminate against the Asians from entering in the more prestigious schools, while the Blacks are allowed acceptance beyond their abilities.

I took the following statistics about math and reading from "Average National Assessment of Educational Progress (NAEP)

scale scores of 12th-grade students, by race/ethnicity: Selected years, 2005–2015

Race	Mathematics	Reading
Asians	171	297
Whites	160	295
Hispanic or Latinos	139	276
Black	130	266

While searching for the above statistics, I found a ton of information on why Blacks are doing so badly because of race discrimination. The excuses never end. Math and English grammar are considered discriminatory. Chicago school district wants to eliminate history from its curriculum. While soon, California will not use exams for admitting students to colleges. They do all these in the name of Equity. Better said mediocrity. Instead of applying an excellent curriculum, we reduce the standards so the blacks don't appear to perform so poorly.

In China, excellence is number one in their society. How are we going to compete with the Chinese?

And what is the incarceration rates among the four races, https://www.prisonpolicy.org/graphs/raceinc.html, https://www.visualcapitalist.com/visualizing-u-s-population-by-race/

Race	Incarceration rate per 100k	Percentage of US Population
Asians	115	5.6 %
Whites	450	60.1 %
Hispanic/Latinos	831	18.5 %
Blacks	2,306	12.2 %

The Blacks represent 12.2% of our population, at least in this survey, and have the highest incarceration rate per 100,000 people.

The race with the highest prison population are the blacks per the graph taken from Pew Research from 2017: https://www.pewresearch.org/fact-tank/2019/04/30/shrinking-gap-between-number-of-blacks-and-whites-in-prison/

Race	Share of US Prison Population	Share of US Adult Population

Whites	30 %	64 %
Hispanic/Latinos	23 %	16 %
Blacks	33 %	12 %

The data speaks for itself. The Blacks have exceeded the Whites in prison, although the white population is five times larger.

And what is the situation about the police shootings, the reason of being for Black Lives Matter?

The following graph is taken from Washington Post, a Bastion of Leftism,

https://www.washingtonpost.com/graphics/investigations/police-shootings-database/?itid=lk_inline_manual_5

Race	**Population in the US**	**Number Killed**
Others	49,000,000	240
Whites	197,000,000	2,886
Hispanic/Latinos	39,000,000	1,057
Blacks	42,000,000	1,507

As you see the 2,886 Whites are killed by police versus 1,507 of Blacks. Whites are killed 1.9 times more than blacks. But everyone is screaming that blacks are killed disproportionally more than the whites. By population yes, but not by total numbers. Equity cannot be applied here.

When it comes to murder, let's see who is killing who? The following numbers are taken from FBI data for 2019:

https://ucr.fbi.gov/crime-in-the-u.s/2019/crime-in-the-u.s.-2019/tables/expanded-homicide-data-table-6.xls

Victims		**Offenders**			
Race	Total	White	Black	Other	Unknown
White	3,299	2,594	566	56	83
Black	2,906	246	2,574	23	63

According to this data the Whites and the Blacks have the most murders. I realigned the numbers by races.

3,299 Whites are killed by 2,594 Whites and 566 Blacks.
2,906 Blacks are killed by 246 Whites and 2,574 Blacks.
6,205 Victims are killed by 2,840 Whites and 3,140 Blacks.

The Blacks have the largest number of killers, 3,140, and they killed almost as many of their own Blacks, 2,574, as the Whites, 2,594, killed Whites. Considering that the Black population is 46 million, while the White population is 236 million, or 19% of the White population, these numbers are hard to comprehend. The reason and excuses are explained at nauseum by others, justifying the killings and assigning blame on everything but the real reason.

So, what is BLM doing about this? According to Don Lemon, BLM is concerned about white cops killing blacks. White cops killed 13 blacks in one year. What is worst, 13 blacks killed by white cops, or 2,574 blacks killed by blacks? Is this Systemic Racism? Or Black Lives Don't Matter to Black Lives Matter?

Why are the Blacks so unfortunate? The answer shouted to us on every Mainstream Socialist Media, MSM, channel is *racism*. Is it? Why are the Asians doing so much better, aren't they discriminated against as a race? How about Hispanics? They are doing better than the Blacks, although many Hispanics are immigrants, legal or illegal, and do not benefit as the Black population does in all aspects of entitlements.

Blacks are as intelligent as Asians or Whites. We all have the same intelligence given to us by nature, God.

Looking at the pervious data, there is only one explanation, and it starts with the Black Society's family structure and culture. Look at the Asians; family integrity, hard work, discipline, and purpose make them the most successful. That's the culture all other races should emulate, including whites.

America has bent backward to accommodate and help the black society. Constitutional amendments for blacks. Massive welfare programs for housing and nutrition for blacks. Affirmative Action and racial quotas for blacks. Discrimination against other races for entering higher education in favor of blacks. Criminalizing words and actions on behalf of the blacks. Why didn't the black society get ahead? There were no such privileges afforded to Asians, Latinos, Native Americans, and other races. And the Leftists call this Systemic Racism instead of Black Privileges. Some black scholars say that black families were better off under segregation than they are now. That's what the welfare system did to them.

The Liberals, Progressives, Leftists, or Marxists have destroyed the Black Society. Unfortunately, the Black Society continues to be used and abused by the Socialists, and the Black Society accepts and supports the Black Lies Matter, which could care less about blacks.

As long as the Black Society thinks that they are victims, exploited, discriminated, persecuted by the police, victimized by our justice system, and are entitled to free benefits and stuff, nothing will change in their lives. Regardless of the Critical Race Theory outcome, I dare to say, they will be in the same predicament fifty years from now. And just the way the War on Poverty destroyed the Black society, the Critical Race Theory will do even more damage to them.

In the news by David Muir on ABC World News Tonight on 10/27/20, commented about what Jared Kushner said:

> What we've seen in the black Community, which is mostly the Democrats, President Trump policies are policies that can help out people that want to break out of the problems they're complaining about, *but you cannot want for them to be successful more than they want to be successful.*

That's right. Jared Kushner commented about President Trump helping the black community with his policies, but if the black community does not want to be successful, there is nothing to be done. It is as when a horse doesn't want to walk to the water trough to drink. The farmer brings the water to the horse, but the horse doesn't drink. So, what can the farmer do? What can we do? Equity is their answer, which is a formula for disaster.

All the above facts don't matter, and thousands of excuses are told by scholars who know a lot about less and less. Bottom line, what can be done other than pointing fingers at each other. From the previous data, it is evident that the culture and family structure of Asians is at the core of their success. Therefore:

1. If the Welfare system is maintained, it should reward the construction of families, not penalize them.
2. The vouchers for school choice must be instituted.
3. All young blacks committing crimes and caught by the police should be sent to trade boot camps, not to jail.

This sounds like a socialist remedy. It might, but *tough love* gives results.

As long as the Leftists are allowed to sow hatred in our society, the blacks will suffer. If the blacks will not stand up and say: "I am responsible for *my faith*," nothing will change.

Chapter 13. The Communist-Fascist China

There has never been in human history a situation as it is now when a nation allowed another nation to transfer, copy, or steal its industrial technology and production as it happened and happens between the USA/Western World and China. The transfer of economic power that has occurred between the Western World countries and China is bizarre. Every nation wants to keep, protect, and enlarge its industrial base, employment, and technology. However, contrary to the obvious, the United States has willingly, or companies have coercively given away its industry and Intellectual Capital to China.

China has the largest population on Earth, and the Chinese people are hardworking and disciplined. That is very admirable of them. At the same time, the United States economy has been hallowed out, and our industrial employment diminished. Senator Dianne Feinstein praised China, and therefore the Chinese Communist Party, for how much progress it made to eliminate poverty, ignoring the fact that it has impoverished the US workers at the same time. In "McMafia: A Journey Through the Global Criminal Underworld" by Misha Glenny, analyzes the world's criminal organizations. Guess who the number one organized criminal entity is? China. This is on account of how much Intellectual Capital that country has stolen from the United States.

The US Capitalists salivated at the prospect of developing China and the enormous market it could become. They pushed to include China in the World Trade Organizations, WTO, in 2001, and the world has never been the same since. The politicians praised the move, bringing China into the "brotherhood" of Nations. But, instead, they brought in the Chinese Dragon.

China used to be a Communist-Socialist country, and as long as Mao lived, there was no way to end that faulty ideology, which would have caused the collapse of Communist China shortly after 1989. Fortunately for China, it had practical communists among them, and they became the cheap labor market of the world, achieving prosperity. Deng Xiaoping recognized the fallacy of Marxism when he said:

> *It doesn't matter whether a cat is black or white, as long as it catches mice.*

It doesn't make any difference if the Chinese economy becomes capitalist if it improves their economic situation. Under Deng Xiaoping's leadership, he opened China for business after 1982, offering its millions of cheap laborers to the outside world, the one asset they have plenty of. People don't work hard for the glory of Communism-Socialism, but will work harder when they gain something for themselves. Therefore, the Chinese Communist Party kept its political power but converted economically from Communism-Socialism to Communism-Fascism, (aka National Socialism.)

The difference between Marxism-Socialism and National-Socialism is that the Fascists do not confiscate the wealth of the wealthy citizens in their country, allow capitalism under the party's control, but confiscate the wealth of other countries. But China did not invade any country. Of course not. It doesn't have to invade the United States as long as it can take away the US industry and employment and bring it to China. No need for occupation. Besides, China owns a sizeable chunk of our debt. Why invade when they can foreclose?

Although China has many billionaires, they do what the CPC tells them to do, or else. Therefore, I find it ridiculous when I hear on the news that so and so Chinese students or scientists, or businessmen have relationships with CPC and the Chinese Military. Make no mistake, all Chinese nationals are responsible and obligated to serve China and the CPC.

According to Wikipedia:

China has been the fastest growing economy in the world since the 1980s, with an average annual growth rate of 10% from 1978 to 2005, based on government statistics.

In 1980, the Chinese economy was $191 billion, while in 2019, it was 14 trillion. Without a doubt, China has become an economic powerhouse. It has a strong industry, through the acquisition of all the Western technology. The Chinese scientists are making breakthroughs with the technology they gained or stole from us, getting ahead of us.

Is there anything that we buy that isn't made in China? It didn't become apparent how much we depend on China's manufacturing until the pandemic of 2020 when we didn't have enough masks and protective clothing. That should have been a wake-up call, and we as a country need to correct that deficiency in all areas of manufacturing if we don't want to jump when China says jump or die when China keeps the supplies for itself.

When President Trump began negotiations with China regarding trade, the Mainstream Socialist Media hollered how restricting imports from China will hurt us, especially the poor, their usual mantra. Same hypocrites said nothing when our middle class lost their jobs to China, becoming the new poor and dying from opioids overdoses. So, we behold to China now. But wait a minute, when it comes to the relationship between supplier and customer, who has more leverage? The customer has all the leverage, and we, the Americans, are the customers. What will happen to China if America stops buying from them? In 2020 China's economy slowed down because the rest of the world stopped buying. We have the power, but our Corporate-Bureaucrats will continue selling the rope to China, with which China will hang us. The Chinese economy is sensitive to American buyers, and they feel the immediate increase or decrease in our buying habits. One article I read in the New Yorker illustrated how a sneaker manufacturer selling to Americans on Amazon saw its sales decrease because of the pandemic and then increase within days after the US Government paid the incentive checks out to the Americans. Americans spent our American incentive dollars to help Chinese workers.

Should we be worried about China? Or believe Joe Biden:

"C'mon man, China is no competition for us."

China has infiltrated our economy, political system, and academic institutions through sweet business deals, donations, and outright bribes.

The Majority leader in the Senate, Mitch McConnell, is married to a Chinese woman, Elaine Chao, the daughter of a Chinese magnate doing business with China. How much is China influencing him?

California Representative Eric Swalwell had an affair for many years with a Chinese woman, Fang Fang, and helped him raise money for his political career and elections. How much is China influencing him? Do the Chinese have embarrassing pictures of Eric and Fang in bed? You bet they do.

Dianne Feinstein had a Chinese spy working for her for 20 years. Was she kicked out of the Senate? No. Her husband is doing business in China. How much is China influencing her?

Joe Biden, our current president, tops them all. His son Hunter Biden traveled to China with his dad on Airforce 2 and conducted personal business in that country. He returned home with a Chinese fund worth $1.5 billion. At 10% commission, you can only imagine how much money he and the Biden family stand to make. The morons accused Donald Trump of being Putin's man. Joe Biden is definitely Xi Jinping man. How much is China influencing Joe Biden?

I saw a video clip about a conference in China discussing the return of good days after Donald Trump is out of the office and "their man" Joe Biden is in the White House. Yes, the United States still matters, but for how long? The Mainstream Socialist Media, as directed by the Democrat Socialist Party Politburo and the dishonest politicians like Adam Schiff and Eric Swalwell, are constantly reminding us about the Russian threat. In this case, I would have to paraphrase Joe Biden, "*C'mon man, Russia is no threat to us*." Direct the public's attention to an imaginary threat like Russia, with an economy smaller than Italy's, while China is taking over quietly. The writing is on the wall, and it reminds me how the Roman Empire collapsed by having corrupt politicians and collapse of its culture.

China is populous, its people are hardworking and disciplined, and their leaders are National-Communists, just like Hitler and the NAZI-Germany were in the last century. As a result, the Chinese Communist

Party will make China the most significant power globally, and they will have the largest military, largest economy, the strongest currency, and foreign influence unmatched by the United States.

World War II in the Pacific happened because Japan wanted to be the Pacific Ocean Power. China has the same aspirations, and it will become the Pacific Ocean Power. Unlike the United States, whose policies change with each election's winds, China is a one-party state and has a leader for life. Their goals are obvious, and their plans extend for 100 years, rather than four years like ours. Here we see the difference between Democracy and Totalitarianism. Is Totalitarianism superior? Yes, if we let democracy and freedom die.

In my travels, I'm amazed how much the Chinese have expanded their influence over smaller and weaker nations using economic help and loans as a new form of colonialism. China is all over Africa, and the Pacific Island states. In Western Samoa, the Chinese built a brand-new government building for that island country, with Chinese workers, of course. Chinese-owned Landbridge Group leases and operates port Darwin in Australia for a 99-year lease. How long will it be before it leases and operates the Port of Los Angeles, or Long Beach? In the Western African countries, the Chinese have large plants making fish meals to feed farm fisheries in China. How do they make the fish meal? They fish any fish from the Atlantic that may not be tasty for consumers, and churn the catch in a yellow protein powder as fish meals to feed farmed carp or salmon. The local fishermen's yield has been wiped out. No fish will be safe from extinction, while all fish becomes a source of protein mining. Even the sharks are in danger from the Chinese fishermen. The shark is not an edible fish, but for whatever reason, their fins and tails make a "delicious" soup, as far as the Chinese prefer. The sharks are caught in nets, their fins and tails cut off and then thrown back in the water, where they will die soon, unable to swim.

The wildlife in Africa is in peril from the poachers who kill Elephants and Rhinos for their tasks and horns, respectively. Rhino horns are used as an aphrodisiac in China. I guess China doesn't have enough people. They kill an entire animal for a horn that could be cut off and then will regrow. The seahorses around the Philippines waters are overfished by the Filipinos to be sold to the Chinese, for medicinal purposes. Like most Asians, the Chinese eat everything, including bats and pangolins, as we found out about the wet markets in Wuhan. Wait until the Chinese start killing whales or dolphins, if they haven't done so already. Unfortunately, the wildlife on land and sea is in more danger than ever before.

The Communist-Socialists countries have polluted the environment with impunity. In the USSR, Siberia, in 1957, at Mayak nuclear complex, while building their atomic bomb, a tank of radioactive waste exploded and the radioactive plume extended for over 200 miles. Entire towns and villages disappeared off the map. The people were relocated just as it happened at Chernobyl. In Socialist Romania, the sludge from a mining operation flooded a valley and drowned an entire village. Only the steeple of the church protruded out of a lake of sludge. China fires up a coal power plant every month, and we have to reduce our pollution? The Democrats and Leftists present themselves as the environment champions instead of the biggest polluters, with China leading the way.

But wait, we did the same thing; why blame China? Yes, we're guilty, but we also wised up and try to correct our past mistakes. The Chinese economy is growing, and don't want to agree on any restrictions. The Climate Change agreement is a perfect example of how the Chinese behave. That's the reason why President Trump withdrew from the Paris Accord, and President Biden re-joined. Saving our planet is a good thing, but not when the US has to cut most of our emissions, at enormous cost, and pay other foreign nations to cut their emissions, while China, India, and Russia will not, on the pretext of being developing nations. Cutting pollution in China is easy to accomplish. Stop importing anything from China that pollutes and bring the manufacturing back to our country while we still cut pollution as promised. But this is the dirty secret. We cut our pollution by exporting the polluting industries to China. As I mentioned, certain industries may not become clean industries, ever.

China's military ambitions are clear; at first, it dominates the South China Sea and then the Pacific. They are expanding their Navy and now have aircraft carriers. They are taking over uninhabited islands, some in the water territories of other nations, and transform them into military bases. To become an economic power, China must become a military power as well, and they are making substantial progress. One of their long-time goals is to invade Taiwan and annex it. The United States protects Taiwan through agreement. But considering that China has a friend in the White House from 2021 to 2024, I wouldn't be surprised if China will not invade Taiwan during President Biden's administration. And if they invade, what will the US do? What did the US do when China broke its promise about democracy in Hong Kong? Nothing. Also keep an eye on North Korea; nothing emboldens Kim Jong-un, the supreme leader, than a weak American President.

China is already in space, being the third nation to send a man in space in 2003. They also landed on the dark side of the Moon. There are plans to send a Chinese space station into orbit in 2022. Following that, they intend to land on the Moon. China's space success was built at the beginning with Russian technology. With technical information obtained through spying on the US Space technology they advanced to the point of landing on the dark side of the Moon. Exploring space is good for all humanity, but just like the Soviets, the Chinese Space program and the military are one and the same. In 2007 China launched a missile that blew up their own low-orbiting satellite, creating debris that could be dangerous to other satellites and disrespecting international agreements.

However, all that I mentioned above pales compared to what China is doing to our freedom of expression. Our Democrat Socialist government is misleading us by saying that Russia is our enemy and not China. Aside from nuclear weapons, Russia is insignificant compared to China, the real villain. The MSM obediently promotes the same lies and says nothing about how China is ruining us. Hollywood makes movies that are self-censored to appease China. If they don't, China will not allow those movies released in China. The NBA, making vast fortunes from telecasting the basketball games in China, is completely under the speak-no-evil-about-China rule.

China keeps Chinese expatriates or Americans in fear of expressing any damaging thoughts about the Chinese Communist Party. The following is from the New Yorker Magazine article "Ghost Walls" of April 12, 2021, about how the Chinese Foreign Ministry views any political dissent:

> Fear permeates the émigré [Chinese] community. As a recent Freedom House report notes, "China conducts the most sophisticated, global, and comprehensive campaign of transnational repression in the world." Its tactics have ranged from digital intimidation and threats of lawsuits to unlawful deportation. Recently, Xi Jinping's government took an unprecedented step: sanction Western academics whose work on Xinjiang [province in China where the Uyghurs are politically persecuted] it found objectional.
>
> "They will have to pay a price for their ignorance and arrogance," the Foreign Ministry declared.

They make direct threats against people who dare to speak up. A person was told by a Chinese woman in Washington:

> She said, "If you get poisoned, do you know how to treat yourself?" the threatened person responded, "Why should I know that?" She replied, "You know the Chinese government is very powerful. You could die in a car accident, or get poisoned."

We heard about Russian dissidents that Kremlin poisoned. China will do the same and more against whoever speaks against them. The Chinese digitally stole the federal government employees' information. Who knows how they'll use that information in the future? But they have plans. As China grows more powerful, the Chinese Communist Big Brother will watch you, here in your home country, the USA, just as they watch a billion and a half people in China.

From the same article, "Ghost Walls," of April 12, 2021, I discovered that China is actively engaged in genocide and re-programming of the Uyghur (non-Chinese) people. In Xinjiang province, the Uyghur people are mass incarcerated to teach them Mandarin Chinese, indoctrination in the Marxist-Leninist-Maoism ideology, forced to divulge other people who object to the Chinese government, and asked to write in Chinese a self-denunciation document. The Uyghurs sent to prisons or camps are called "students" to be re-educated. They put many of them in forced labor until they learn the communist, correct way of being Chinese citizens. Before they release the Uyghurs, their DNA is sampled, and their pictures taken, which are entered in giant databases for street cameras to recognize them in the future and if they need to be arrested again. Re-programming and Genocide in the 21st century? It happens in Communist-Fascist China today.

What we feared about Hitler and his NAZI-Socialist party of Germany was the ability of a totalitarian government, with a strong industry, hardworking, diligent, educated, and disciplined people to start a war of conquest as the supreme race. If it weren't for America, NAZI-Socialist Germany would have conquered the USSR and become a world superpower instead. The United States and the Soviet Union were engaged in a cold war for 44 years, a war between Freedom and Tyranny. Fortunately, the Soviet Union was not an economic superpower, and it ended.

Communist-Fascist China is the equivalent of NAZI Germany with a totalitarian government, a strong industry, hardworking, diligent, educated, and disciplined people of one and half billion, almost five times that of the US population. After their incredible industrial success and the decay of the American superpower, the Chinese people will believe that they are the master race. We cannot deny the results of their success. Believing that they are the master race hasn't happened yet because the Communist Party takes all the credit, and the individual is unimportant. The party is supreme, not the people. But even that could change. Although China has not achieved the per capita wealth of the United States, and its military is not equal to ours, it is a matter of time, at most a decade, before Communist-Fascist China will be the ultimate superpower on Earth. All this happened because we wanted cheaper jeans, T-shirts, and sneakers. And then TVs and iPhones.

If I sound like I'm bashing China, I'm not bashing the Chinese people. They have a right to prosperity as any other nation on Earth. Instead, the blame goes to the Chinese Communist Party and their Communist-Fascist government that wants to make China into a superpower at any cost, at full speed, damn the human rights, freedom, environment, and the wildlife.

What do we need to do? Stop buying Chinese products and bring the industry back to America.

President Kennedy. They considered President Kennedy a weak president and sent nuclear missiles to Cuba. President Kennedy was not soft and, in 1962, imposed a naval "quarantine" that was, in fact, a blockade. The Soviets retrieved the missiles.

As Jimmy Carter was our President, the Soviet Union invaded Afghanistan in 1979 without fear of retribution. Jimmy Carter didn't do much, aside from boycotting their Olympics, to dissuade the Soviets from occupying that country. What could he have done short of war? Major economic embargo. Later, Afghanistan was engulfed in a civil war, and the Taliban eventually won, allowing Al-Qaeda to set camp in the country and strike against the United States; Nine-Eleven 2001 was the result.

In 1979 the Sandinistas, a socialist guerilla supported by Cuba, ousted dictator Anastasio Somoza and instituted a socialist government in Nicaragua. Somoza may have been a dictator, but he was a reliable ally of the United States. So, what did Jimmy Carter do to help Nicaragua stay free from socialism? Nothing and Nicaragua became a socialist country, struggling even today to be free from under Sandinistas and dictator Daniel Ortega.

In 1979, the Iranian Revolution or the Islamic Revolution overthrew Shah Mohammad Reza Pahlavi, and Ayatollah Ruhollah Khomeini formed an Islamic republic, calling the United States the great Satan. President Jimmy Carter declared himself a good friend of the Shah and could have supported him to defeat the Islamists. But Jimmy Carter was a coward and did no such thing, and the Shah was overthrown. Worse yet, when the Shah needed medical treatment in the US, Carter did not allow him in. The Shah died in exile shortly after.

To make the matter worse, on November 4, 1979, a group of Islamic revolutionaries, claiming to be students, took over the American Embassy in Teheran and took over 60 Americans hostages. Negotiations and a military rescue mission failed to release the hostages. Finally, the captors freed the hostages on January 21, 1981, after President Ronald Reagan delivered his inaugural address and replaced Carter. The hostages were held captors for 444 days and not liberated until Ronald Reagan became the President. It was not a gift to Reagan but fear of what President Reagan could do to Iran. Power promotes respect.

Iran continues to be an Islamic Republic, a Theocracy, and the Ayatollahs are determined to become the Middle East superpower, determined to build nuclear missiles and destroy Israel. All these developments happened because Jimmy Carter was President, one of the worst President in the modern age, although Joe Biden is working hard to take that title from Carter.

President Barack Hussein Obama II,

44th President, 2009 to 2017, Democrat Party.

President Barack Obama is a Democrat Marxist. He made no bones about hiding his Leftists allegiances, but the MSM covered it very well. He still is a populist President, endowed with charm and eloquent speech. However, he is the first President who hates America, the country of his birth. His hero was his father, Barack Obama Sr. from Kenya. Although a married man, his father married Barack's mother Ann Dunham, and had nothing to do with raising Barack Jr., seeing him only one time when Barrack was ten years old.

His mother's second husband was Lolo Soetoro, a Muslim from Java, and Barack lived in Jakarta, Indonesia, for about four years, learning in Muslim schools. Despite the lack of parental contact with Obama Sr., Barack accepted his father's anti-colonial beliefs, and in turn, he hated America, the symbol of white colonialism. As an adult and married to Michelle, they attended Jeremiah Wright's congregation, who professed hatred toward America. However, that did not dissuade him from politics, and it culminated with his election as the President of the United States, beating Hillary Rodham Clinton.

President Obama had a two-track policy, make America Socialist, enforce equity in government hiring, and destroy the USA as a superpower. Make America one among equals, not superior as we are and should be.

His most known achievement toward socialism is the Affordable Care Act, the Obama Care, which he was able to pass in the first two years of his presidency when the Congress was Democrat-controlled. Luckily for us, he lost control of Congress after the 2010 election and was kept in check by the Republicans. That didn't dissuade him from passing socialist executive orders.

His pro-Muslim inclinations were well known, bowing deep and long to the Saudi Arabian king. He had a stance of indifference to Israel and had a great affinity towards the Arab nations and Iran in particular. With the help of John Kerry, the US Secretary of State, he reached the Iran nuclear deal preliminary framework agreement in 2015. Iran could continue to enrich uranium but was subject to international inspections. In exchange, sanctions on Iran were lifted, and Iran prospered by selling its oil and gas.

In another hostage situation exchange deal, President Obama gave Iran $1.8 billion. The first installment was $400 million of cash to free the hostages. Iran is good at hostage taking. Thanks to President Obama, Iran was free to prosper and get $1.8 billion as a reward. What does Iran do with that money? Finance terrorism in the Middle East and send rockets to the Palestinians to attack Israel.

President Joseph Robinette Biden Jr.,

46th President, 2021 to present, Democrat Party.

President Joe Biden is a Democrat and a charlatan. Why a charlatan? Joe has no character and stooped as low as it took to become the President of the United States. As a President, this man is dangerous, not because of his intellect, which he has none, but because of his ego. He tried several times before for the presidency and failed. In 2020 he was the best alternatives for the Democrats between Bernie Sanders, a declared socialist, and many other liberals. He gave the impression of being the center candidate for the Democrat Party.

If Joe Biden has an ideology, it is inconsequential to his desire to be called President. And not only the President but the most progressive President. I don't think Joe Biden is progressive, but he will be whatever it takes to achieve his goal of being a historical figure. I am convinced that he won the election because of fraud. Why am I saying that? The zeal by which the Democrat party and the Mainstream Socialist Media denies wrongdoing, not allowing the verification of the results, and destroying anyone of importance if they mention electoral fraud. Mass mailing of ballots is inherently prone to fraud.

He will do significant damage to our country if he ends his term or Kamala Harris succeeds him. Why?

The illegal mass migration across our southern borders. There is no doubt that the Democrats want to expand their undocumented democrat voter numbers by changing the population make-up of our country. President Joe Biden obliges. Hundreds of thousands of immigrants crossing unobstructed in our country, not screened for Covid 19, helped to resettle throughout our country at our tax expenses and while undermining our poorest Americans' jobs and wages. Not to mention the additional strain put on our social programs by the illegal children.

President Biden surrounded himself with Obama's operatives who make the executive decisions for him, decisions that scream Socialism. He wants to make a name for himself by enforcing Critical Race Theory and eliminating Systemic Racism, where there is none. Equity is paramount to him, damn the equality. And race purity by eliminating the imagined "white terrorists" from our government and military, declaring that white supremacists are more dangerous than Al-Qaeda and ISIS combined. Commissar Austin, Secretary of Defense Lloyd J. Austin, is engaged in a purge of the radical white supremacists from the military. They performed purges in all Communist-Socialist countries, the most famous being Stalin. Under Stalin, the purged officers were executed; what will they do to our officers?

President Biden is determined to have the entire population vaccinated for Covid-19, including children. Why? What is in those vaccines that he wants all of us to get? In due course of time we may find out. He is determined to nationalize the elections, and continue fraudulent elections, using mail in ballots. When States, like Georgia and Texas, passed laws to ensure proper voting, he called that Jim Crow on steroids and the biggest challenge to us since the Civil War. All this over having to vote in person and showing an ID. The lunatics are running the asylum.

This is what we have become under President Biden, Socialist. President Joe Biden is presiding over a new rein of socialist terror in the Land of the Free.

Book 2. Hitler's Playbook

After I wrote the book "Hitler Was a Socialist," I learned more about socialism than I knew from experience and schooling about what socialism was and the many ways it comes to power. The preferred methods of the past to impose Marxism-Socialism on a country were through bloodshed, revolutions as Russia, Cuba, China, and other countries in Asia have done. Hitler rewrote the book on political power grab through legal elections. Today, more than ever, our country is in jeopardy of becoming Marxist-Socialist, through a great effort of the American Democrat Socialist Party. Surprisingly, the American Democrat Socialist Party uses Adolf Hitler's playbook as the blueprint to introduce and establish full-pledged Marxism-Socialism in the United States of America.

Marxism-Socialism had early roots in America, and after WW I, it became a political force. Luckily for us, our predecessors were vigilant and snuffed out this ideology. However, that doesn't mean that Marxism-Socialism did not have any effect on our government's policies. Windrow Wilson was a socialist. Many of President Franklin D Roosevelt's initiatives were socialist, and he leaned Left. He admired Hitler and Mussolini for their leadership and for solving the economic problems caused by the Great Depression. However, the march toward socialism did not end, and the War on Poverty moved our country closer to that goal.

Chapter 1. Ideology

All movements, political, cultural, social, religious, economic, moral, are based on an ideology, written or unwritten.

What is Ideology? According to Merriam Webster:

> A manner or the content of thinking characteristic of an individual, group, or culture.

In short, it is a set of philosophical ideas that guide us. "The Ten Commandments" is an ideology. Every set of beliefs has an ideology. Without one is like navigating without a compass.

Ideologies according to Wikipedia:

> **Conservatism** in the United States is a political and social philosophy which characteristically shows respect for American traditions, republicanism, and limited federal governmental power in relation to the states, referred to more simply as limited government and states' rights.

Individual Freedom was left out of this definition, which is the most important factor of Conservatism.

> **Liberalism** aims at the preservation and extension of human, social and civil rights as well as the government guaranteed provision of positive rights. It combines social progressivism and to some extent ordoliberalism [German variant of economic liberalism] and is highly similar to European social liberalism.
>
> **Progressivism** in the United States is a political philosophy and reform movement that reached its height early in the 20th century. ... Historian Alonzo Hamby describes American progressivism as a "political movement that addresses ideas, impulses, and issues stemming from modernization of American society.

In other words, keep up with the times, no matter how crazy our society gets.

> **Socialism** is a political, social, and economic philosophy encompassing a range of economic and social systems characterized by social ownership of the means of production. ... Social ownership can be public, collective, cooperative, or of equity.

Ownership of all industry and commerce means State ownership. Collective and cooperative concepts are placating words to prevent a bloody uprising by the peasants. Still, the Communist Party controls those entities through the power of the Police State.

> **Fascism** is a form of far-right, authoritarian ultranationalism characterized by dictatorial power, forcible suppression of opposition, and strong regimentation of society and of the economy.

No. Fascism is not far-Right but Leftist, as I explained previously. Ultranationalism is not a mark of fascism. The USSR was ultranationalist as well as all other socialist countries. After people lose faith in socialism, the next thing the government relies on to stay in power is *nationalism*. Fascism is National-Socialism ideology that is based on Marxism.

> **Nazism** is a form of fascism, with disdain for liberal democracy and the parliamentary system. It incorporates fervent antisemitism, anti-communism, scientific racism, and the use of eugenics into its creed.

Nazism is National-Socialism ideology and based on Marxism. All socialist ideologies disdain the liberal democracy and the parliamentary system. Since Nazism and Communism are based on Marx ideology, communism must be eliminated as the competition. Nazism is a racist ideology.

As I mentioned earlier, Fascism and Nazism are Left ideologies, not as Stalin wants us to believe.

> **Communism** is a philosophical, social, political, and economic ideology and movement whose ultimate goal is the establishment of a communist society, namely a socioeconomic order structured upon the ideas of common ownership of the means of production and the absence of social classes, money, and the state.

In short, the above ideologies can be described in a few words as follows:

Conservatism – Individualism and Freedom, Democracy.

Liberalism - Social and Civil Rights, Statism.

Progressivism – More radical than Liberalism, Statism on Steroids

Socialism – State economic ownership for the "good" of the people, aka the Proletariat Dictatorship.

Fascism – State economic control for the "good" of the people, Nationalist Dictatorship.

Nazism - Nationalist economic control for the "good" of a race of people, Nationalist Dictatorship.

Communism – The Government owns everything, including the individual. Human=Ant=Bee.

The simplest definition of Marxism-Socialism and Fascism is as follows:

Marxism: Socialism with nationalized economy.
Fascism: Socialism with private economy.

I didn't include the far-right ideologies, which are the Oligarchy Dictatorship. We don't have to worry about them in the US.

As you see, it starts with the individual, free to do as God created him or her. Then, as we progress down, the State takes over what the individual is allowed to do based on secular rules and laws until the individual as an entity disappears.

Adolf Hitler described the National-Socialism ideology out in "Mein Kampf." That book became the bible of the NAZI-Socialists, and was the basis for the party's action plan described in the NAZI-Socialism's Twenty-five Point Political Program. It is an expanded version of the Communist Manifesto and parts of the Critical Race Theory (the Aryan race theory.) Hitler's succession to power is an excellent guide for the American Democrat Socialist Party to introduce and establish a full-fledged dictatorship, neo-Socialism, in the United States of America.

The Marxists in the USA don't need to invent a new ideology as Hitler did. They have the ready-made Communist Manifesto to guide them and many other writings by various Marxist-Leninists to augment their ideology, such as the Critical Theories. But, Marxism-Socialism was proven a disastrous ideology. Even the Woke-Zombies would understand that if they would listen to past experiences about Socialism. Unfortunately, the remaining socialist countries in the world like Cuba, North Korea, and Venezuela's emerging basket case adhere stupidly and criminally to the Communist Manifesto.

Jesus says in the New Testament:

> Every kingdom divided against itself will be laid waste, and no town or house divided against itself will stand. [Mathew 12, 25]

Ideologies cannot only inspire the followers but divide a nation as well. The Critical Theory, Feminist Theory, LGBTQ, the Critical Race Theory and others like them are divisive teachings to destroy Freedom.

Since the collapse of the communist economic systems and communism was discredited, the Leftists renamed themselves Liberals, Progressives, Socialists, or even Marxists.

The same horror house under new name and management.

Chapter 1.1 The Communist Manifesto.

1. **Abolition of property in land and application of all rents of land and public purposes.**
Abolition means confiscation of all private, income producing property, businesses, commerce, Intellectual Capital, and so on. Only the Government or the State can own the economy, and therefore exploit the people, instead of the capitalists. No one may "exploit" other people to get rich.
2. **A heavy progressive or graduated income tax.**
Tax the productive, the efficient, the innovative, the enterprising, the hardworking, the risk taker, and even the "lottery lucky" to redistribute any excess wealth. No one may get rich.
3. **Abolition of all rights of inheritance.**
If your parents are rich and somehow their wealth was not confiscated already, all the wealth goes to the state after they die. The survivors will be penniless, just like the rest of us. It doesn't take a leap of fate to wonder why work harder and save for the future instead of spending it all now, or retiring early?
4. **Confiscation of the property of all emigrants and rebels.**
If you decide to flee the socialist state or oppose them, all your properties/wealth will be confiscated, unless you transferred your cash and gold offshore. I possessed nothing before I escaped from Romania, so they confiscated nothing for my crime of defecting.
5. **Centralization of credit in the hands of the State, by means of a national bank with State capital and an exclusive monopoly.**
All financial institutions, banks, including the Federal Reserve will become the property of the state under one National Bank. The money printing machine belongs to the State. No other foreign bank may do business within a Socialist country. Strict control over the country's currency is essential.
6. **Centralization of the means of communication and transport in the hands of the State.**
The state owns all means of communication, like the postal service, public or private, telephone, Internet, TV, radio and Internet media, including Facebook, Twitter, Google, Instagram and all others.

Facebook, YouTube, Twitter, and Google will be a treasure of personal information for the government. All transportation like ships, trains, buses, trucks, highways and railways, and perhaps cars will be the state's property. The State will control all communications and movement of people.

7. **Extension of factories and instruments of production owned by the State; the bringing into cultivation of wastelands, and the improvement of soil generally in accordance with a common plan.**

This is State central planning of the economy. Since all production capability is in the hands of the state, the state must do all the planning. The problem is, do party bureaucrats know better than business owners how to plan for the industry? Never. That's why Socialist economies fail.

8. **Equal liability of all to labor. Establishment of industrial armies, especially for agriculture.**

Everyone Must Work; even if you have enough money or live off the back of your parents or others, you must work to partake in the society's benefits. There will be no free higher education if your parents don't work, or free medical if you don't work. Keep in mind that when they wrote the manifesto agriculture was a large part of the economy, and even that sector must be under the State's supervision.

9. **Combination of agriculture with manufacturing industries; gradual abolition of the distinction of town and country, by a more equable distribution of the population over the country.**

This is social engineering or population redistribution. The state sees that everyone is economically or geographically equal by establishing industries where none were there before. No overcrowding of cities. Not because of health reasons but the people can organize easier in the dense populations of the cities and start riots.

10. **Free education of all children in public schools. Abolition of children's factory labor in its present form. Combination of education with industrial production, etc., etc."**

This is good, free education and abolition of child labor, which has been instituted worldwide (mostly) since then. Unfortunately, the

Liberal American Corporations are the ones accepting child labor in some of the overseas manufacturing plants. Capitalism did not invent child labor. All children throughout the ages in agrarian societies worked along with their parents from sunrise to dusk, during harvest season. That's the reason children have summer vacations.

Chapter 1.2 The Critical Theory.

The Communist Manifesto took the socialism ideology only so far, even with improvements from Lenin, aka Marxism-Leninism. Sure, Marxism-Socialism took roots in Russia, but nowhere else before the WW II. Marx predicted that all industrialized nations would become socialist. It did not happen at the speed the Marxists expected because they didn't consider the increase in productivity under Capitalism and, therefore, an increased standard of living. A new ideology based on Marxism, the Fascism/National-Socialism, was more successful, spreading faster, without destroying the Capitalism.

Something was missing. Enter the new Marxist-Socialist elite professors at Frankfurt School in Germany in the 1920s and 1930s who thought hard and deep and found out what the problem was. Their solution was the Critical Theory. According to Wikipedia:

> Critical theory (also capitalized as Critical Theory) is an approach to social philosophy that focuses on reflective assessment and critique of society and culture in order to reveal and challenge power structures. With origins in sociology and literary criticism, it argues that social problems are influenced and created more by societal structures and cultural assumptions than by individual and psychological factors. Maintaining that ideology is the principal obstacle to human liberation, critical theory was established as a school of thought primarily by the Frankfurt School theoreticians Herbert Marcuse, Theodor Adorno, Walter Benjamin, Erich Fromm, and Max Horkheimer. Horkheimer described a theory as critical insofar as it seeks "to liberate human beings from the circumstances that enslave them."

In their satanic minds, they figured that human beings are enslaved by the political and economic systems that exist now, Capitalism. Never mind that the Capitalism system evolved organically, developed by individuals, and displaced the feudal system where the population's poverty was 99%.

Religion, societal and cultural structures are responsible for keeping us enslaved. No one came from Mars and imposed those structures upon us; we created them. What keeps us believing in false ideologies is the nuclear family structure. Yes, our parents unknowingly are "brainwashing" us to believe in obsolete customs. Therefore, everything must be abolished and re-built a new selfless, collective-citizen to build Communism.

Chapter 1.3 The Critical Feminist Theory.

Since we talk about the nuclear family, we must address the patriarchy issue. Male-dominated society at the expense of the women. We have the Critical Feminist Theory and a few points about it from https://owl.purdue.edu/owl/subject_specific_writing/writing_in_literature/literary_theory_and_schools_of_criticism/feminist_criticism.html

1. Women are oppressed by patriarchy economically, politically, socially, and psychologically; patriarchal ideology is the primary means by which women are oppressed.
2. In every domain where patriarchy reigns, woman is other: she is marginalized, defined only by her difference from male norms and values.
3. All of Western (Anglo-European) civilization is deeply rooted in patriarchal ideology, for example, in the Biblical portrayal of Eve as the origin of sin and death in the world.
4. While biology determines our sex (male or female), culture determines our gender (scales of masculine and feminine).
5. All feminist activity, including feminist theory and literary criticism, has as its ultimate goal to change the world by prompting gender equality.

6. Gender issues play a part in every aspect of human production and experience, including the production and experience of literature, whether we are consciously aware of these issues or not.

This is why Hillary never stops saying *misogynism.* If Bill Clinton controls her, she has the right to say so, but I doubt it. I don't control my wife, but we have a partnership in which we both prosper together.

The insistence that men and women are equal was distorted by the feminist movement. Everyone knows for a fact that 100% of all babies are born by women, and 0% by men. Our prisons contain 91% males and 9% females showing the differences between the two sexes. An agricultural society depended on brute force and was a patriarchal society, but as the industrial revolution progressed and women entering the job market, the patriarchy lost its meaning. With all its advances, capitalism eliminated physical work by using machines, which are controlled by mental work. And when it comes to intelligence, men are not superior to women. Our mental capabilities are the same. When smarts and education come into play, women and men can perform the same jobs. As a matter of fact, there are more women than men enrolled in colleges. When it comes to STEM (Science, Technology, Engineering, Mathematics), according to the National Science Foundation for under 29 years of age, women make 56% of the workforce, whereby for all ages, women make 43%. The sciences category includes social sciences, education, and health, which are dominated by women. In the nursing field, the women are 91%, while men only 9%. For teachers, there are 76% women teachers versus 24% for men.

Only 20% of women are graduating in engineering. What's holding the women back? There are a lot of excuses, and most are fabricated to justify women's exploitation by men. Was there discrimination in the past against women? Sure, but now women are ahead of men in higher education. However, the type of smarts and inclination women have may differ from those of men, as shown by the participation in the various fields. Suppose when women do not excel in a specific field, they are discriminated against, but men are not discriminated against if they are minorities in other fields. Why is this absurd insistence that men and women have to be the same in every aspect?

We are biologically different from conception. I do not accept the LGBTQ bullshit that you are what you believe you are.

Maybe it has to do with nature, why women are attracted to the humanitarian type of professions and men to the technical types. But no. The feminist movement insists that there should be an equal number of men and women in all fields of education and work. In other words, equity. There is absolutely nothing to stop women from selecting their higher education and career, except the way God made us. But not for a moment, I think that women cannot obtain Electrical engineering degrees because it is the hardest of all engineering disciplines. It is a matter of inclination and nature.

So, there you have it, all you male-chauvinists. You exploit women. I don't know about you, but I do what my wife tells me to do. And better do it with a smile.

Chapter 1.4 The Critical LGBTQQIAAPP Theory.

Have you heard of LGBTQQIAAPP? I heard of LGBTQ, but I don't keep up to date with our modern society madness, and I'm sure by the time you read this book, more letters will be added showing more out-of-this-world pervert believes. Who knows, we may find out that dogs are gay or dogs and cats suffer from gender identity. The cats think they're dogs and vice-versa. Will they require surgery?

This theory seems to be a Gender Identity theory. I didn't find a critical theory for this, but I'm sure some queer thinker is working on it. It doesn't matter how small these entities are as a population percentage; we must conform to the minority's wishes, no matter how few they are. I thought the majority rules, but the more anarchy the better for the neo-Marxists.

In my fiction book "The Pregnant Pope," I wrote the following:

> There is a woman in San Francisco who is legally married to her python. At the end of her life and after her snake grows large enough, she wants to be swallowed by the beast. To be one with her snake.

Soon fantasy and reality will be indistinguishable in a socialist world.

Chapter 1.5 The LatCrit Theory

LatCrit is the Latino Critical Theory. Following the lines of CRT, the Latinos, Hispanics, Indigenes of Latin America have their qualms. Unlike the blacks brought by force to the Americas, the Latinos are the descendants of the indigenous people of the Americas, (and the white Spanish invaders, which are ignored.) The Americas belong to them, not to the Anglo-Puritans, white men, who invaded and took away the North American land from the natives.

The bottom line, the LatinX are the rightful owners of the Americas, including the United States. The whites should leave or subordinate to the true owners of this land.

Chapter 1.6 The Critical Race Theory.

The Critical Race Theory is all the rage nowadays. In school, kids are taught that if they're white, they are evil. Think what that will do to a kid's mind. Black kids are told that they are victims because of the white kids. Think how much hatred we instill in that child's mind. Our military considers most white men, if not all, White Supremacists, making every white soldier is a second-class citizen. Employers make their employees take CRT seminars and write apologizing letters for the racist trespasses they might have done in the past. Think what that would do to your self-respect. What's next, self-flagellation if you're white?

The Critical Race Theory completes the Marxism ideology of Neo-Marxism. The abolition of *personal wealth* is at the heart of Marxist-Socialist theory, implying that by abolishing wealth, we lift out of poverty everyone else. But, with fewer poor people in America, there are not enough desperados to change or take over the government. But wait! There is a class of poor people, and what's better yet, this class is easily identifiable: The Black Society.

Why are the Black people poor and don't seem to rise economically like the rest of us? They wrote entire libraries of books on this subject, and that's irrelevant to the Critical Race Theory, just like black lives are irrelevant to Black Lives Matter.

The Critical Race Theory insists that there is one and only one reason the Black Society is not doing well in the United States of America: Systemic Racism.

According the Encyclopedia Britannica,
https://www.britannica.com/topic/critical-race-theory

> Critical Race Theory (CRT), intellectual movement and loosely organized framework of legal analysis based on the premise that race is not a natural, biologically grounded feature of physically distinct subgroups of human beings but a socially constructed (culturally invented) category that is used to oppress and exploit people of color. Critical race theorists hold that the law and legal institutions in the United States are inherently racist insofar as they function to create and maintain social, economic, and political inequalities between whites and nonwhites, especially African Americans.

CRT claims that Systemic Racism is ingrained in the Western Civilization, our institutions, population, schools, laws, culture, and history. The Western Civilization causes the evils listed below:
(https://owl.purdue.edu/owl/subject_specific_writing/writing_in_literature/literary_theory_and_schools_of_criticism/critical_race_theory.html)

- White privilege: Discussed by Lipsitz, Lee, Harris, McIntosh, and other CRT scholars, white privilege refers to the various social, political, and economic advantages white individuals experience in contrast to non-white citizens based on their racial membership. These advantages can include both obvious and subtle differences in access to power, social status, experiences of prejudice, educational opportunities, and much more. For CRT scholars, the notion of white privilege offers a way to discuss dominant culture's tendency to normalize white individuals' experiences and ignore the experiences of non-whites. Fields such as CRT and whiteness studies have focused explicitly on the concept of white privilege to understand how racism influences white people.

- Microaggressions: Microaggressions refer to the seemingly minute, often unconscious, quotidian instances of prejudice that collectively contribute to racism and the subordination of racialized individuals by dominant culture. Peggy Davis discusses how legal discourse participates in and can counteract the effects of microaggressions.
- Institutionalized Racism: This concept, discussed extensively by Camara Phyllis Jones, refers to the systemic ways dominant society restricts a racialized individual or group's access to opportunities. These inequalities, which include an individual's access to material conditions and power, are not only deeply imbedded in legal institutions, but have been absorbed into American culture to such a degree that they are often invisible or easily overlooked.
- Social construction: In the context of CRT, "social construction" refers to the notion that race is a product of social thought and relations. It suggests that race is a product of neither biology nor genetics, but is rather a social invention.
- Intersectionality and anti-essentialism: These terms refer to the notion that one aspect of an individual's identity does not necessarily determine other categories of membership. As Delgado and Stefancic explain, "Everyone has potentially conflicting, overlapping identities, loyalties, and allegiances" (CRT: An Introduction 10). In other words, we cannot predict an individual's identity, beliefs, or values based on categories like race, gender, sexuality, religion, nationality, etc; instead, we must recognize that individuals are capable of claiming membership to a variety of different (and oftentimes seemingly contradictory) categories and belief systems regardless of the identities outsiders attempt to impose upon them.

There you have it, folks: The White Men are *evil, and racists* and we must destroy Western Civilization since especially African Americans are affected and cannot succeed.

The Critical Race Theory claims that *Equality* is *Racism*. In reality *Equity* is *Racism.*

According to "Critical Race Theory: What it is and How to Fight it" and article by Christopher F. Rufo, it says:

> There are a series of euphemisms deployed to describe critical race theory, including "equity," "social justice," "diversity and inclusion," and "culturally responsive teaching." [37]

We must apply "culturally responsive teaching." Our education is racist, and we must change it. They force the Critical Race Theory on all our schools from kindergarten and up. The school curriculum needs to be revised. They must make the white kids aware that the whites are the exploiters; they take advantage of "white privileges." What do you think this teaching will do to the white kids' sense of self-respect? Instead of integrating we are separating ourselves by race through hate.

Mathematics is challenging; therefore, it is discriminatory. Let's eliminate math in schools. English and grammar teaching too. And American history is out the window. And what kind of history are the kids supposed to learn? Not Western history, which is white-racist. Some demented professor at Oxford wants to eliminate music notations. White men developed during colonial times the Western music notation, and it is Racist. Lowering college entrance exams or eliminating them will be applied in California. When you have less able students, do you flank them? Or reduce the curriculum so they can pass. The intelligent and bright become as ignorant as the stupid ones.

The Critical Race Theory is not only taught in our schools but at our employment locations. The indoctrination must be complete, just the way it was under socialism. Your employer, especially in a large company, will schedule seminars for you and your coworkers and preach the Critical Race Theory. If you are white, you are the oppressor, the racist, and committing micro-inequities just by being white. If you are a white male, you are a white supremacist and should feel guilty for your white male privileges. You'll be asked to confess some racial sin that you may have committed in the past or present, even write a letter to a fictitious woman, or gay, or black man or woman apologizing with deep sincerity for your misogynistic, homophobic, or racist behavior you had or even

thought. Very important, this is for your own good. *Shame and guilt* will correct your faulty thinking.
This is beyond Socialism; this is Communism.

A reasonable person would think that the Critical Race Theory and its concerns about the black people is the manual for helping an inferior race, which cannot rise from poverty. We must lower educational standards to be equitable to all, especially the black kids, to succeed in school. They will press the employers to hire even more blacks than already they do regardless of their skills or education. Equity is the New Law of this land, and we must change the entire socio-economic structure to correct the situation. Change it to what? Socialism.

Would black people want to be considered inferior as CRT states? The Critical Race Theory is not only racist but insulting to the Black people. The proponents of CRT and Systemic Racism argue that black people are not incapable. But the white race, the legal system, laws, the political system –democracy–, and capitalism make them unable to succeed. Therefore, we must change everything according to Marxism-Socialism to level the playing field. Bullshit! Leveling the playing field is discriminatory against the achievers, regardless of their skin color.

A new ideology, Neo-Marxism, emerged to guide us and attain Socialist Globalization. What they needed to start a revolution is the Villain.

Chapter 1.7 The Villain.

A movement must always have a villain; otherwise, who are you going to hate and try to destroy? Love is not enough. A religion-based only on love won't succeed. Hate is mandatory and a much more effective ideology. *Marxism is the ideology of hatred.*

The capitalist is the villain for all classical Marxists. That evil, wealthy men who owns the capital and exploits the workers in their factories, while keeping all the profits for their benefit. They live in splendor, while the *proletariat* live in squalor.

But improved technologies, pursued as a necessity by businesses, had improved everyone's life. Although the capitalists have never gained the image as benefactors for humanity, they rouse little hate to cause revolutions. Some of the proletarians have become educated and understand the reality of how economies work. Besides, many proletarians dream of becoming bourgeois themselves, so hating wealth is counterproductive.

Hitler chose the Jew as the evil enemy of the German people. The Jews enriched themselves during WW I, and continued to get more prosperous after the war, he said. At the same time, the German people toiled for a meager piece of bread. Exterminate these evil people, and the Germans will be prosperous again. Thus, the Jew became the villain.

Who should that villain be in America? The **Villain** is the **White Man.**

Yes, folks, if you are White, Christian, Heterosexual, and worst yet, a Man, you are the villain and the reason of suffering for Black people, they claim.

The Jew of Nazi Germany in America today is the White Man.

The Critical Race Theory based on Systemic Racism was carefully and patiently planted in our minds, mainly to the younger generations by the American School System. The Critical Race Theory is pure hate, and it works wonders.

Do you see Systemic Racism in your everyday life? I, for one, do not. If I'm right, the Critical Race Theory and Systemic Racism ideology will turn this country upside down. If most people see what I see this ideology will collapse, but not before causing much turmoil and even deaths.

The Critical Race Theory and Systemic Racism is the neo-Marxism ideology, and the White Men are the Villains. Therefore, we must eliminate or reprogram them.

Chapter 2. Indoctrination and Propaganda.

Propaganda can get a political party only so many followers, but indoctrination will get the party fanatic members. Hitler said:

> *Even the smallest minority can achieve a mighty result if it is inspired by the most fiery, the most passionate will to act.* [14]

Hitler brainwashed the German people to believe that National-Socialism is the savior, and only the fanatics are *the most fiery, the most passionate will to act.*

The radical Marxists began indoctrinating the students on college campuses about Marxism in the 1960s. Through the Democrat Socialist Party, the American Marxists' first strategy was to make the Republican Party, the conservative party, an outcast party. It took them decades to incite so much hatred against the Republicans that some people recoil when the Republican name is mentioned as if it is the NAZI party. Evilly and well done, Democrats.

The second tool used to combat the opposition was the implementation of Political Correctness. Say or write the wrong words, and they shame you or fire you. And they do this oppression without the government's police help. Immorally done, but effective, Democrats.

The third tool is to use the word *fascist*. On account of Hitler and the NAZI-Socialist party and diligent work by Hollywood, the Nazis and the Fascists are universally hated. We hate most the Nazis or Fascists on the account that they are an extreme Right-wing ideology. We learned that the Nazis or Fascists are racist. It plays well in the Systemic Racism propaganda.

But, as I explained, the Nazis and Fascists were/are Socialists, Leftists.

Chapter 2.1. American Universities: The Marxist Indoctrination Machine

> *America is now ill with a powerful mutant strain of interwind ignorance, anti-nationalism and anti-intellectualism.* "The Age of American Unreason" by Susan Jacoby.

I'll have to agree with the above statement, although the book speaks to the liberal-progressives to show how the religious fundamentalists and the conservatives cause ignorance and anti-intellectualism. However, if viewed from the Conservative point of view, most people are ignorant and anti-nationalist because of the poor state of our schooling system and the Socialists. The educated elites who purport to know what's good for us created anti-intellectualism and equity. And look where the Socialists who dominate our schooling system have led us: ignorance, anti-nationalism, and anti-intellectualism (on account of not being able to reason.)

And so, they have reduced our school system to a Marxist dogma indoctrination institution, where truth is what you are told and not what reality is. As a result, America and Western civilization are racist, homophobic, misogynist, White men supremacy, and religion-dominated.

Who are those Marxist-Socialists, who destroyed our educational system, and how did they do it?

Marxist brainwashing is accomplished through hate, guilt and lies.

In the book "The Breakdown of Higher Education - How it happened, the damage it does and What can be done" by John M. Ellis explains in brilliant detail how the Leftist indoctrination in our higher education schools began, took hold, and continues unabated. I recommend this book for a more in-depth understanding of how a minority of radical son-of-a-bitches have brainwashed generations since the 1960s.

The Students for a Democratic Society (SDS) were only 200 of them, held a congress at Port Huron, and they decided to obtain political power by infiltrating the universities. They stated:

> While two-thirds of mankind suffer under nourishment, our own upper-class revel amidst superfluous abundance. [1; pg48]

John M Ellis continues:

> ... political radicals are the very last people we should ever want to have running our universities: their values are the reverse of academic values. Yet they now control academia. [1; pg55]

If you are unaware of what Marxism represents, it is Internationalism, among the many things it professes. The modern-day word for it is *Globalism*. The statement above makes the USA responsible for poverty and hunger in the world. SDS continued:

> Although mankind desperately needs revolutionary leadership. America rests in national stalemate... its democratic system apathetic and manipulated rather than 'of, by, and for the people.' [1; pg48]
>
> The economy itself is of such social importance that its major resources and means of productions should be open to democratic participation and subject to democratic social regulations. [[1; pg49]

Democratic is the code word for *Socialism*. When the Leftists accuse the conservatives of being anti-democratic, they say: the conservatives are against Socialist "democracy" or totalitarianism.

Later on, at Berkley, the Free Speech Movement started the current that we see the results today. There was Free speech in America, but the radical students wanted to bring their radical Leftist politics to the University Campuses. Among the early participants were Mario Savio, Alan Haber, Tom Hayden–Jane Fonda's ex-husband–, Sandra (Casey) Cason, and others. SDA was behind their movement.

Whatever the SDS wanted was not democracy but imposing themselves on the society for *our* "better" good:

> ... this would not really be a democracy, but rather a dictatorship of the enlightened, as they imagine themselves to be. [1; pg48]

Lenin decreed that communism was the *dictatorship of the proletariat*. But the dictatorship SDS wants is not of the ignorant proletariat but the *intelligentsia*, the elite scholars' dictatorship. Have you heard about the *elites* in this country, the so-called *intellectuals*? The ones that haven't work a "sweat-day" in their lives, racquetball excluded, the ones that are not held accountable over what they teach and how successful the students are after they graduate, the ones being paid good wages, living comfortably with no worry of being fired, unless they're conservatives.

These Leftist professors have plotted since the 1960s to *transform* our country into the Marxism-Leninism Utopia. These are the people who are destroying our country in the name of equity to bring misery, tyranny, and poverty to all of us.

About education Lenin said:

> Give us the child for 8 years and it will be a Bolshevik forever.

Hitler, Lenin's socialist "cousin", was of a similar opinion when he said:

> This new Reich will give its youth to no one, but will itself take youth and give to youth its own education and its own upbringing. [40; pg 249]
>
> The German youth, besides being reared within the family and schools, shall be educated physically, intellectually and morally in the spirit of National Socialism . . . through the Hitler Youth. [40; pg 253]

Indoctrinate and brainwash the people from a young age to believe religiously in Marxism-Socialism, or Nationalism-Socialism as the case was for the NAZI-Socialism. Thus, the citizens of the older generation will pass on, as they wish in the USA today, just as Oprah Winfrey wished that the older, white generation die away.

Early on, brainwashing the young people from the first grade was impractical in the US. The socialists didn't have the power and cooperation in imposing their curriculum on the teachers, especially when the kids were under their parents' tutelage. The parents had a say on what their kids learned. But once the kids matured, 18 years or older, and still receptive to new information, the indoctrination began in colleges and universities.

By now, so many people who graduated from the Socialist Indoctrination Institutions have become the teachers of K 12, and the brainwashing is happening from the earliest age, even teaching the kids about BLM, a Marxists organization. Seeing my grandson's books, the books he learns from, makes me cringe. For government and citizenship, they learn from a booklet "The US Constitution: Then and Now." Learning about the Constitution should be good, but that's not the intent of this booklet. White men in white wigs wrote the Constitution, and it had to be *amended* to include the rights of the Black people. That's not too bad, except it is racist, comparing the Constitution as it was written originally versus the correct way as it should be. I would have no problem if this booklet were called the Constitution and the emancipation of Blacks. Instead, they teach the kids a distorted interpretation of the Constitution where whites are villainized, even marginalized. At the same time, the blacks are disproportionately elevated to new, unearned status. A distorted history.

They taught to hate Christopher Columbus because he discovered the Americas. He brought with him the death of millions to natives of the New Land and white domination. They even call that genocide, as if Columbus decided to discover the new continent and exterminate the natives. And if Columbus would not have discovered America, someone else would have done soon after him. The Chinese and Vikings discovered the Americas before him, but their discovery didn't hold.

In contrast, the more advanced civilization of 15th century Europe did. It is always the case when a more advanced society comes into contact with a primitive one. Even today, if we discover a new primitive culture on Earth one way or another, we would influence it. And that's the way it is, no matter how noble we want to be.

What would happen if we find microbial life on Mars? Do we stop landing there and exploring the planet? Or not go there so we wouldn't contaminate Earth upon return, which would be the right thing to do. Should we stop admiring Neil Armstrong as the first man to step on the Moon? In a hundred years from now, the Moon will be an unfamiliar landscape than it is today after humanity undertakes mining there, with trails crisscrossing the landscape. Neil Armstrong is the destroyer of the Moon. How crazy is that? Just as crazy as calling Christopher Columbus an instigator of genocide. This is to be expected from Marxism; it is an ideology of antagonism and hatred.

According to John M Ellis, this small group of radicals, SDS, managed this incredible feat because of fortunate circumstances. The war in Vietnam was one of them, causing a lot of dissent among the young people, questioning the reason for going to war against communism. Unfortunately, the young people did not understand that the Korean and Vietnam wars happened because of the strategic failures of Franklin D Roosevelt during WW II. He did not follow Churchill's advice and attack Germany through the Danube river basin, stave off the Russians, keep them within their border, and thus preventing Stalin from spreading communism in Eastern and Central Europe, and later on, in Asia. Instead Roosevelt attacked through Sicily. It was expedient, but it caused the future bloodshed in Korea, 40k, and Vietnam, 58k dead.

The Civil Rights Act of 1964 prohibited discrimination in public places, provided for integrating schools and other public facilities and made employment discrimination illegal. Title IX the federal civil rights law protects people from discrimination based on sex in education programs or activities that receive Federal financial assistance. There is nothing wrong with the Civil Rights Act or Title IX. However, there are always unwanted consequences coming from good intentions.

And finally, the expansion of colleges and universities to accommodate the baby boomers' educational needs. They erected many new colleges and universities over a short period, and those schools needed professors. But, unlike before when staffing the universities took a methodical approach of who will be hired as professors, this time the selection process couldn't handle the needs for new personnel, and the SDS graduates were eager to fill the positions.

John Ellis explains:

> ...our... splendid academic institutions and their virtual takeover by radical political activists – people with no real interest of academic thought, teaching, or research,

> who wanted instead to use their positions to promote their extreme political ideology. [1; pg 47]

There you have it, undermine the foundation of academia based on logic, reason, research, and indoctrinate the young minds in the worst political belief that has caused so much suffering and death, Marxism.

After the passage of the Civil Rights Act, the emphasis on campuses was to increase the number of minorities attending higher education, which was good. However, when you admit quantity over quality, *diversity* in academia replaced *excellence*, and mediocrity replaced the level of academic eminence.

Furthermore, John Ellis states:

> The arbiters of diversity were not intellectual giants of the campus, but instead political radicals – the intellectual mediocrity. They were the ones who now led the way and could demand that their judgments be the basis of policy. [1; pg66]

They don't do that in China.

I am a firm believer in education for all, especially minorities, to gain higher education and break the cycle of poverty. However, the professors on campus knew the situation and did nothing. Just pass them through, and after they graduate, they're unemployable. How discriminatory is that? Eventually, the *get-free-pass* encounters the real world, and there is no Diversity Board to protect the minorities outside the universities.

Title IX dealing with sexual discrimination had a different impact on universities. Someone had to be the watchdog and make sure that young women were not sexually harassed or discriminated against. John Ellis gives an example of what happens when a new watchdog operates on campus, and he states:

> Until quite recently, the Title IX office had a staff of only one. Then, within a period of three years, that individual increased the size of her office to five investigators plus support personnel – an astonishing percentage increase in so short time.
>
> But an office devoted to sexual harassment has the opposite incentive: the more sexual harassment there is, the more the office is needed, and the more it can grow and throw its weight around.

> They are now crucial part of the way in which political radicals exercise power on campus, and in which identity politics now strangles academia. [1; pg65]

The universities have changed from an institution of learning to that of an *indoctrination machine*. The professors are no longer in charge, but political activists and bureaucrats masquerading as professors.

Besides the increase in the watchdog bureaucracy and to promote equality and racial unity, new subjects appeared in the curriculum of the universities such as Women Studies, Black Studies, Ethnic Studies, and many others. I checked my Alma Mater, CSULB, to see what they offer today under the College of Liberal Arts:

- African Studies, where among other subjects you can learn Swahili. And I suppose all the other courses may prepare you for a job in Africa. But for job opportunities there are: Social Scientist • Social Worker • Counselor • Teacher • Archivist • Journalist • Public Relations Consultant • Community Organizer • Recreation • Law • School Administrator • Linguist • Parole Officer • Probation Officer • Editor • Writer • Urban/Regional Planner • Public Policy Administrator • Foreign Policy Officer • Researcher –of whatever.
- American Indian Studies, the job opportunities are: American Indian Affairs • Social Scientist • Archivist, Social Worker • Journalist • Counselor • Teacher • Public Relations Consultant • Community Organizer • School Administrator • Linguist • Law Parole Officer • Probation Officer • Editor • Writer • Urban/Regional Planner • Public Policy Administrator • Foreign Policy Officer • Researcher.
- Women's, Gender, and Sexuality Studies, B.A., but there are no jobs listed for this degree.

Social Worker and Community Organizers seem to be proper jobs. Barack Obama's only job was Community Organizer, and he became the President of the United States. The fact is that the above and other such "studies" did not exist before 1960. African studies started in 1968. They invented these studies in search of students, with no productive aspect whatsoever, mandated by the Civil Rights Act and Title IX. It never stops to amaze me in how many ways the government is screwing its people.

What do women learn in Women's, Gender, and Sexuality Studies? All I see is how much women hate men. The following from Wikipedia about *Toxic Masculinity*:

> The concept of toxic masculinity is used in academic and media discussions of masculinity to refer to certain cultural norms associated with harming society by men. For example, traditional stereotypes of men as socially dominant and related traits such as misogyny and homophobia can be considered "toxic" due to their promotion of violence, including sexual assault and domestic violence. In addition, the socialization of boys in patriarchal societies often normalizes violence, such as in the saying "boys will be boys" concerning bullying and aggression.

It's true that throughout the world the men dominate. In the modern age, brains, not brawn, are what's needed in the economy, and the dominance of men diminished. But instead of reconciling our differences, they blame the men for everything. Who is teaching these classes? Socialists with their hostile and hateful ideology. In their minds, there is nothing good in our culture, and they must break it and remake it in the image of utopian Socialism and political correctness. The Great Reset, they call it.

There is a book which I will not name the title, that advocates genocide against all men, and prevent any human males from being born. It even has suggestions on how a society of women can procreate and have sex without men. How demented is that?

In the California Universities Institution, there are 285 thousand students and 227 thousand staff. That makes 1¼ students per employee. I call this a *royal* education. At a rate of 20 students per class-professor, the institutions would need 14,250 professors. What are the rest of 212,750 employees doing, besides administrative and maintenance of campuses? And you wonder why the tuition is so expensive? It takes money to support a socio-political-indoctrination bureaucracy.

Universities are the institutions to teach young minds *How to Think* based on facts, logic, and reason. But, instead, the universities have become the institutions to train young minds *What-to-Think* based on Marxist ideology.

I watched a movie, which I recommend seeing, "God's Not Dead" by Pure Flix Entertainment. It depicts what happens in an American University Philosophy class. The professor asks all students to write on a piece of paper "God's dead," sign it and forward it to him. If you cannot write that statement, that student must defend their point of view in front of the class, and the jury is the class' students. If he/she fails, his/her grade will be reduced by 30%. One student cannot accept this falsehood and writes, "God's Not Dead." The punch line is when the student asks the atheist professor, *"Why do you hate so much something that you believe does not exist?"*

See the movie and see what happens.

The professors and teachers continue the perpetual indoctrination of all the young minds. What was once a bunch of radicals in academia, now all teachers and professors are even more radical. The teachers prepare our kids to be good socialists. When they enter the workforce, the Marxist philosophy will become the predominant political belief.

According to foxbaltimore.com, in 2017, in 13 Baltimore City High Schools, there were *zero* students proficient in math. So are the kids dumb, or the teaching quality has come down? All school districts in the USA are showing the same poor learning results. Per the study from pewresearch.org, out of 71 countries, our education ranks 38th overall.

From investopedia.com:

> The Organization for Economic Cooperation and Development (OECD) compiled educational data ... in 2015, the United States spent approximately $12,800 per student on elementary and secondary education. That is over 35% more than the OECD country average of $9,500. At the post-secondary level, the United States spent approximately $30,000 per student, which was 93% higher than the average of OECD countries ($16,100).

The post-secondary level is college, and we spent approximately $30,000 per student to teach our young people useless and counterproductive knowledge and Marxist beliefs.

And if you think our schools produce people who cannot count, read or write, the universities are as bad, as John Ellis notes:

> Only 41 percent of graduate students tested in 2003 could be classified as "proficient" in prose – reading and understanding

> information in short texts – down 10 percent points from 1992. [1; pg102]

Michael Gorman, president of the American Library Association and a librarian at California State University at Fresno, said:

> Only 31 percent of college graduates can read a complex book and extrapolate from it. That's not saying much of the remainder. [1; pg102]

It means 69% of graduates cannot "read a complex book and extrapolate from it?" And these graduates will be the future professionals that will lead our country. They were and are not taught "*How to think*" but "*What to think*." For the socialist manipulators, that's not a problem; too much knowledge and ability to reason is dangerous for their cause.

Socialism needs followers, not thinkers.

Chapter 2.2. The Woke Zombies

Unfortunately, all these Woke people have become indoctrinated zombies, brainwashed in *What to Think*. A zombie will act on what they are programmed. Reason and logic are not acceptable to them.

The younger generation is angry and hateful toward our country and the flag for which is stands, hateful of the Western civilization and White men, hateful of our founding fathers and our history, hateful toward the Free-Market-Capitalism, which elevated the world's population standard of living to unknown levels until our modern times. They oppose freedom and free speech if it's disagreeable with what they think. They believe in the lie called *Systemic Racism*, and above all, they believe in Socialism, which is the most disastrous political ideology ever invented by men.

What is this Woke thing? According to the Wikipedia:

> **Woke** is a political term originating in the United States referring to a perceived awareness of issues concerning social justice and racial justice.
>
> ...woke had been adopted as a more generic slang term broadly associated with left-wing politics, socially liberal and cultural issues (with the terms woke culture and woke politics also being used). Its widespread use

since 2014 is a result of the Black Lives Matter movement.

We send our kids to college to get an education. Instead, they learn adulation of the worst possible ideology in the world—Marxism, which is based on lies, lies, and more lies. Even my 40-some-year-old daughter became a *Woke Zombie*.

Why do I call them Woke zombies? Because they are so indoctrinated, brainwashed, that no amount of reasonable discussion can persuade them, worst yet they do not want to hear anything contradictory to their beliefs. Facts and truths are false. What their Marxists professors told them is the ultimate truth. They believe what the Socialist Mainstream News tells them, one-party opinion propaganda. Our history is wrong. The evil which caused all this is the *White Man and the Western Civilization*.

As I said my daughter is a Woke Zombie, and I tried to understand her beliefs. Although she has a master's in education, she is unable to articulate her reasoning, other than she will *not be selfish*. I understood that to mean: she is *guilty* for benefiting from white privileges. We paid for her college, she wasn't allowed in for free, no questions asked as other minorities were accepted with paid scholarship. I asked my son-in-law, a lawyer, to explain what is Critical Race Theory. He forwarded me articles, which I already read. I wanted his thoughts, got no answers. The problem is their inability to discuss or elaborate on their beliefs, because they don't have full and contradictory facts.

The people who poisoned their minds are the neo-Marxist Academia and our educational system. Not all educators, but many fanatics who dominate our education. Those fanatics are the traitors of humanity, of America and Freedom. But how did they do it? Igniting a love for Marxism is difficult considering the vast proof of its disastrous effects. Love is powerful, but *Hate* is more powerful to influence people. Hitler used hatred for great advantage. The American new-

Marxist Academia used it to great effect as well. But hate of what? Our country, the *United States of America*.

It started with the Vietnam war. The images coming from the war, showing the bombing and the destruction of Vietnam, kids running naked from their burning village was repulsive. Compounding those images were the death of American soldiers, barely adults; our youth was dying for a hard-to-understand reason; Freedom. Free people do not understand freedom until they don't have it anymore. And who was responsible for all the mayhem? Our country, the United States of America. The fanatic neo-Marxists used the hatred of America to begin their brainwashing, in full accordance with the teachings of Marxism, which is *the ideology of Antagonism and Hatred*.

When I went to college in the 1970s, I was amazed about the antagonism against the United States within the university campus. My wife graduated in political sciences. The books she had to read were nothing else but pure vitriol against America, our country, Imperialist America, interventionism in Latin America, the ruling families, capitalism and imperialism consequences to the detriment of the world. The communists in the USSR or Romania could not have written more hateful books about America than the American professors. And we let them do it because of our Liberty, which they abused to the maximum.

Hitler used hatred against the Jews to promote the National-Socialist party. The Marxists did the same thing in America. Promote hatred against one's country, our country, against the white exploiters. From there, it's just a springboard to introduce Marxism that is "peaceful and good for all people." It is that simple. Skillfully using *hatred, shame, and guilt*, the Academia convinced our youth to turn against our country. And then came the Critical Race Theory, tailor-made to hate, shame, and assign guilt to the white people and the Western Civilization.

Chapter 2.3. Propaganda.

The NAZI-Socialist party embarked on a continuous campaign of promoting their ideology. Their newspapers and speeches showed how badly the German people subsisted compared to the Jews, the ruinous sanctions imposed on Germany, and the war reparations. The NAZI-Socialist Party was to correct the abysmal situation in Germany if they came to power. Germany for the Germans.

Hitler said:

> We are National Socialist fanatics. . .. We know only one interest and that is the interest of our people. [14: Munich Speech May 1, 1923]

Propaganda must be delivered with the most eagerness and passion for instilling in people the message. He was not joking about fanaticism. A few good fanatics are worth one hundred lame followers.

Hitler's job was to consolidate and add as many members as possible to the National-Socialist movement. Here it is in Hitler's words from *Mein Kampf*:

> Today, when the ballot of the masses decides, the chief weight lies with the most numerous groups, and this is the first: *the mob of the simple and credulous.*
>
> The art of propaganda lies in *understanding the emotional ideas of the great masses* and finding, through psychologically correct form, the way to the attention and thence to *the heart of the broad masses.* [13: pg 242, 180]

Emphasis added.

For the American Marxists, socialist propaganda was futile, considering what was going on in the world since WW II in the European Communist Block. Communism's reputation was eroding fast, and by 1989 it completely collapsed in Europe. Pro-Marxist propaganda was not useful anymore. The American people would have laughed at the American Marxists should they have embarked on old-style propaganda used by Hitler or the old Communist-Socialists.

The Russian communists tried to promote the Marxist cause by taking over Hollywood and producing movies that would influence the people. They tried and failed to control the Black communities in the 1950s.

Instead, they undertook a more insidious Marxist propaganda—indoctrination through Education. Promoted by no other than John Dewey, who learned from the USSR and Stalin's educational system.

Chapter 2.4. The Media and Hollywood: How They Lie to Us

In the Socialist News and Media, the journalists and editors are primarily *liberal or outright socialists*. Conservative journalists were all fired, and if they tolerate one such openly declared conservative on TV or newspapers, it is a *token* conservative on their staff to prove that their institution is fair and unbiased. As our universities pump out more and more Leftist journalists, the entire industry has become an extension of the Democrat Socialist Party, a journalistic propaganda machine.

In his book "Left Turn" by Tim Groseclose states:

> …a little bit of liberal media bias can make us more liberal, which causes us to seek more liberal media outlet, which causes us to become more liberal, and so on. [6; pg18]

In the former communist-socialist countries, the indoctrination in Marxism-Leninism is conducted in the media, in schools, and at work. Yes, comrades, at least once a week, there were political meetings at the place of employment to ensure that we stayed obedient serfs to the Communist Party. Without realizing it, today, they brainwash us in Marxism if you watch the Socialist Mainstream Media: ABC, CBS, NBC, PBS, MSNBC, and CNN. Do you listen to the radio? Then they indoctrinated you. Do you read newspapers: the New York Times, the New Yorker, the

Washington Post, and others like those? Then they indoctrinated you.

But wait, there are conservative TV channels like FOX News, Newsmax TV, and OANN TV. Those channels are the enemy of socialism, and they try to shut them down, prevent advertisers to promote on those programs and delist them from DCP. There are conservative newspapers like the New York Post and the Wall Street Journal. There are conservative radio shows, buckets of them, like the late Rush Limbaugh (replaced by Charlie Kirk,) Dennis Prager, Sean Hannity, Larry Elder, Ben Shapiro, and Tammy Bruce, among many others. So yes, there are conservative radio shows/hosts because the Socialists have appropriated most of the TV.

As Tim Groseclose remarks:

> The problem is that our opinions and educated guesses are based almost entirely upon information we learn from the media. [6; pg20]

And that is so true. What we know and believe was carefully distilled and promoted to us. To distinguish what's true or not, you must get your news from two different sources, liberal and conservative. Do you wonder why President Donald Trump got mauled in every news segment? He's the enemy of Socialism, and he must be eliminated.

When I mentioned to some of my brain-washed friends and relatives that I listen to the late Rush Limbaugh, I got funny looks, which makes me feel as being back in Communist Romania, where I was listening to Radio Free Europe and Voice of America. Those stations were illegal to listen to, and I had to listen in secret. This is America today, where I feel like a dissident under socialism when I listen to conservative radio talk shows.

Hollywood movies are one of the best propaganda institutions. No wonder the communists tried to infiltrate the Hollywood studios. Upon the end of World War II, defeating the Nazi-Germany, the Soviet Union and Communism were the heroes in the world. Unlike

Hitler, we did not discover the atrocities and murders, 50 million deaths, the USSR committed against their people.

In 1947, the House Un-American Activities Committee in Congress began conducting hearings to discover communist subversives, operating under Moscow's direction and control, who infiltrated our government and the Hollywood as well. Stalin was confident as the winner in WW II that America was ready to have a red revolution and communism take over. One target for the communists was the Hollywood establishment. Unfortunately for the communists, senator Joseph McCarthy, an anti-communist, started investigations again into the communist subversion in the United States in Hollywood. He ousted many communists or perceived communists from the studios, and delayed the communism advancement by at least ten years. Because of the Leftists, he became the black hat politician, and they named McCarthyism after him for the practice of making accusations of subversion or treason without "proper evidence." In New Yorker magazines of Aug 3 and 10, 2020, McCarthy is villainized anew. The socialist media is adamant about destroying this patriot's memory and serve as an example against anyone who will attack Communism-Socialism in the USA. They don't have the power to arrest their opposition yet, but when that time comes, get ready for the socialist concentration camps, American gulags in Alaska perhaps.

In 2005, George Clooney wrote, directed, and played a role in the movie "Good Night, and Good Luck" about Senator Joseph McCarthy's investigations against the Hollywood communists. George Clooney is a self-described *liberal*, meaning socialist, abhorring the conservatives. He made the movie an homage to the expelled communists from Hollywood and villainized Senator Joseph McCarthy's fight for our freedom. This and other anti-freedom, anti-American films made by other Leftists (calling themselves liberals) contribute to the people's image that America is bad, the conservatives, the right, the Republicans are evil. People believing in God are dumb and backward.

You may think that you have seen no movies from Hollywood lauding Communism-Socialism. That's true. There is not much good to say about this horrific ideology, unless such movie is a dark satire. The movies made in Hollywood are to show how terrible the conservatives are or how criminal the American soldiers are in

Vietnam, a la Oliver Stone, or Iraq and Afghanistan. Creating hate against everything that is right and works for us pushes us to the Left.

The Media: TV, Radio, Newspapers, online media disseminated through the Internet, and Social media have more powerful control over us than the Communist-Socialist press had in the heyday of Communism-Socialism. One of the ultimate goals of communism was to know and control the thoughts of the citizens, mind control. They were ahead of their time in their intentions. But today's technology can facilitate *thought-control*, a dream come true for the Communist-Socialists.

Fake News is the usual news we hear on TV, radio, and newspapers. But what does "Fake" mean? Not reporting all the news, reporting only part of the news, reporting the news with mini-editorials built in, distorted news, or outright lying. There are also editorials and commentaries masquerading as news. And then there is entertainment, pretending to be political commentators like Bill Maher or Jon Stewart, or those "Night" shows with Stephen Colbert or Jimmy Fallon, and the rest. Most of everything in the Media and the shows on TV are Leftist, just short of being completely Socialist. They are also anti-American. The only TV programs of the Right are Fox Channel, Newsmax TV, and OANN.

Here is an example of how they report the news on TV, on our National Airwaves.

Laura O'Donnell on CBS news said about the damages by BLM protests and the insurance costs on September 15th, 2020:

> … could be the *highest insurance pay* in history. The protest in late spring, were *mostly peaceful,* are damage, looting and arson will cost one to two billion dollars in claims that's according to the Insurance Information Institute.

Mostly peaceful protests caused one to two billion dollars in insurance claims? The highest ever? Thank God we didn't have violent protests; it would have bankrupted the insurance industry and America. This is blatant Fake News describing the protests *mostly peaceful* on all MSM news. Reporters in the field reported mostly peaceful protests, while fires were raging in the background and looters coming out of stores with their arms full of stolen merchandise. Laura O'Donnell is a pretty, talking head, reading from the teleprompter what the Leftist producers wrote. If she and all other newscasters don't want to report the Fake News, there is a line circling Manhattan wanting their jobs. But do they think that we're that stupid, not understanding the reality we see with our own eyes?

News by David Muir on ABC World News Tonight on 9/25/20 said:

> *Unnamed* sources telling ABC News at this hour that the President doesn't intend to pay any merit to supreme court pick and the president would like a vote before the election… a great political issue for him and GOP senate leadership *do again his bidding*. The judiciary committee headed by Lindsey Graham planning hearings for the second week in October with a vote possibly coming before election day or shortly thereafter *despite that ABC poll*, which shows a strong support, 57% of the American public, *that's a lot of republicans too*, think that the next president, the president elected in November should fill the empty seat.

Is this news or editorial? Favorite word for the Fake News: *Unnamed* or *anonymous*. Under this pretext, they can report anything they like. The GOP Senate, *do his bidding again* [Trump's], insinuating that President Trump does not have the constitutional right to appoint anyone to any post during an election year, which he does. But, wait, it's not only the insinuated illegality but most American people, 57%, polled by ABC, think that the next President, [hopefully Biden at the time] should appoint the next Justice. Better yet, some people thinking that way are *republicans* too [not only democrats.]

During the riot at Capitol Hill on Jan. 6, 2021, four people died. A Capitol security shot sand killed one woman, two protesters had heart attacks, and the demonstrators allegedly killed one Capitol police officer Brian Sicknick, by being "*bludgeoned with a fire extinguisher*," screams CNN. Sometime later, it was found out that he died from a heart attack next day because he was "*sprayed with hair spray*," corrected the MSN. Both reports were lies, masquerading as news. Brian Sicknick died of a heart attack the next day after telling his mother he felt OK after the riot that evening. The Mainstream

Socialist Media, MSM, should not report lies when they don't have the facts. But Socialism is all about lies.

Considering that MSM is reporting from the same "memo," it makes you wonder who is coordinating all this misinformation? Is all this news or Leftist propaganda ordered directly from the Democrat Socialist Party Politburo? It must be.

A Pew Research for the first year of the presidency has shown the following negative reporting for Clinton, Bush, Obama, and Trump in terms of negative, neither, and positive.

President	Negative	Neither	Positive
Clinton	28%	44%	27%
Bush, W	28%	49%	22%
Obama	20%	38%	42%
Trump	62%	33%	5%

What did Obama do so well to deserve 42% positive and only 20% negative? Does ISIS, Lead from Behind, Benghazi, Fast & Furious, IRS targeting conservative organizations, Bowe Bergdahl swap, Solyndra, Uranium One, Iran Nuclear agreement, Clinton email scandal, FISAGATE, unmasking of Trump's people and leaked to the Media, allowing the Russians to intervene in our 2016 elections, $1.8 billion in sanctions lifted and $400 million given in cash to Iran, and many others qualify as ***good***? The Mainstream Socialist Media definitely didn't care about Obama's faults. And he was so *lovable*.

There is another thing to comment for the above survey, since 1993, for Clinton, the Media has shifted to the extreme Left, and although his sexual transgressions were ignored, his star doesn't shine much, but not because of Monica Lewinsky. He is the one that threw in jail so many black criminals, who now need to be let out of prisons. He is the one who supported cuts in Welfare. Bad, bad, bad.

During the pandemic, President Trump's negative coverage went up to 92%, peaking to 99.5% because of the Covid-19. All this after what President Trump has done for our economy, sending military hospital ships to New York and Los Angeles, building massive mobile hospitals to care for patients, and instituting Operation Warp Speed to speed up development, production, and distribution of the Chinese

COVID-19 vaccines. For which, not surprisingly, Joe Biden is taking all the credit.

There was a Total War against President Trump in the Media. New York Times reported they obtained a leaked document from IRS showing that President Trump paid only $750 in federal taxes. If this info was leaked by an IRS employee, that's illegal, but it is an *unnamed* source. Then what's the big deal about a Real Estate billionaire paying only $750 in taxes. It is not illegal, totally within the IRS code. Bloomberg, Buffet, Musk, Bezos, and Soros paid $0, zero, taxes in some years, but MSM does not talk about them.

In the late 1980s, my wife and I paid zero taxes for many years. We owned several properties, and the loss and depreciation canceled all our taxes. IRS audited us, and it turned out that in the year we paid taxes, I made a mistake by not carrying past losses, and IRS owed us a $400 refund. I like that kind of audits.

If you think that the Media is not anti-American, what do you think when Washington Post, another Democrat Socialist Party flag newspaper, said upon the death of Abu Bakr al-Baghdadi, the leader of ISIS, was an "austere religious scholar." This man and his organization committed atrocious crimes, including beheading Americans. Washington Post gives him an honorific title. This is like calling Hitler after his death "the austere political leader."

The Marxists have penetrated even science shows like Nova on PBS. What is wrong with the TV screen photos taken from the program "A to Z How Writing Changed the World" from Nova show on PBS below?

If you see nothing wrong, you are not a Marxist or knowledgeable in that ideology. That is very good, I may add. Look at the same picture below identifying the pervasive way the Marxists are planting subliminal messages about Socialism.

Mao and Lenin's books are depicted in this documentary's introduction, which subject was about how and where writing was invented. Those socialists couldn't find any images of Western writing except that of Lenin and Mao, both of them are mass murders. They might as well have included Mein Kampf and Hitler, he was a socialist too.

This is the pervasive way that they manipulate us, indoctrinate and brainwash by the neo-Marxists that have infiltrated all sections of our society.

Before the automobile was invented, people used to walk, used carriages and horses, or use public transportation when it became available, and we made eye contact with one another when crossing each other's paths. Then the automobile became a common method of transport, and we gave into *road-rage* and SUVs for safety. We could give other fellow motorists the finger and feel perfectly safe and satisfied that we taught them a "lesson" for cutting us off. So, we see each other at a distance, surrounded by our bubble vehicles. Sometimes some would reach in the glove compartment, pull a gun, and shoot at the offending motorists. Would we have behaved that way while walking?

And the phone before we could trace the caller, the anonymous calls we could give swearing at one or even giving death threats. Or send letters with malicious intent. All this is possible under the disguise of anonymity.

We live in a strange time. Until the Internet, we taught we were civilized, polite, considerate, respectful, and all the other noble attributes we humans have. Think again. On the Internet, through which erroneously assumed anonymity, one can tell another person the most hateful things one can say, including death wishes. Over the Internet, we have complete anonymity, or so we presume, using a real or fake name and blast everyone's comments on Facebook, blogs, or Twitter. Are you surprised at the animosity we see on Facebook from people we know, or on blogs from people we don't, or on book reviews on Amazon from people we don't know and are under real or fake names?

If we as people could kill another human without being known and escape punishment, how many people would kill or be killed? It is only the fear of being discovered and punished that prevents some of us from killing a myriad of people we dislike or hate based on what they say. How about one's perceived enemy, competitors, offenders, or just deplorables? I don't think humanity would have survived if we would have had such ability to kill without recourse. Instead, we shame, disgrace, embarrass, humiliate, dishonor, insult or threaten with words over the Internet.

And then there are the Digital Communist Platforms: Google, Facebook, Twitter, YouTube...

The ultimate attack on our freedom and minds comes from the Digital Communist Platforms. Why do I call them *Communist*? It resembles what communists would do, censure, spy, and delist us, as the Infernal Digital Media has done.

YouTube takes down videos that "god YouTube" considers antagonistic or "fake news" or disagrees with the Leftist rules. I wouldn't mind this policy since YouTube is a business, but YouTube is a monopoly. Who died and made YouTube the Czar of truth?

Have you had a posting on Facebook taken down? I had, and why? The Facebook "Committee of Marxist Truth and Lies" deemed my post misleading, untrue, spread malicious lies, and many other mortal-online-sins reasons. In short, Facebook, Twitter, YouTube, Instagram, Google, and many such online media are taking away our First Amendment right. And they are not the government yet; they are monopolies protected by the law from lawsuits to infringe on our First Amendment.

Twitter and Facebook had the audacity of canceling President Trump's accounts. So what world do we live in? A Socialist world.

As far as I heard, Google is the biggest violator of our freedom. When you search for something, the first pages show Leftist information. Google's algorithm steers you away from any information belonging to the Right. Yes, the information is there but buried under other pages of irrelevant information. And then there is the manipulation of our decision on how to vote. According to Ronald E. Robertson, Google could influence 20% to 80% of the undecided voters. Considering the small margin to win in the elections, Google has become a *king-maker*.

I searched for my name "Sandru" on Google. It is a Romanian name from the Transylvania region. Considering that I published 16 books, I have a website, I have art websites, and my name appears in many YouTube videos I should appear at the top. On what page do you think I finally appear on? Page five, under "Dumitru Sandru Webpage." What other "Sandru" names appear on the previous pages? Most of them doctors named Sandru associated with medical centers.

So why am I complaining? I'm not famous enough. That wasn't the case a few years back, not until the Communist Digital Platforms figured out that I am a conservative, all taken from my Facebook posts and my book "Escape from Communism." After publishing "Hitler Was a Socialist," they demoted me further down the pages. This is pure Communism-Socialism, and Google has the power to do what it wants. That's why I stopped using Facebook and Twitter, and I try as much not to use the Digital Communist Platforms.

What's even more criminal is what Amazon, Apple, and Google did to Parler. Amazon shut down their servers, Apple removed Parler App, and Google does not find Parler. There is more to this illegal monopolistic destruction of a competitor, but it is too lengthy to explain.

The Internet is a tool, and it is up to us how we use it. Still, Google, Facebook, YouTube, Twitter, and others like them are tools with evil minds masquerading as good for us.

Trump's legacy is how well the economy did during his four years of administration, reflected by the historic low unemployment rate, which the Mainstream Socialist Media, MSM, grudgingly mentioned about, and the Stock Market, which the MSM quickly points out that only the rich benefitted. Well, I'm not rich, and my 401k retirement plan did well.

The biggest lie about the economy is that Obama performed better than Trump. According to MarketWatch article, Jan 20, 2021, by William Watts, under Obama, the S&P 500 went up 13.8%, annualized, while under Trump, only 13.7%, annualized. Here is a good example of "Figures Don't Lie, But Liars Do Figure," and although the figures don't lie, the figures presented are ratios, percentages, which compare two numbers. Here is an example: take 100 and increase it by 50%, and you get 150. Now, take the 150 and increase it by 49% this time, and you get 223.5. The 50% is bigger than 49%, or so it appears. But, if we look at the increase in absolute numbers, real numbers, the 50% reflected an increase of 50 points, but the 49% reflected 73.5 points. So, the 73.5 points are larger than 50 points, although the percentages are saying otherwise.

The above example of how they're lying to us is abundant in the news articles. For example, the figures in the following table represent the actual return of the two presidents based on the S&P 500 index, from the inauguration dates of Trump and Obama:

President	**S&P 500**	**Increase**	%
Obama Total	827 - 2,271	1444	87.0%
Trump One Term	2,271 - 3,854	1,583	69.7%

Percentage-wise, Obama did spectacularly well, however, Obama was in office for eight years, where Trump was just four years. But the real eyeopener is that under Obama, the index grew by 1,444 points during eight years from a historic low, while under Trump, the index grew by 1,583 points during four years after the market recovered. It doesn't take a genius to realize that if you invested in the Stock Market, you made more money under Trump, in half the time.

And Time is Money.

Chapter 2.5. Black Lives Matter and its Platform

The Systemic Racism trumpeted so loudly by the MSM is a lie.

Black Lives Matter is Black Lies Matter.

I have seen no such "systemic racism" in real life. I worked among blacks, in the past, I went to school among blacks, I shop amongst blacks, I live in a city with at least a 20% black population. My neighbor on the right is black with a house that's bigger than mine. On my street of 12 homes, there are three black families. And I live in a nice neighborhood, but also in the Socialist Republic of California.

Race relations in society achieved the best level before we elected Barack Obama, the President of the United States. However, after he was in the office, racial relationships began to deteriorate. Not because the whites became racists, but because the blacks showed more racism toward whites with the prodding of white Leftists. This attitude is not only in society but also when encountering the police. How dare a white police officer stop a black man for a traffic violation or when acting suspiciously? I've seen many videos showing black men fighting the police and ending up dead. And it is all due to the lack of respect the Black society has for the Law, and consequently the police gets involved.

As explained in their demands, the Systemic Racism that the BLM claims to exist is about financial inequality. But is it true because of systemic racism, the black population lags all other races? The data I showed previously does not support that claim. The black population makes up 13.4% of the total US population, yet it has less than 1% of the total wealth. Why? There are many reasons, and they act as excuses instead of reasons for the poverty rate. A preferential system admits black people in universities to the detriment of Asians and Whites. Employment is not denied to *qualified* black people. My wife worked in Human Resources most of her life, and her employers were actively searching for qualified black employees to hire. It was an EEO, Equal Employment Opportunity, requirement. But it was hard to find *qualified* black people. The black people are at the bottom of wealth possession not because of their race, as Critical Race Theory claims, but because of their *culture*. Until that changes, nothing will improve, even under Socialism.

Patrisse Cullors, Alicia Garza, and Opal Tometi are the founders of Black Lives Matter. Patrisse Cullors claims that "We are trained Marxists." And yet, she's buying houses worth millions of dollars. This is typical for all Marxist demagogues; they blame the rich while they line their pockets.

This is what Karl Marx thought of blacks:

> ...that the common Negro type is the degenerate form of a much higher one ... a very significant advance over Darwin.

Marx affirmed Darwin was right on the evolution of species and that the common Negro is a less evolved human. Shocking, but true of what Karl Marx, the Socialist, believed.

BLM is a Marxist-Leninist movement. That is not advertised, and many people believe they stand against police killing black men. BLM thinks Marxism-Socialism will eradicate racism. They will have a rude awakening if that comes to be. In a Totalitarian system, dissenters, like BLM, will quickly be eliminated, arresting their leaders and making their crusade illegal.

Black Lives Matter is a Marxist organization demanding the institution of Socialism in this country. BLM might as well be called Black Leninists Marxists. BLM does not care about black lives, even though it is based on the death of black men at the hands of the white police. Nor do they care about how many black men are killed by black men. Black Lives Don't Matter to BLM. They don't care about improving the Black society by helping them succeed as all the other races have done. Their goal is to succeed by taking from others, just as Socialism does, and as the blacks have done under the War on Poverty program.

The following is the BLM platform. Their demands from Wikipedia and my analysis:

Demands

1-End the war on black people -

I never thought nor I found any evidence, other than the lying MSM that there is a war against black people. This demand is to emphasize the victimhood beliefs.

Seeks to resolve: "the criminalization and dehumanization of Black youth across all areas of society";

If you commit a crime, in a law and order society, the society expects punishment. If not, we will have a lawless society, anarchy. As far as *dehumanization* of black youth it is not the society who imposes that stigma on the blacks; the black youth criminals bring it upon themselves. All the shootings, killings, and robberies and mayhem seen on TV reinforces that notion. MSM called the BLM demonstrators "mostly peaceful demonstrators," while behind them we see breaking, destroying, looting, and burning of property. Ariel Atkins, an [BLM] organizer, told NBC Chicago:

> That is reparations. Anything they wanted to take, they can take it because these businesses have insurance.

The looting and stealing are *reparations*? We live in anarchy, and the blacks are contributing to it.

There is no excuse for how young blacks behave. Sure, the Marxists blame everyone else and specially the White people for their behavior, except the culprits themselves. I can call a black man a decent young man, but if he burglarizes me, robs me, shoots me, and kills his own kind every night in the streets, I reserve the right to *refuse* calling him a *human being*. You don't demand respect; you earn it.

Stop committing criminal acts and they'll get respect.

Seeks to resolve: capital punishment;

There are many people who are against capital punishment. This is a matter of the society at large to decide. And since we are in a democracy, as of right now, the society decides on capital punishment. If the blacks commit disproportionately more capital crimes, they suffer the consequences the most.

Seeks to resolve: money bail and court surcharges in court proceedings;

This again has to do with crime, and as long as being released on bail without consequences, what are the chances that the criminals will return to court to face charges? Almost none. And therefore, the police have to chase the perpetuators and arrest them to bring them to justice. More money, the taxpayer money, and more chances of having violent encounters and shooting by the police. Many Liberal District Attorneys, DA, are releasing the demonstrators caught committing crimes, without bail or charges. Next day they return to do the same thing. Instead of neutralizing the criminal behavior, the Liberal DA encourages it. We instituted the bail based on being presumed innocent, and be able to earn a living while awaiting trial. The criminals earn a living by committing crimes, and releasing them without bail facilitates them to commit more crimes. Look how crime exploded since 2020.

Seeks to resolve: use of past criminal history to determine eligibility for housing, education, licenses, voting, loans, employment, and other services;

Once you commit a crime and go to prison you are marked for life, preventing you from obtaining a job, therefore most times perpetuating the criminal behavior because all other alternatives are closed. Society is entitled to know, if engaged in any transaction about one's background. Should we eliminate a negative mark on one's record, which prevents that one to prosper in a civilized society?

As an example, take the financial credit score ratings. Based on the formulas used by financial institutions, each one of us has a credit score, from the 500s to the 800s, from poor to exceptional. If you don't pay your debts on time, or default on a loan you get punished, and lenders will not finance you, or if they do, it will be at a higher rate. In case you get foreclosed you won't be able to borrow for a mortgage for seven years, regardless how well you pay your other debts. I think we should base the criminal record on the same principles: forgiveness over a period, for exemplary behavior.

Most crimes happen in a moment of passion when one is young. It should not punish them for the rest of their lives after they served their punishment. What I'm proposing is a rating of "M" for misdemeanor and "F" for felony followed by a number. The numbers should decrease over the years of exemplary behavior and gainful employment. In the end, when the number following the letter M or F gets to zero, we expunge the criminal record, clearing all criminal past.

I agree, we must give all people who committed mistakes a second chance to prosper, while the society is protected as well.

Seeks to resolve: the war on Black immigrants including the repeal of the 1996 crime and immigration bills;

Under Bill Clinton's administration "The Illegal Immigration Reform and Immigrant Responsibility Act of 1996" was passed to enforce the immigration laws, and punish illegal immigrants for being here illegally or committing crimes while in our country.

This demand is racist against all other races, except black. Also, this demand could be here on the account of Opal Tometi's parents who illegally immigrated to the US from Nigeria. This is a matter of the Immigration Law. No one group should be preferred over another. The Democrat Socialist Party has trampled the Immigration Laws. The Democrats want to call the illegal immigrants as undocumented immigrants. Another alternative is to call them undocumented Democrat voters. A country's prosperity can be maintained only with enforceable immigration laws that favor *our nation and our people*.

Seeks to resolve: the war on Black trans, queer and gender nonconforming people;

This demand is here on the account of Patrisse Cullors who is queer, and Alicia Garza, both of them being activists in the L.G.B.T.Q. community. Is there war against black trans, queer and gender nonconforming people? Aren't all L.G.B.T.Q. free to do as they please?

This is to emphasize the victimhood beliefs. There is no war against black trans, queer and gender nonconforming people. This is a fabricated lie. And if it is true? Do we need more laws than we already have?

Seeks to resolve: the mass surveillance of Black communities;

I didn't know that the black communities are masses surveyed like the white communities. BLM may not think they are *radical*, but they are, considering what they did, and if we don't meet all of their demands, they'll burn down our cities. And where do they get the idea to *burn down our cities*? They took this from the operational manual of Soviet Communists when they tried to infiltrate and caused dissent among the black society earlier on.

Per the information from "Color, Communism and Common Sense" by Manning Johnson, citing an excerpt from "Why Communism?" by M. J. Olgin (Official Communist pamphlet instructing members in revolutionary strategy) the following is said:

> Workers stop work, many of them seize arms by attacking arsenals. Many had armed themselves before... Street fights become frequent. Under the leadership of the Communist Party the workers organize Revolutionary Committees to be in command of the uprising. Armed workers... seize the principal government offices, invade the residence of the President and his Cabinet members, arrest them, declare the old regime abolished, establish their own power... [16; pg18]

Seems familiar after the riots we had in the summer of 2020?

All radicals regardless of color are surveyed. Therefore, they want to prevent security forces from knowing what BLM is plotting. If FBI and other intelligence organizations would have done a better job, nine-eleven would have been prevented. And so future mayhem that BLM might cause.

Seeks to resolve: the militarization of law enforcement;

Stop the militarization of law enforcement goes hand in hand with defunding the police. This is a goal of the neo Marxists-Leninists when time comes to rise there will not be any forces to oppose them other than the military, if the military will have not been indoctrinated by then.

Seeks to resolve: the privatization of police, prisons, jails, probation, parole, food, phone and all other criminal justice related services;

What does the privatization of those services have to do with anything other than saving money and providing a better service. Why are Government control over those institutions and services preferred? The inmates control many such places. Would private ownership change that situation? Most likely it will.

Seeks to resolve: public jails, detention centers, youth facilities and prisons in their present conditions.

There is a point to be made here. Detention centers by any name remove the criminals from the society and punish them by restricting their freedom. Instead, the detention centers have become universities for training and producing more criminals. It punishes, while dehumanizes an individual. And after they release a detainee, where does he start in life? He is older, learned more criminal skills, but not working skills. Crime is their only alternative.

For non-violent criminals the detention centers should be rehabilitation and job-skill training centers. Even if they build a wall, demolish it afterwards, and rebuild it again, the detainees will learn the masonry skill. We can apply other trade skills as well. But that will cost money, and why help a criminal improve his life when a law-abiding youth has to pay for himself to learn a skill? Society will have to decide on this issue of what is better, more crime or more productive citizens. Give them skills and they may never commit crimes again. I hope.

2-Reparations for the:

"systemic denial of access to high quality educational opportunities in the form of full and free access for all Black people";

This is BULLSHIT. Since the 1960s the American society and school system have bent backwards to accommodate and admit black students in universities. In fact, the American Universities in their socialist zeal have and are engaged in racial discrimination against Asians and Whites. The result is: graduating students that are poorly educated, educated in useless subjects and consequently are unemployable. As attested earlier the graduated *don't know how to think*. Going to university will not make one smarter if one doesn't understand what one's studying.

Reparations for the: "continued divestment from, discrimination toward and exploitation of our communities in the form of a guaranteed minimum livable income for all Black people";

Continued divestment from the black communities results from the high crime and riots in those communities. Businesses are reluctant to invest where crime is high. Every time there is a riot they burn the businesses down. I read an article in "the New Yorker" magazine, my source of mostly Leftist information, discussing how there are no businesses in high-crime areas, and the only retail stores seeming to exist in those communities are the "Dollar" type stores. That is a poor choice of shopping for people in any community, but that's the only choice for blacks after they burned down the supermarkets. What's worst, they frequently rob the remaining stores. If business people cannot operate and make a profit, they'll not invest in those areas. And who is responsible for the bleak reality in those areas? The criminal blacks.

Guaranteed minimum livable income for all Black people is a socialist demand, or Equity. How can any business provide that if they cannot operate profitably their businesses? BLM has the impression that businesses are sitting on a stash of cash, unwilling to pay the black people *minimum livable income* because they are black. In a free economy demand and supply decides what are the prices to be paid. They don't pay employees for what they demand, but for what skills they have and how many jobs are available.

The only solution is: learn a skill, work hard and stop destroying your own neighborhood.

Reparations for the: "wealth extracted from" the black communities "through environmental racism, slavery, food apartheid, housing discrimination and racialized capitalism in the form of corporate and government reparations";

This should be a major problem for a "trained Marxist" like Patrisse Cullors. The Communist Manifesto intends to eliminate individual wealth. I guess she is a "trained Marxist," but money talks, and Marxism BS walks.

But let's "agree" with this demand. All wealth is derived from work, and the black slaves contributed to the wealth of the plantation owners without compensation. How much should the compensation be? Reparations for slavery in the United States are under consideration and according to Wikipedia the following it is said:

> Economist Robert Browne stated the ultimate goal of reparations should be to "restore the black community to the economic position it would have if it had not been subjected to slavery and discrimination". He estimates a fair reparation value anywhere between $1.4 to $4.7

> trillion, or roughly $142,000 (equivalent to $153,000 in 2019 money) for every black American living today. Other estimates range from $5.7 to $14.2 or even $17.1 trillion. Rapper, T>I, supports reparations that give every African American $1,000,000 and that slavery caused mass incarcerations, poverty and other ills.

As of 2019, the black population was 44 million people or 13% of American population, and considering the high estimate of $1 million for each one, the amount needed will be $44,000,000,000,000, that is 44 trillion dollars. America's wealth in 2018 was $98 trillion dollars. The compensation would be 45% of the country's total wealth. In 2019, the American population was 328 million, and based on these figures, the nation's wealth per individual is about $300,000. What would justify 3.3 times more compensation for the black people than the rest of us? Nothing. One million compensation for each black person is preposterous.

Another amount considered above is $153,000 per person, and multiplied by the black population, it would come to $6.7 trillion. The compensation will be up to the American people, or better said, the Democrat Socialist Party. Although 99.99% of all Americans did not own slaves or profit from slavery, each man, woman, and child will have to pay $20,524 in extra taxes, including the black people.

If this happens or not, there are many questions to be answered. How about compensation for the Native Americans? We took an entire continent from them. For Latinos, who even today are paid lowest wages to pick the harvest from the fields? How about all the nations in the world that claim that we "robbed" them of mineral resources? And while we're at it, in the name of all the people in Central and Eastern European nations who lived for 44 years under communism enslavement, I place a demand on the USA to compensate those nations for allowing the Soviet Union and Stalin to occupy and convert them to socialism, compliments of President Franklin D. Roosevelt, of course.

There could be no end to demands from the potential victims, real, imagined, ridiculous, or bizarre.

The compensation of $153,000 will be have to be taxed, and therefore each black individual will get around $100,000, or less.

What will the impact be on our economy? Over four trillion infused in the economy will cause major inflation.

How wisely will each black recipient use their reparation amount? The chances are high that most people will blow the entire amount in less than a year. A *decent* Mercedes-Benz or BMW can cost $100,000.

Poor people do not know the value of money, only the reward of spending it. And in the end, all that money will end up in who's pockets? The ones who know the value of money, most of them the so-called "exploiters." Yes, but many blacks will live a better life for a year.

And after that, what?

The black people will be back where they started, as poor as before, but owning a Mercedes-Benz, and costing them $1,000 per year to maintain. While the rest of the population, 328 million, will have to live with $20k less, each.

Reparations for the: "cultural and educational exploitation, erasure, and extraction" in the form of, among other things, "public school curriculums that critically examine the political, economic, and social impacts of colonialism and slavery"; and

Since the 1960s there has been nothing else but rewriting the public-school curriculums to educate our kids about the exploitation of colonialism and slavery. Under the Communist-Socialist school system (always over-critical of the US, capitalism, imperialism, colonialism.) I had less education about colonialism and imperialism evils than the kids in the US. In my opinion, the US schools went overboard on these subjects contributing to the hatred of white race and of our country. And this trend is speeding up.

the demand the state and federal levels require "the United States to acknowledge the lasting impacts of slavery, establish and execute a plan to address those impacts".

This is adding insult to injury. Slavery was a common thing throughout ages. No one in the past ever considered abolishing slavery until the 18th century when the Western White Society started the abolishment of slavery. Whites killed whites to emancipate the black slaves. The Blacks would have stayed slaves if it wasn't for the Whites, and the Whites were not the first to enslave them. In 1981, the last country to abolish slavery was Mauritania in Africa. How about a thank you to the Whites, instead.

Today's American people have made extraordinary advances and spent enormous amount of money in race relationship arena. Today's people have nothing to apologize for. If the black people want to get self-respect through white people's apologies or kissing the boots of black men, it won't bring self-respect for any black person. Self-respect comes from within, not from others.

3-Invest-Divest:

Reallocation of federal, state, and local government funds from "policing and incarceration to long-term strategies for education, restorative justice services, and employment programs."

As far as education, the US spends more than any other country on education and yet our kids are poorly instructed. According to the Boston Sun – https://www.baltimoresun.com/education/bs-md-nations-report-card-20180409-story.html – the following results from current education in Baltimore:

> Baltimore City students scored near the bottom in reading and math compared to children in other cities and large urban areas on an important national assessment given in 2017, according to scores released Tuesday morning.
>
> In fourth- and eighth-grade reading, only 13 percent of city students are proficient or advanced. In fourth-grade math, 14 percent were proficient and in eighth-grade math 11 percent met the mark, according to the National Assessment of Educational Progress, a federally mandated test from the U.S. Department of Education.

Black teachers taught those kids, in a city with a black mayor, and nine of the fourteen council members are black. No white oppression or systemic racism there. Throwing more money at the education won't solve the problem.

However, there is a solution: Vouchers for private schooling, which the Democrat Socialists oppose because the teacher unions oppose it. The teacher unions, strong supporter of the Democrat Socialist Party, care more about the teachers than the students. No matter how much the black parents want a better education for their kids by implementing vouchers and private education they'll get none as long as they vote Democrat.

As far as employment, or lack of, which is at the root of all poverty problems, learning a skill is the only solution. Employment without skills won't happen in a Free-Market economy. So far most of the young black men and women lack skills, and it doesn't seem to be a rush for self-improvement. Should we run our schools like skill-producing institutions, like boot camps to ensure education and skill acquirement? Perhaps it should apply to all young kids going to high school, and are caught in the streets committing crimes.

The decriminalization, immediate release, record expungement, and reparations for the disparaging effects of both the "war on drugs" and "the criminalization of prostitution" on black communities.

I addressed this above, and a solution offered. However, automatic erasing of all records is the equivalent of emptying all jails and prisons. The crime will soar, just as it happened in the 1990s and later in 2020 based on the hysterical reaction of Democrat Socialists DAs and Mayors to defund the police and release the arrested criminals without bail.

"Real, meaningful, and equitable universal healthcare"

Despite the opposition by the Republicans, something has to be done about healthcare. But *not government run health care,* which will be a disaster for everyone. Why? Does a bureaucrat who cannot be fired perform better than a private employee? Let your own health decide what's best for us: Higher taxes, long lines and poor treatments or what we have today.

A constitutionally protected right to a "fully-funded education"

A constitutionally protected right? What were the writers of these demands smoking? We have free education from K to 12, and it is not written in the Constitution. If they mean higher education, like college and university, that cannot happen. It will be a waste of money to produce more poorly educated graduates, with skills that are not productive and therefore unemployable. It also comes down to who will pay for that education? The people who don't go to college and work. Not fair for the rest of us. Besides higher education will generate more socialist brainwashed people.

Divestment from the "use of fossil fuels and investment in community-based sustainable energy solutions."

This is Pie-in-the-Sky. Also, it is associated with the demented "Green New Deal." Why so? People who ask for sustainable energy solutions do not know what energy is, how it is produced and used. Yes, I would love a new form of clean energy, but there is nothing that can replace fossil fuel today. Because we don't have a solution to abandon the fossil fuels, the economy, all economies, will go into contraction, causing more poverty for all. And what does "*community-based sustainable energy solutions*" mean? Communist-speak.

Cuts to military expenditures and a reallocation of those funds to "infrastructure and community well-being"

These are pacifist aspirations, unrealistic in our world. Nations don't behave like neighbors. They behave like thugs. A weak military country invites aggressive moves from other nations, like Russia, China, Iran. This request is shortsighted and foolish.

4-Economic Justice:

Redistribution of wealth through a "progressive restructuring of tax codes at the local, state, and federal levels."

They took this from the Communist Manifesto, Point 2.

A heavy progressive or graduated income tax.

This is what Barack Obama and other Marxist-Socialists call redistribution of wealth. This rule is one among many rules why under socialism the economy and the poverty level reach new lows. Socialism brings only poverty and misery, but *equally and equitably distributed.*

Employment programs that specifically target the "most marginalized Black people" in order to promote economic equality.

See what I said about skills and employment above. Also, this is very similar to another socialist system, the "NAZI-Socialism's Twenty-five Point Political Program" Point 7 that states:

> Every citizen has a job. We think that the government's first job is to make sure every citizen has a job and enough to eat. If the government cannot do this, people who are not citizens should be made to leave Germany.

Replace German with black people and you're in tune with Hitler's NAZI-Socialist party.

It is also in alignment with Point 10 of the same program that states:

> Every citizen should have a job. Their work should not be selfish, but help everyone.

Do you still have doubts that Hitler was a Socialist?

"A right to restored land, clean air, clean water and housing and an end to the exploitative privatization of natural resources."

This is Rule 7 in Communist Manifesto:

> Extension of factories and instruments of production owned by the State; the bringing into cultivation of wastelands, and the improvement of soil generally in accordance with a common plan.

Right for workers to organize in both the public and private sector.

Don't we have unions and the right to organize?

Restoration of the Glass-Steagall Act.

Whatever. Why would BLM care what the private economy is doing? Private ownership of the economy is to be abolished, anyway.

"An end to the Trans-Pacific Partnership, and a renegotiation of all trade agreements" with an increased focus on the interests of workers and communities.

Isn't this what President Trump has done to bring the jobs back from China? Is President Biden doing the same?

Increased support for "the development of cooperative or social economy networks."

This item is in the spirit of Rule 1 from the Communist Manifesto, the nationalization of the economy. They have applied it to all European ex-Communist-Socialist countries and failed catastrophically. "Cooperative or social economy" is managing by committees, mediocre ideas are undertaken with no one responsible for the outcome.

"Financial support of Black alternative institutions."

Not sure what Black alternative institutions are, but they should get the same financial support as well other race groups receive. Again, this is racist.

Increased protection for workers in poorly regulated industries.

Protection for workers is paramount to our industrial workers. That's why OSHA – Occupational Safety and Health Administration – exists.

5-Community Control:

Implementation of "democratic community control of local, state, and federal law enforcement agencies."

We live in a democracy and the citizens vote for candidates to represent us, therefore we have community control.

"End to the privatization of education."

They wrote this entire platform to improve the lives of black people, and yet, this very demand defies logic. Charter schools outperform public schools, and from what I heard, responsible black parents want their kids to advance and be successful and want vouchers to send their kids to private schools. Short of protecting the Teachers Unions, the other reason for not wanting the black kids to learn better is the basic principle that Socialism don't want *thinkers*, only *ignorant followers*.

Communal participation in "budgeting at the local state and federal level."

We have democracy in this country, and the people elect state and local officials. Why do we need another level of *communal* bureaucracy? Socialism.

We disrupt the Western-prescribed nuclear family structure requirement by supporting each other as extended families and "villages" that collectively care for one another, especially our children, to the degree that mothers, parents, and children are comfortable.

This is BULSHIT. After decades of *War on Poverty*, black families have almost achieved this demand if we consider that 72% of all black babies are born out-of-wedlock. Their "success" is reflected by the fact that black males go to jail five times more than white males. The US incarceration rates in 2010 by race per 100 thousand people was:

Race	Incarcerations	Single Parent %
Black	2,306	66 %
Latin	831	42 %
White	450	34 %
Asian	115	22 %

The interesting fact about the above data is that the lower the incarcerations, the higher the nuclear and expanded family are among those races. Then why is BLM proposing such an idiotic idea? Are the blacks wanting all races to fail like them?

The reason is simpler; the dissolution of nuclear families is a prerequisite to making the new Communist ~~Man/Woman~~ Entity under the Communism ideology. Therefore, BLM wants to transcend socialism and go directly to Communism.

6-Political Power:

"End to the criminalization of Black political activity."

Unless the black political activity is not causing harm, why would this even come up. We don't live under J. Edgar Hoover's FBI.

Termination of super PACs and the implementation of "public financing of elections."

BLM has received tens of millions of dollars in donations from individuals and businesses. What are they doing with that money? Acting as a super PAC for the Democrat Socialist party.

Establishment of "full-access guarantees, and protections of the right to vote for all people."

All people have the right to vote based on their beliefs. Only US citizens can vote, otherwise, we're not a country. Without proof of the right to vote like an ID, one should not be able to vote. You cannot do much without an ID in our society, but when it comes to voting, not having an ID is discriminatory. Are they saying that the black people are so dumb that they cannot get an ID? I think not.

"Full-access to technology" through the implementation of "net-neutrality and universal access to internet."

Everyone has access to the Internet, so what's the problem? Is the Internet discriminating against the black people, and how does it know that?

"Protection and increased funding for Black institutions." This should apply to all races not just Black institutions.

I'll have to say that they wrote this platform as if we would still be in the 1960s, completely ignoring the progress we made in this country on race since then. It ignores that the black people have received more benefits and benefited mostly over other races in the US. They have brainwashed many white people to believe in *Systemic Racism* against black people.

The failure is not because of our society, but the black community that has not made an effort to grow and prosper like most American people. They feel they failed because of us, especially the white people, when in reality, they failed because of themselves. This platform is nothing but an entitlement demand, the *give-me* belief because we did them wrong, and Socialism will correct that. Unless most black people stop thinking like victims instead of achievers, nothing will change, no matter how much society will give them. The entire black society's culture and values have to change; otherwise, everything will stay the same with non-stop protests, property damages, fires and looting, and backlash from the rest of the population.

Then what BLM stands for? Not killings of blacks. That is a smokescreen. Black Lives Matter has a neo-Marxist Socialist political agenda using the Communist Manifesto, Critical Race Theory, and the Race Card to bring Socialism to America.

Chapter 2.6. ANTIFA Subdue and Intimidate the Opposition

Hitler established the Brown Shirts, the infamous SA, or Sturmabteilung, or Storm Troopers, for protection, intimidation, and promotion of his ideology. In the beginning, they were used to protect themselves against the communists, which had similar "Storm Troopers" and were attacking the Nazi speeches and events. The SA turned up to be a very useful tool for the Nazis, especially as an intimidation organization and for demonstrations.

The American Marxists established the Antifa, Anti-Fascist, organization to fight any Right-wing demonstrations or propaganda. In their black attire, the violence they provoke, they are nothing else but a Fascist organization despite the red "Hammer and Cycle" symbol. But then Fascism is a Leftist ideology anyway. Antifa, a fascist organization that pretends to be anti-fascist that fights fascism. Their ideology according to Wikipedia:

> Individuals involved in the Antifa movement hold anti-authoritarian, anti-capitalist, anti-fascist, and anti-state views, subscribing to a varied range of left-wing ideologies. A majority of adherents are anarchists, communists, and other socialists who describe themselves as revolutionaries, although some social democrats and others on the American Left, among them environmentalists, LGBTQ and indigenous rights advocates, also adhere to the Antifa movement.

In reality, Antifa, in appearance and actions, does not differ from the Nazi Brown Shirts or Italian Fascist Black Shirts. Antifa organization is a Fascist, Socialist, Communist, and anarchist organization all rolled into one to fight *Fascism*. Their ideology and purpose are to fight against all those of the Right ideology, in their mind the Fascists. For example, during the BLM demonstrations, they were the ones who provoked and facilitated the BLM protesters breaking windows, starting fires, and inciting others to commit acts of violence, including murder. They are organized, commit mayhem and they hide among the naïve demonstrators.

What's surprising is, Antifa recognizes that the Fascists have parallel ideology as of the Marxists and accuse the Fascists of stealing and adopting the Socialist ideas. Hitler accused that Marxists stole the name *socialism* for their purpose. But it doesn't matter; they're all Socialists.

Antifa's members are mostly white, middle-class Americans and spoiled brats whose brains are underground. Our country is a prosperous country with upper mobility, and poverty is not an issue, aside from what Southern Poverty Law Center, a racist-socialist organization, says. Therefore, Antifa is fighting racism, neo-Nazis, white supremacists, and far-right extremists, patriarchy, homophobics, Islamophobics, and Christians. This is not much different from the BLM platform. As far as islamophobia, it just shows you the hypocrisy of their ideology. Muslims are religious and conservative, but that doesn't matter as long as President Trump banned certain Islamic countries from entering the United States, they're pro-Islam.

The so-called *Systemic Racism* is a big lie, but they believe it as true. The American neo-Nazi party has 500 members, from what I found online. KKK, white supremacists, and far-right extremists may have 5 to 8 thousand members, which is hardly a threat.

But this "racism" seems to have been increasing since the election of Barack Obama in 2008. Why? They elevated racism as the "*sin*" to eliminate and hatred toward those perceived as racists. But you don't combat racism with racism. The hatred toward the white people has escalated and became more evident in 2021 with Joe Biden in the White House. Not all white people have been brainwashed to believe they are racist, and they react with mixed emotions when accused of being racist or denied opportunities because their skin color, not qualifications, matter. There is an undeniable covert war on the white people in America. Antifa, mostly white, are at the front.

Who really are the Antifa members? As I mentioned, they are primarily *white people*. Mostly young, but not all. Mostly educated – indoctrinated– but not all. Many have jobs, professional jobs. They are trying to do "justice," fighting minority groups of the Right. Their entire strategy is to combat Fascism (conservative, White people) and prevent it from spreading. That's why every time there is any gathering of the Right, it's met by Antifa with screams, jeers, provocations, harassment at work or place of domicile, doxing, and violence if necessary.

Antifa's motto is:

> We [Antifa] go where they [the Right] go.

Wherever a Right-wing group, like the Boogaloo movement, Proud Boys, Patriot Prayer, and others gather, they go to counter-protest and provoke them or prevent that gathering from taking place. Their actions have frightened the municipalities and prevent Right wing gatherings. Prohibition of free speech.

What they do is prevent *free speech*. In their opinion according to the book "Antifa" by Mark Bray:

> ...that free speech absolutism, like many kinds of rights absolutism, is impossible in a society of overlapping interests. [30: pg. 145]

How else would we communicate when we are in a society with *overlapping interests*, but through *Free Speech*? And talking about absolutism, Antifa is all about *absolutism*.

This prohibition against free speech is not only in the public spaces but on campuses where Right-wing or conservative speakers are prevented from speaking. The Constitution affirms our right to free speech, but not all free speech is acceptable to the Marxists, and they claim you have the right to free speech as long it is not hateful or hurtful speech. Antifa states that anything the Right mentions is hurtful. Well, everything Antifa and the Marxists say is hurtful to me and others like me. Free speech does not mean it can only be agreeable speech. Considering how much I hate Socialism and Communism, I will insist that they can assemble and speak freely.

And if only agreeable and ethical speech is allowed, *who would decide that*? In the Socialist countries, the Communist political censors, enforced by the power of the police, did that. Antifa insists that they have the right, as private citizens, to ban the free speech of the Right. Just because our Constitution guarantees free speech, meaning the government cannot obstruct free speech, Antifa, a non-government organization, can prevent and block free speech. However, since they are blocking free speech on University campuses, which get money from the government, they don't have the right to do that on any public or government-supported institutions. Unfortunately, they have free rein in the Marxist Universities and of the Democrat Socialist Party-controlled cities and states like Oregon and Washington.

The Marxists and Antifa's strategy ensure that you hear only the Left's opinion, and MSM and many private companies now comply. An example is Amazon. Yes, I was able to publish and sell my book "Hitler Was A Socialist," but when it came to advertising my book, the Amazon Marketing Services that provides the advertising blocked me. It was obvious what was going on. Amazon is based in Seattle, an Antifa town, and most likely, their members work for Amazon. A book with such title as "Hitler Was a Socialist" is blasphemy to the Marxists. Out of discussion. Yet, I invented nothing but researched and quoted what Hitler said and what the NAZI-Socialists did, which was Socialism. And believe me, I know what Socialism is and what it does. Eventually, I wrote to Bezos, and they relented, and I could advertise. But, typical of Marxists, they were determined to destroy my book, and the Marxists ganged together and gave me one-star reviews without reading the book or providing logical criticisms, except slogans. All comments were ignorant, dogmatic messages.

My book, "Escape from Communism" was prevented from being advertised by Amazon Marketing Service. In an e-mail they stated:

> Please remove this content from your ad. The portion of your custom text that needs to be corrected is "than the Socialist slavery."
>
> Yours sincerely, The Amazon Advertising Team

Scouse me, but I lived in that hell, and I was a slave, and I have the right to call Socialism slavery.

This very book "Freedom Trumps Socialism: How the Democrat Party is Using Hitler's Playbook to Make America Socialist" is prohibited from being advertised on Amazon. The reason:

> Your ad contains content that is not allowed for advertising. Please remove any content related to political campaigns, elections, or political issues of public debate; that <u>advocates for or against a politician or a political party</u>; or that personally attacks a political figure.
>
> Yours sincerely, The Amazon Advertising Team

My ad had no words only the cover and the full title. Therefore, in the United States of America a writer is prohibited from writing against (Democrat) political party. This happens only in Socialism.

Despite their attempt to silence me, my books sell and I urge you to buy it and read them. Freedom fighters need information. (If you want to make the Marxists suffer, give my book five stars.) You'll learn a lot about Socialism as Hitler applied it, which now the Democrat Socialist Party follows.

I couldn't find a membership number for Antifa, and they have a decentralized organization based on cells in different cities and countries. Why are they organized this way and not as a hierarchal organization? From my education under socialism, in my young days, I know that all clandestine and illegal organizations, like those of the communists, organized themselves in cells with limited contact among the cells. The reason, in case the police caught one of their members and confessed, it limited their knowledge about the members to that cell only. However, that doesn't mean they are headless. Specialists conduct indoctrination and instructions in how to create mayhem.

Antifa, a domestic terrorist group, will not be in any danger from the police or FBI, as long as Joe Biden is the President and the Democrat Socialist Party is in charge.

There is no surprise that young people join Antifa. As the saying goes:

> If You Are Not a Liberal at 25, You Have No Heart.
> If You Are Not a Conservative at 35 (or 45), You Have No Brain.

The Marxist professors brainwash the young people attending colleges, and Antifa actively recruits on campuses. As long as this continues, socialism is winning.

Some Antifa members are adults with jobs, as reported in the New Yorker Magazine about how AG Barr was overreaching by catching and prosecuting protesters. Two of those arrested were *lawyers*. The police found Molotov cocktails ingredients in their van. They saw one of them on video, throwing a Molotov cocktail through an unoccupied police car's window.

Another of these Antifa protesters was an older man. On TV, this older man, in his 70s, approached the police officers seemingly to appease them. One of the policemen pushed him out of the way, and he fell flat on his back, injuring his head and bled. That didn't look good. Until the truth was unveiled, that older man was an Antifa member. I guess his brains never caught up with him. His appeasement gestures were an intent to scan and collect the radio frequency used by the cops with his smartphone and inform the Antifa coordinators. They would redirect demonstrations at locations where the police were absent.

On TV as well, I saw how an Antifa member deposited a pallet of bricks in a street, near a BLM demonstration, and called his associates to pick up the bricks. Smashing businesses' windows is easier with bricks that otherwise would be scarce to find in any city's downtown.

Antifa tactics are to push as close as possible to the line before their actions become criminal. When they are among crowds and with their identities masked, they'll gladly smash windows, set fire to businesses, or even kill. When the Republican convention was held at the White House, Antifa and BLM quickly surrounded it, demonstrating against imagined fascists. What was even worse is the participants at the White House, on their way after leaving the White House, were harassed, being verbally abused, spitted on, and water was thrown on them. These anarchists harassed senator Rand Paul and his wife Kelley as they walked back to their hotel. Luckily, the DC police gave them some protection and didn't get hurt.

Another form of harassing free citizens is by doxing. According to the book "Antifa," an Antifa group in Omaha doxed Cooper Ward, co-host of *The Daily Shoah* podcast, and this is how they did it:

> Antifa Nebraska printed thousands of flyers with his name, photo, and information on his Nazism and plastered them around town, forcing him to drop out of college, take down his social media, and go in hiding. [30: pg. 115]

Cooper Ward was a Nazi, but that is not illegal. But Antifa ruined his life. How would you like, without being a Nazi, to be doxed by being a conservative, voting for Trump? To me, that is a political crime.

The entire summer of 2020 was on fire by the demonstrations of BLM and Antifa. Night after night, hundreds of the hoodlums demonstrated until the wee hours of the morning. One would wonder, aren't those people employed, do they have a job to attend during the day? Of course, the pandemic nullified attending work, but it takes money to show up, and most times, many of these people were not local. Were they that rich to afford travel and accommodations? No, they were not rich but were recruited and paid to demonstrate. I saw a video that showed this man in his thirties explaining that he was a professional demonstrator. "Where would you apply for such a job?" the interviewer asked, "On George Soros website." I checked and didn't find any place on that site to apply for a demonstrator job. But, there was an enrollment box to receive e-mails and news e-letters. Sign up, and in due time you'll be offered to demonstrate for free and later get paid. A friend of mine told me that when there were demonstrations and riots in LA, the demonstrators were accommodated at the Four Seasons in downtown LA. That takes a lot of money. But, hey, Soros has billions.

The question remains if Fascism is nonexistent in the United States, who are these Fascists? Antifa and the Leftists consider Fascists anyone who is religious and believes in God, patriotic, hardworking to better themselves and their family, believes in the Constitution, Democracy, and Freedom, and are White race, especially white men.

Do you believe in God, family, Constitution, Democracy, Freedom, are you a patriot, hardworking, and White? Are you one of those deplorables? If you do, you are that *Fascist*, according to them.

We, the white people, are the equivalent of Jews of Nazi Germany who must be re-programmed or eliminated.

Chapter 3. Infiltration.

Hitler felt the bitter taste of defeat in 1923 with his disastrous Putsch in Munich. It landed him in jail, and they barred him from public speaking for many years. A serious blowback for the NAZI-Socialists. What he realized was that taking over the government by force was not possible in Germany. Therefore, he changed his tactics and vowed to gain power through democratic elections. But he needed allies, especially in the Police, judiciary, and the Military. Those government bodies could crackdown on his party and send him back to Austria and the NAZI members in jail. He successfully infiltrated the government bureaucracy, police and justice. But not the Military, which had a code of conduct not to be involved in politics.

As for the Deep State, the Bureaucracy, he formed a parallel government with Nazi members, emulating the actual government. Then, when the NAZI-Socialists would come to power, he would have a Nazi Deep State ready to take over the old government.

The American Marxists have done the same. They infiltrated the Deep State, the government bureaucracy, and the Justice Department. By appointing Liberal Judges to the American courts, the American Marxists had been successful at eroding our Constitutional rights. And of making laws of their likings. Our police and the military are different.

The neo-Marxists have infiltrated the Justice Department and FBI, the federal police. The reason is relatively simple. To be an FBI agent, one must have a college degree. Therefore, the younger, college graduated generations have been indoctrinated in Marxism. Do you see why the FBI was spearheading a coup d'état against President Trump, using the fabricated Russian collusion as the reason. The FBI may become the future Political Secret Police in the United States.

The local police officers don't have to have college degrees to become police officers. Although, they need to graduate from police academies. They escaped the Colleges' Marxist brainwashing. Also, they are down to earth and deal with the life realities in the streets every day, unlike we do in our living rooms. Because the neo-Marxists did not infiltrate the police, they must destroy the police as we know it and remake it, *re-image* it as the Leftists say. Do you see now why they want to *defund* the police? The police shooting of blacks, armed or unarmed, has caused great fuel for the propaganda against the White police officers, although there are many Black police officers as well. Most of the black people killed have criminal records or are engaged in crimes when a shooting happens. Most of the black men killed do not obey the orders from the police and act as if they are above the law, and fight the policemen who are trying to arrest them.

I saw a dashcam video where a white policewoman attempted to arrest a black motorist. As she was trying to handcuff him, he turned around, hit her in the face, and knocked her down. Then he straddled her and began punching her in the face. After he got tired, he departed in his car. The condition of the policewoman, I don't know. The police officers confront violent criminals every day, and they could be killed without warning. And if there are more blacks killed, it is because the blacks commit more crimes than any other race group. The

Washington Post shows that in 2019, the police officers shot 13 unarmed Black and 25 unarmed white men.

George Floyd's death is not part of the above statistics. He was a convicted criminal and tried to use a fake $20 bill at the store in front of which he died. George Floyd's death shows in what a bind the police are in when attempting to arrest an out-of-control criminal, drugged beyond limit, and dies in a picture-damning situation under the officer subduing him. You're damn if you do, you're damn if you don't.

But that's not important. The police are the *Evil* that persecutes the black population. False. The police are trying to keep the peace while risking their lives for all of us.

Anarchy will rule in our streets with a diminished police force. Even the "abolish the police" malcontents will scream for more police when their neighborhoods will not be safe. The socialist's plan is to break something that works just to be replaced with their socialist design of State police. The Democrat Socialist Party agenda is to federalize the police, retrain it and re-image it.

The military infiltration will be discussed in a later chapter.

Chapter 3.1. Infiltrate the Educational System.

The young minds are most malleable to accept any ideology. Unlike in the US today, the German universities were more inclined to accept the NAZI-Socialist Propaganda before Hitler became a dictator. After Hitler was in power, all schools became NAZI-Socialists indoctrination machines, just as ours are today.

The American Marxists have succeeded in infiltrating our education institutions. They have complete control in most universities, and all professors that are not Leftists don't get a chance to teach. They are not hired. One's political affiliation determines eligibility to be a professor today, not competence. The American Universities have become Marxists indoctrination machines. The Marxist indoctrination has begun at all levels of education, from K-12 to college. Hitler would be proud of them.

Chapter 3.2. Infiltrate the Media.

After WW I, Germany had a democracy and free press. Most newspapers in those times were affiliated with one party or ideology, depending on who owned them. Other than the official Nazi newspaper, "Völkischer Beobachter" Hitler was unsuccessful in infiltrating and taking control of the media until after he became a dictator.

The American Marxists had a spectacular success in infiltrating most media, newspapers, TV, Social Media, and Hollywood. Except for conservative talk shows, and FOX News TV, NewsmaxTV, and OANN. The indoctrination of the American public is in full force. Hitler would have only wished to have achieved such success before he took power in Germany.

On March 16, 2021, Robert Aaron Long, a white man, attacked three spas or massage parlors in Atlanta and killed eight people. Six of the victims were Asians, and the MSM (CNN, MSNBC, etc.) howled about the anti-Asian crime spree committed by White men. But, in reality, racial hatred did not motivate the killing spree.

Some miscreants attack Asians in the streets because of the Coronavirus, prompting Congress to pass anti-Asian racism laws. Except, most of the Asian attackers are Black. Didn't see or hear about that? That's because the MSM is not interested in the truth but only spreading hatred against the white men.

On March 22, 2021, in Boulder, Colorado, an allegedly white man shot and killed ten people. CNN declared emphatically the threat we face from White men. Except, the shooter, Ahmad Al Aliwi Al-Issa, is a Syrian, and he killed ten White people, one of them a police officer. There were no Asians killed, but the attack still shows the evil of guns. This news was beyond Fake News.

But wait, the victims were ten white people killed by an Arab. No one mentioned anything about that as a "Muslim terrorist." Those ten people were just a bunch of *deplorables*, and it doesn't fit the MSM agenda of spreading lies and hatred against White men. These are two examples of how the neo-Marxists, controlling the Mainstream Socialist Media, are constantly twisting the news to show how bad the White men are. This is their Socialist campaign of spreading hatred.

Chapter 3.3. The American Labor

Surveys show that 44% of the American people view socialism favorably. To me, this is a DISASTER, considering the crimes Socialism has committed throughout the world. People who didn't experience life under socialism, or didn't learn about it, are prone to repeat history with dire consequences. When 44% of the people believe that socialism is good, we're doomed.

How could this subversive Marxist philosophy take over the people's minds?

> *Repeat a lie often enough, and it becomes the truth*, said Joseph Goebbels, the NAZI-Socialist minister of propaganda.

Therefore, if lies are taught in schools and introduce no contradictory information for critical thinking, lies become the truth.

I've got many 1-Star reviews on Amazon for my book "Hitler Was A Socialist," and one such 1-Star reviewer said:

> This author doesn't understand what socialism is and how it's uplifted people out of poverty globally.

Think about it? *I don't understand what socialism is*? Being born and lived under socialist tyranny, with all its political oppression, misery, and poverty. How misinformed can this person be to say that Socialism "uplifted people out of poverty globally," instead of knowing that socialism destroyed every nation it controlled. The Western Civilization's *Capitalist System uplifted people out of poverty globally*.

This reviewer and all other such "pretend reviewers" did not buy or read my book. Their comments attest to their limited knowledge of the subject. They learned their biased opinion from Marxist professors that socialism is wonderful. Hitler could not possibly be one of them, but he was, and all Socialists are alike. Be that Marxist-Socialists or National-Socialists, or Fascists.

The students more prone to fall prey to leftist ideologies are those graduating from the schools of humanities: Business, Social Sciences, Political Sciences, Psychology, Communication, Journalism, Visual Art, Performing Arts, and Education. In 2018, there were 1.9 million bachelor graduates. Out of these, 926 thousand were from the school of humanities. If we take these graduates and multiply by 30 years, we get 28 million workers in America today. There may be over 28 million believing what their Leftist professors taught them, but for simplicity, let's use 28 million workers who have the most influential jobs in our country. These are the professors and teachers, politicians, civil service bureaucrats, union leaders, activists, agitators, community organizers, news and media, Hollywood producers, writers, and Corporate-Bureaucrats. Those are the people who can influence the rest of the population, and they have done so for decades.

Talking about the writers who, in most cases, are Leftists, I must remind them what happened to the writers in the Soviet Union during Stalin. The book "The Soviet Writer's Union and Its Leaders: Identity and Authority Under Stalin" by Carol Any, Northwestern University Press, proclaimed in 1932, the union [writers] began with 2,200 members. By the time Stalin died in 1953, they had arrested 2,000; three-quarters of whom they had executed or perished in labor camps.

In the 2016 election, they surprised us how many votes socialist Bernie Sanders received in the primary. According to Wikipedia, Bernie received 43% of the Democrat popular vote. Most of the votes came from young people, recently indoctrinated in socialism. A Gallup poll from 2018 showed that among the democrats, 57% have a favorable view of socialism; results of our education today. Some don't know how to write and read, but socialism will be their salvation.

As John Ellis mentions:

> These figures should make us sit down and take notice: more than half of 18-to-29-years-old now look favorably on a political system that has brought misery wherever they imposed Marxism, while our own country has achieved remarkable success by avoiding socialism. It is a system so unpopular with people who

> lived under it that brutal dictatorships rely on violence to keep it in place when their people come to understand real-life under socialism. [1; pg113]

I personally attest to the tyrannical system that socialism is, not to mention that anywhere socialism takes over, the killing of innocent people who opposes socialism follows. Two hundred million people were killed by communism-socialism throughout the world, and they're not done yet.

The *Fear* that a citizen experience under communism-socialism is indescribable. I know Romanians who got visas to visit Italy. While in Rome, they planned to defect, but they were scared shitless to defect fearing, while in a free country, the long arm of the secret police of Communist-Socialist Romania.

In 2020 Joe Biden won the Presidency, and soon after he revealed his policy, it was as if Bernie Sanders and Alexandra Ocasio-Cortez threw up all over it. Joe Biden has shifted to the Left into socialism and wants to put his mark as the Critical Race Theory champion. The Democrat Party and all people voting democrat are voting for socialism.

Do you wonder why the BLM protesters were as many whites as blacks? Those white people were young, recently indoctrinated, and idealists. But eventually, they will climb the ladder of professional life and influence American politics and culture. Why are the celebrities and enterprises donating millions of dollars to Black Lives Matter? Apple, Google, Amazon, Microsoft, Nike, Walmart, and many other big companies donated or committed hundreds of millions of dollars to BLM. Those that were young once have climbed the corporate ladder and are showing their allegiances to BLM and Socialism. I want to remind those Marxist corporate executives of what Lenin said:

> The Capitalists will sell us the rope with which we will hang them.

Only the capitalists, one may think, will be hanged. No. As the executives of corporations racking huge salaries and bonuses, they'll suffer the same fate. So, they should choose the ropes and the trees in advance for fine hangings, unless they convert to Socialism.

The socialist indoctrinated people are part of the government at every level, from the city councils to the Federal Deep State bureaucracy. They determine what's good for us, and they will carry out all socialist initiatives with enthusiasm. How else could the fraud perpetrated in the 2020 election take place? With the help, participation, and complicity of the workers at the poll places and vote counting.

The Woke Zombies are now part of Corporate America. True, the businesses need to adapt to market trends, and if the markets move to the Left, so will the businesses. However, when corporations decide to ban a company's product because its owners expressed "unclean" views of the Right-wing, Socialism is here. An example is Mike Lindell and his company My Pillow, which Big Stores like Kohl's, Bed Bath & Beyond, and Kroger's banned his products. Any business needs a broader distribution channel for its product. Limiting the distribution channels limits the business's viability to prosper.

Or Coca-Cola Co. and Delta Airlines blasting Georgia legislature for the new Voting Law the State Legislation passed. Everyone, including Joe Biden, condemns the law as being against minority voters. They passed the law to make sure there will not be a fraud as it was in 2020. The law bars no one from voting except non-citizens and anyone without ID. The law increased the period to vote, before the election, but not after. The Democrat Socialist Party and their corporate lackeys are against preventing fraud, as fraud is their only chance to stay and gain total power.

Welcome to Socialism, comrades.

Chapter 4. Crisis

Political transformation happens during a crisis.
If there is none, create one.

And then came the Great Depression of the 1930s.

When Hitler joined the National Worker's Party movement in 1919, he was number seven. By 1932 the Nazi-Socialist party had 450,000 members. Many fresh recruits came from other parties, including the German Socialist party. The Great Depression devastated Germany, and Hitler took advantage of it. He didn't create the Depression, but he used it masterfully. In the 1933 election, the Nazi party received 17 million votes, gaining 288 seats, or 44%, in the Reichstag. What impact did the Great Depression have on Germany? Five years earlier, in the 1928 election, the Nazi-Socialist party received 810 thousand votes for only 12 seats in the Reichstag. That's what a crisis can do, elevated the Nazi-Socialist party representation in the Reichstag from 12 seats to 288.

The American Marxists control the Democrat Party, and that party has 47 million members or 31% of the American population. Republican membership represents 25% of the population. But the Democrats want more, as 41% of the voters are Independents. Their goal is an absolute majority in all branches of government, preferably a supermajority like the Democrat Socialist Party has in California legislation. But they cannot achieve that without new adherents to their cause or an increase in popularity. President Trump proved he can *Make America Great Again*. He had a high chance of being reelected in 2020, but...

Bill Maher said early in Trump's presidency:

> Pray that we have a recession in 2020 or Trump will be reelected again.

Something had to be done. MSM did its best to denigrate President Trump, but it could do only so much. They needed a crisis to change the rules:

Enter the Communist-Fascist China, Wuhan, Covid-19, Coronavirus Pandemic.

Governor Newsom of California said:

> With this pandemic, we'll have an opportunity to transform America.

After the 2020 election Chuck Schumer said on TV:

> Now, we'll change America.

Klaus Schwab, WEF chairman, said:

> The Pandemic represents a rare but narrow window of opportunity to reflect, reimagine, and reset our World.

As more news became available about this virus, more and more it looks that scientists developed it, and the United States paid part of the research via CDC funds. Then as it happens in a mystery novel:

> A scientist says he's found 13 Wuhan coronavirus sequences that were deleted from a US database - and claims they're a 'goldmine' for research into the virus' origins.
>
> [https://www.yahoo.com/news/scientist-says-hes-found-13-131605072.html]

They are covering their tracks.

Communist-Fascist China, Wuhan, Covid-19, Coronavirus Pandemic is the equivalent of Hitler's Great Depression. The Democrat Socialist Party exploited the pandemic to the fullest, as if they anticipated it.

Chapter 4.1. The Communist-Fascist China, Wuhan, Covid-19 Coronavirus

Dr. Anthony Fauci said back in January 2017 that the Trump administration would face a surprise disease outbreak. Was he expressing an educated guess, or he knew something else?

The 2020 Covid-19 Pandemic started in China as most viruses start, like influenzas, and it spread throughout the world, killing millions. The Communist Party of China did not like the virus to be called the Wuhan virus, which's bad for business, and told World Health Organization, WHO, to use another name. So, we now have Coronavirus, or more scientifically named Covid-19. How can the Chinese do that? Simple, China bribes most of the officials of the UN organizations, and it has WHO in its pocket, including its director Tedros Adhanom. Where is the proof? Occasionally, you hear scandals about these bribes. Still, it doesn't take a genius to figure that all third world country representatives at the UN, and other organizations like FIFA, just like the politicians in their home country, are corrupt and easily bribed and controlled. China does not claim to be holier-than-thou, like the United States, and gets what it wants with money under the table. China rules.

Was it a man-made virus created at Wuhan Virology Laboratory and used as a biological weapon, or a natural virus that Chinese shoppers in the wet market acquired from bats or pangolins? Was it leaked from the Wuhan bio-labs not too far from the market, or they gave the animals infected by the virus from the lab to be sold in the market for a quick yuan? Was it developed by the US and then contracted by Anthony Fauci et al. to Wuhan Biolabs to continue the experiments on the Coronavirus?

In 2020, the official position is that the virus was natural, jumping from bats or pangolins to humans in the wet markets in Wuhan. But there were significant doubts that was the case.

Chinese virologist Dr. Li-Meng Yan claims that the virus is artificial made in the Chinese Labs. She defected to the US for protection, her mother disappeared in China, and Twitter suspended her account. She also mentioned that this virus is not natural, including the mutations it evolves into. The MSM did their best, including many scientists, to cover up and stop rumors that this virus escaped from the Wuhan Labs. Only the wet markets were suspected. Why? To cover up that the virus was man-made, released for nefarious intentions.

The Mainstream Socialist Media, MSM, is criminal along with the Democrat Socialist Party on how they mislead and deceived us about this pandemic. Many more people died by staying at home, isolated, or because their cancer was not diagnosed in time, as it happened to a good friend of mine. How many businesses closed forever, and how many people became poorer because of the political lie perpetrated on us? And Joe Biden promised to lock us up because he *listens* to science. Science is only one element to resolve this pandemic. We still don't know the whole aftermath of locking up the entire population.

The Mainstream Socialist Media, with continuous lies and omissions, divided us instead of uniting us. People dying meant nothing to them, considering that all they wanted was to get rid of Donald Trump at all costs. They, including the Digital Communist Platforms, DCP, did everything possible to hype the dying, keep us in our homes, and prevent us from hearing about any alternative solutions to prevent and cure the Wuhan, Covid-19.

There seemed to be a definite conspiracy to prevent finding alternative medicine for this virus. Hydroxychloroquine, a malaria medication, also known as Plaquenil that Lupus patients take, became a forbidden medication, prohibited to many doctors for prescribing it to their patients. Many doctors offered alternative points of view about what we should do or blew the whistle on reporting deaths as Covid-19. DCP deleted from YouTube any such information. How about Facebook deleting postings that did not follow the party line about the virus? They deleted some of mine. Who is deciding what's good for the citizens of this country? DCP like Facebook, Twitter, and YouTube, and the Democrat Socialist Party Politburo. If you die, you are collateral damage.

However, we must ask: Why did Communist-Fascist China allow infected Chinese people to travel to other countries?

Once the Chinese found that the virus was lethal, they wasted no time locking up the entire Hubei province and protecting the rest of China from the virus. They enforced the lockdown with brutal, communist effectiveness. They sealed infected people in their apartments until they died or healed. And the Chinese had fewer cases and deaths. Are the Chinese better equipped to deal with the virus they created, are they a superior-virus-resistant race, or better liars? Or, being the originators of the virus, they minimized their fatalities. China must not look weak and lose face in the World.

Why was the virus released in the rest of the world? Was it a mistake, a deliberate act to sabotage our economy and President Trump's reelection, an act to show who's the boss in the world, or other nefarious reasons?

There are certain facts that we know:

- The Democrat Socialist Party has moved quickly to use the pandemic and steal the elections in 2020 by introducing mail-in voting. How prepared in advance were they, or just quick opportunists?
- Why was the pandemic started in 2020 and not in 2018 or even early 2019? How far in advance did the Communist-Fascist Chinese prepared for its release, and who in the US collaborated with them?
- Is the virus natural or artificial? They conducted experiments with this virus in the US and Wuhan Labs. Was it an accident or an excellent ploy planned in advance?
- Or was the virus intentionally released to stop President Trump, an enemy to Communist-Fascist China and the Democrat Socialist Party?

In 2021, we discovered that the virus was released from the labs at Wuhan, infecting personnel and infecting others outside and the world. Dr. Fauci provided funds for experimenting on Coronavirus in the Wuhan Labs despite President Obama prohibition of the experiments. Dr. Fauci used a third party to channel the money to Wuhan. The Chinese scientists continued to experiment and enhance the virus to be more infectious. Most scientists declared that the virus was natural and not man-made. However, they didn't analyze it or directly know "how and what" Wuhan Labs did. The Chinese Communist Party gave an orientation trip to select western scientists to prove no mal-processes. It was not an investigating trip but a sight-seeing, managed by the Communist handlers.

But those people are scientists; they are incorruptible. Hardly. Scientists are people just like anyone else. In China, the scientists do as told by the Chinese Communist Party. In the West, they do as told by the people who grant them the money. If there were no grants, many scientists would starve. Climate Change is an obvious example of scientists voicing their "informed opinion" that men made pollution jeopardize Earth. The grants they receive were to prove that hypothesis. But, they received no grants for finding other causes, or is Climate Change another historical occurrence that happens with or without mankind's involvement. And so, it is with the Covid-19.

We know that Dr. Fauci sent money to Wuhan to continue experimenting on Coronaviruses to make them more lethal. I am not saying that Dr. Fauci is complicit in releasing the pandemic in the world, but he was instrumental. It is almost certain that the virus escaped from the labs, as many Chinese scientists got infected and died back in late 2019. Infected Chinese could travel out of China, spreading the virus to the world. The Chinese lied to WHO, and WHO lied to us when they told us in early 2020 that the virus was not infectious, making sure that it will spread to the US without people taking earlier precautions. Any other form of cure, rather than isolation, was not permitted, and whoever dissented was shut out by Digital Communist Platforms, and MSM ignored them or ridiculed them. Over 600 thousand people died from Covid-19. The measures taken by the Democrat Governors to keep the most vulnerable sequestrated in Nursing homes caused more deaths. Wearing masks was enforced even though Dr. Fauci and Surgeon General Jerome Adams stated that the masks would not protect us. Even after they developed the vaccines, through Operation Warp Speed instituted by President Trump, and people were vaccinated, we still had to wear masks. Why? The vaccine was ineffective, and we could get sick; the virus was crawling on us like fleas and potentially infect others, or the love of command and control by our politicians cannot be abandoned. Fortunately, the infections and deaths are down, but everyone must be vaccinated, and they could require a passport to travel. Why? What's in the vaccines that all of us have to be infused with?

In my opinion, the Covid-19 was a deliberate and intentional deployment of a bio-weapon for political reasons to destabilize the United States of America, prevent Donald Trump from being re-elected, and facilitate the Democrat Socialist Party to take over the government of the USA just as Hitler used the Great Depression to gain political power.

Chapter 4.2. Elections.

Any ideology without political power is meaningless. Hitler knew his game, and he didn't make it a secret. All along, he declared that democracy was destroying Germany and only a powerful party, pro-German, would restore Germany and its people to glory and prosperity. His goal was complete control of the government, and he strived for total control. Unlike Stalin, who used electoral fraud to impose Socialism on the Eastern European countries in the late 1940s, Hitler could not do that and had to win honestly.

In the elections of 2020, the Democrat Socialist Party had to win the Congress and the presidency. Unfortunately, the Pandemic opened the door to fraud, and they took full advantage of it.

Communist Joseph Stalin knew how to conduct electoral fraud, saying:

> It's Not Who Votes That Counts. It's Who Counts the Votes! *Joseph Stalin*

And so, the American Marxists and the Democrat Socialist Party won the elections of 2020. They have the majority in the House, fifty-fifty split in the Senate, but Kamala Harris as the VP and president of the Senate gives the Democrats a majority in Congress. The President is a democrat, and the Democrat Socialist Party controls two of the three branches of government. The Supreme Court is marginally conservative, but not by much considering that Chief Justice John Roberts, Jr. is shifting to the Left. This is not the first time the Democrats have so much power, but the American Marxists did not control yesterday's Democrat Party. In the past, they played fair by the Democratic and Constitutional rules to benefit the United States and its people. This is not the case today as the Democrat Socialist Party wants to re-image America into a totalitarian, socialist state under their command.

Some say the national election of 2020 was the most corrupt election ever in the USA. The facts are plain as they can be. The fraudulent elections were possible by allowing voting by mail. There is nothing wrong with mail-in voting, as long as a voter requests an absentee ballot. And when the requester is eligible to vote, not an illegal, undocumented Democrat voter, or a dead person, who always votes democrat, then the ballot is mailed to his/her domicile. It is a one-on-one relationship, one person, one ballot/vote. The electoral body of each state makes the voting laws.

Instead, the Democrat officials made an unlawful decision to send absentee ballots to everyone, if they requested it or not. The shotgun-approach. There was no verification that the recipients had the right and willingness to vote; or other people would vote in their place. The only verifications were the signatures on the envelopes containing the votes. But verify against what proof? From DMV? That's a lengthy process. The signature verification was inconvenient and was dropped, and even not having a signature was not a reason for dismissing that ballot. Everything that came into the polling place was accepted, legal or illegal or late.

The ballots must be cast by a certain date by mailing and by in person voting. Anything arriving after the voting date must be discarded. They changed the rules and accepted all the mail-in votes, even after the voting date, in some places by even a week. This is gaming the system. As it was in the 2020 election night, Donald Trump was ahead by a large margin, but then the "necessary" votes continued to come in to annul his lead and make Joe Biden the winner. The ballots came in, many of them with only one vote, just for Joe Biden. Once they separated the ballots from the envelopes, there was no way to verify their legality.

In Georgia, after they told the observers that the counting was completed and the observers left, the poll workers pulled suitcases full of ballots from under the tables, and the counting continued. And they caught this on surveillance tape. The State officials and the Democrat-Socialists were quick to deny the video, stating that the counting had to go on throughout the night. Sure, but why were the Republican poll watchers told that they were done counting, and only after the poll watchers left, they pulled suitcases from under the tables? In other cases, the poll workers counted the ballots twice. The Socialists never stop cheating.

And then there were the voting machines, which were guaranteed, full-proof against cheating. No Russians could infiltrate and corrupt our votes in favor of Donald Trump. There was no need for any

Russian; there were plenty of Democrat Socialist operatives that could alter the machines. The vote counting machine is a piece of hardware controlled by software. Modify the software and change the counting. The software can ignore many of Trump votes or count Trump's votes as Biden's votes, or the algorithm keeps track of the votes and changes the final votes in favor of Joe Biden's. Recounting the votes through the same machines may not return the same results. And they could discover no fraud without analyzing the software. And recounting was not permissible.

The tragedy in the 2020 election is not necessarily the fraud committed by the Democrat Socialists but by the rules that were adopted without legislative approval. When the Republicans challenged the rules in court, the Pennsylvania Supreme Court, in this case, found nothing unconstitutional about the rules that were in clear violation of the State Constitution. Unfortunately, the legislative bodies in many states allowed outright fraud. The Supreme Court of the United States committed the ultimate crime against the United States Democracy by refusing even to hear the cases when the violation of the Constitution was clear.

When we don't enforce the Constitution, the Democracy of our country is in peril.

If electoral fraud is allowed in the next elections, we will become the United Socialists of America.

Chapter 5. Eliminate the Opposition

Hitler did not have a majority in the Reichstag. So, he entered into a coalition with other like-minded parties to rule as the majority and become the Chancellor. However, Hitler depended on the coalition party, and that was not his plan. He wanted total power to conduct the policies of Germany as a one-party State without debate or interference. And that is the beginning of the Nazi dictatorship. How did he do it?

The following is a quotation from "Hitler Was a Socialist":

> On February 27, the Reichstag burned down, and the arsonist was allegedly Marinus van der Lubbe, a Dutch Communist. Much later it was suspected that Goering had orchestrated the event. The burning of the Reichstag prompted the issuance of the Enabling Act of 1933, which gave Chancellor Hitler the power to enact laws without a Reichstag vote. Hitler wasted no time outlawing the German Communist Party, a deadly adversary. [10; pg:115]

Under the threat of Communism, the arson at Reichstag was the last political straw for most Germans. With Adolf Hitler the new Chancellor of Germany, the NAZI-Socialists acted quickly to pass the Reichstag Fire Decree, which canceled many of the German people's civil liberties. The Enabling Act of 1933 annulled the German Constitution and the Chancellor, Adolf Hitler, obtained dictatorship powers, after which he shut down the Reichstag legislative body. After that, Germany had only one legal, political party, the National Socialist German Workers Party. The opposition, the Communist and Socialist parties became illegal, and their members were hunted down, imprisoned, and/or executed. Hitler and the NAZI-Socialists, by law, could prosecute and silence all the opposition, be that clergy, scholars, Jews, or other moderate German citizens. The NAZI-Socialist party was the only party allowed in Germany.

After the fraudulent elections of 2020, the American Democrat Socialist Party has complete control over the United States government. It has a slim majority in Congress, but considering how scattered and inept the Republicans are, the Democrat Socialist Party can do just about everything they want. Just like the Nazi-Socialist party was a united voting bloc in Reichstag, so is the Democrat Socialist Party. Nancy Pelosi, a natural-born tyrant, made sure she has complete control over the Democrats by using old, tried, and successful Communist methods: *Fear*. Anyone who steps out of line will not get any committee assignments or financial help for reelection. It's simple, and it works.

Any outcome from now on would be speculation, as no one can predict what the American people, while still able to vote in supposedly fair elections, may do. Maybe in 2022, the Democrat Socialist Party will lose in Congress. However, the Presidency will still be in their hands, either with President Biden or Kamala Harris. Or they will maintain the majority, and what they'll do is turn our country into a Totalitarian Socialist State.

Chapter 5.1. January 6, 2021 – the Capitol Riot

The Capitol riot on January 6th, 2021, is the equivalent of the Reichstag fire in Germany of 1933.

On January 6th, the freedom-loving patriots came to the Capital to listen to President Trump's speech and demonstrate against electoral fraud. President Trump gave a speech addressing the Electoral fraud and said:

> We have come to demand that Congress do the right thing and only count the electors who have been lawfully slated. I know that everyone here will soon be marching over to the Capitol building to *peacefully and patriotically make your voices heard.*
>
> *We're going to walk down to the Capitol, and we're going to cheer on our brave senators, and congressmen, and women*. We're probably not going to be cheering so much for some of them because you'll never take back our country with weakness. *You have to show strength, and you have to be strong.*

> "Something's wrong here. Something's really wrong. Can't have happened." And we fight. *We fight like Hell, and if you don't fight like Hell, you're not going to have a country anymore.*
>
> *So, we're going to, we're going to walk down Pennsylvania Avenue ... and we're going to the Capitol, and we're going to try and give...* The Democrats are hopeless. ... But we're going to try and give our Republicans, the weak ones because the strong ones don't need any of our help, *we're going to try and give them the kind of pride and boldness that they need to take back our country.*
>
> *So, let's walk down Pennsylvania Avenue.*

This speech and the following assault on the Capitol by an angry mob, while the address was ongoing, triggered the Mainstream Socialist Media as instructed by the Democrat Socialist Party to declare that act as an Insurrection, a violent uprise to overthrow the government of the United States.

There is a big difference between an insurrection and a riot. An insurrection is planned in advance with the specific goal of overthrowing the government. It has a political leader(s) and a large following of *armed* insurrectionists. They must attack key government departments and political posts at once. They must take control of the media, police, and military if possible. An insurrection is an act of sedition, treason. No government that survives such an act will let the insurrectionists go free. Execution and years in prison are the punishments.

Was this an insurrection? Not by a far stretch of the imagination. This riot, for the Democrats, was the Reichstag fire during Hitler's time.

Who was the leader? President Trump, they claim, was calling on the people in DC to march to the Capitol. There is nothing in President Trump's speech that told the crowd to storm the Capitol and do what they did, just march to the Capitol and support the Republicans to stand up and defend our democracy. I realize that some words; *we fight like Hell,* could be construed as violence, but it just reminded the demonstrators never to give up. *We fight like Hell* was used by the Democrat Socialists Kamala Harris, Nancy Pelosi, Chuck Schumer, just to name a few, and no one objected to the word *fight*. Unless President Trump says it.

During the address, a band of desperados attacked the Capitol, overwhelmed the sparse security, and caused some mayhem inside. The rioters did not hear the words: *I know that everyone here will soon be marching over to the Capitol building to peacefully and patriotically make your voices heard,* because they were already at the Capitol. And even if they had heard that these people were mad as hell and wouldn't take it anymore. In a Democracy, people protest peacefully to voice their objections, and the government must address their grievances. Electoral fraud was their grievance, which the government ignored and insisted there was no fraud. They claimed the elections were legit because the Democrat Socialist Party has control over the Legislative and Executive branches and no opposition.

But President Trump did not take the lead to conduct any insurrection. The invaders of the Capitol were ordinary citizens concerned about what the Democrat Socialist Party will do. No one on the ground took the lead and orchestrated a takeover. It was just a mad mob who pushed against the Capitol police, broke windows, and entered the Capitol, or in some cases went in thorough open doors. (Not shown by MSM.) The rioters were not armed, and the only shot fired was from a security agent killing Ashli Babbitt. Yes, the rioters reached the deliberation chambers, but they evacuated the legislators to safety by then.

Eventually, National Guard came, and they dispersed the rioters. It is a sad moment in our nation's history when a group of people has to attack our democratically elected government for grievances that the elected officials ignored.

The Democrat Socialist Party and a few traitors on the Republican side and the Mainstream Socialist Media and the Digital Communist Platforms monopolies were quick to denounce the President as instigating the riot and called it an Insurrection. Thus, it was a perfect storm to eliminate, oppress, and undertake a NAZI-Socialist style measure against the opposition party, the Republicans.

But an *insurrection* was not. An insurrection happened in France in 1789 on Bastille Day. An insurrection occurred in 1917 when the Bolsheviks stormed the winter palace and took the Czar and his family hostages. An insurrection happened in Italy in 1922, when Mussolini and his Fascist Party took over the government power, although it was bloodless. Insurrection occurs when a group of people plan and act to take over the control of that country by any means necessary.

On January 6th, there were no such things, but the US government, although spooked, is safe and still in power. And thanks to fraudulent elections, it well-positioned the Democrat Socialist Party to do what they want. If there had been an insurrection, the attackers would have been better organized, well-armed, and the members of both houses would have been taken hostages. And then there would have been negotiations, bloodshed, and capitulation by the rebels. But after breaking windows and damaging some parts of the Capitol, the rioters dispersed when additional enforcements arrived. There were not even gun battles.

It turns out that the FBI knew about what was going to happen. The FBI monitors the extreme groups, especially of the Right, and understood the ramifications of having hundreds of thousands of angry people descend on Washington. Sure, there have been large demonstrations in the Capital in the past, but none so antagonistic to the Federal Government as these demonstrators were. And yet, the early warnings did not raise red flags with all law enforcement bodies in DC.

How incompetent could the FBI be? Not incompetent at all, but complicit.

FBI is competent enough to plan a coup d'état against a legally elected President, and along with that, created chaos for our country for two-and-a-half years. It is competent to get away with their crime, and no one in the FBI ended up in prison. FBI is competent to excuse Hillary Clinton from any legal repercussions for using classified material on her closet, private server. It is competent to cover up and not to investigate the Biden's family and their criminal activities. Instead, the FBI, along with the Democrat Socialist Party, allowed the riots to take place. They were complicit as much as Hermann Göring was in the Reichstag fire.

Two thousand security officers protected the Capitol, not all on duty when the riot started and hardly sufficient to stop a mob of tens of thousands invading from all directions. No security officer guarded the Capitol Rotunda. The heads of the Capitol security organizations pleaded for National Guard to come to the rescue, but they refused for ambiguous reasons. Even if the Capitol was not burning, this was a major disaster. It took until 8 PM for help to arrive and disperse the crowd. By then, the required and expected damages happened. The Democrat Socialist Party could have been as giddy as Adolf Hitler after hearing about the Reichstag fire, he said: "Now I've got them!"

What's even more troubling, President Trump asked the Pentagon to post 10,000 national guards in DC. The Pentagon declined or let the request get lost in the bureaucratic shuffle. It was imperative that the Capitol be unprotected for the expected riot to create the perfect storm for the Democrat Socialists against the Republicans and freedom.

Let the Capitol fall, and then we, the Democrat Socialist Party, will have full power to do what's necessary to eliminate the opposition and pass socialist laws. Expel Republican lawmen who objected to the election results would be a bonus. The Big PACs stopped financial support to the lawmen who did not declare their complete approval of the fraudulent elections. Comrade AOC proposed reeducation camps for the Republicans and their kids, which is not different from what happened in the Communist-Socialist Soviet Union and NAZI-Socialist Germany. Reeducation is ongoing in Communist-Fascist China.

The Democrat Socialist Party is working hard to eliminate any opposition from the Freedom-loving patriots. For one, they ordered the FBI to hunt down the rioters, declaring them *domestic terrorists*. This means that the FBI will keep those who cannot be charged on watch lists and prohibited from flying by placing them on the No-Fly list. Second, they proposed to try Donald Trump on sedition charges. Third, the State of New York convened a grand jury to charge criminally Donald Trump and his sons for wrongdoing, regarding the valuation of assets for loan and tax purposes. New York Attorney General Letitia James, probably financed by George Soros for election, is leading the political persecution against our formal President. She campaigned, promising that she will bring Donald Trump to trial if elected. That is a political trial, not a criminal one. Nothing will stop them, and they must keep the conservatives under constant fear.

The campaign of eliminating politically the Republican party will continue. They will scrutinize the Republican representatives for every impropriety they commit or might commit. Even if they are squeaky clean, anonymous individuals will denounce them for some wrongdoing. Or, after what they tried to do to an honest and upstanding citizen like Justice Brett Kavanaugh, a nut job of a woman will accuse any Republican, with no one else collaborating her accusation, of sexual harassment.

As the Democrats increase their power, they will continue to pressure conservative representatives to quit, as they intended with Rep. Marjorie Taylor Greene of Georgia. Thankfully, she fought back and took no crap from the socialists. This kind of pressure on the Republican politicians may soften them and destroy the Conservative Party, eventually.

Or, the Republicans will stand up and defend our freedom.

Afterward, the national guard installed barbed wire fences to protect the Capitol, the government. They stationed twenty thousand or more National guards around the Capitol. Are we a democratic country anymore when the majority political party, the Democrat Socialist Party, our government needs protection from its people? The Democrat Representative Steve Cohen, in my opinion, a clown, demanded that the guards pass a *purity test* to make sure that there are no White Supremacists among them and attempt a palace coup against them. This is a fine example of Socialist thinking.

This is a rather bold accusation against the Democrat Socialist Party to knowingly allow the riot to happen and call it an *Insurgence*. The truth may never surface, but what's real is how the Democrat Socialist party used this tragedy to consolidate its power, just like Hitler did in Germany in 1933.

The Democrat Socialists are out for blood. This was the time to get rid of once and for all of President Trump and his followers. So, they passed the second Impeachment, accusing President Trump of inciting the "insurgency." The word *fight* was what "compelled" the crowd to attack the Capitol. And to make sure that the President cannot use the First Amendment to declare his innocence, the Democrat Socialist controlled House of Representatives proclaimed the President could not hide behind the Constitution. But wait, what does the First Amendment say?

> *Congress shall make no law … abridging the freedom of speech*, … or the people's right peaceably to assemble, and to petition the Government for a redress of grievances.

Congress just violated the Constitution by making a quasi-law eliminating President Trump's freedom of speech. The Democrat Socialists representatives and ten traitor Republicans, one of them Rep. Liz Cheney of Wyoming, voted to Impeach the President. The Senate acquitted the President, but seven traitor Republican senators, not surprisingly, Remocrat Mitt Romney, voted for Impeachment. What the Democrat Socialists wanted most of all was to prevent Donald Trump from running for President, ever.

Regardless of whether there was an insurrection and the legalities behind the Impeachment, one central question arises. Do we still have democracy in our country?

As far as I understand, Democracy is a political system where the citizens of a country agree *voluntarily* to elect their representatives and follow the rules of the majority elected. If the majority does a good job, it gets reelected again, otherwise, the opposition replaces them. For 245 years, the transition of government took place peacefully. But for the inauguration of President Biden, the democracy had to be enforced at gunpoint. Thirty thousand National Guards were present in the Capital and around the Capitol to ensure that "democracy is enforced." It never happened before January 2021. It happens all the time in Dictatorship and Totalitarianism. Those regimes are in power because they command the guns. In a working democracy, the people don't uprise. They petition the government for a redress of grievances and the government responds.

Every petition submitted by citizens to inquire on the election irregularities or fraud was met with derision. The refusal by judges to allow lawsuits, refusal by the government officials to act, including Republicans, and threats that if they don't stop saying "fraudulent election," there will be consequences had *consequences*. The riot. But, worst of all, the refusal of the US Supreme Court to hear their plea when there was a clear case of Constitutional violation in Pennsylvania signified the end of our democracy.

What kind of banana republic are we? A Democrat Socialist republic of one-party rule, elected by fraud.

Mussolini remarked about democracy:

> Democracy is beautiful in theory; in practice, it is a fallacy. You in America will see that someday.

I think we are at that pivotal moment in our country to fix it or accept slavery. Military troops protecting the government is not Democracy.

Chapter 6. Normalization

Chapter 6.1. Never Lose Power Again

The End Justify the Means. Niccolò Machiavelli

A-Ensure perpetual election as the supermajority party.

The Number 1 task for the Democrat Socialist Party is to assure their reelection as a majority in perpetuity. They have announced many of their actions in advance, and it may not come as a surprise what they plan to do.

The Democrat Socialist Party will try to legitimize the fraudulent methods of voting used in 2020, passing anti-democratic laws. As I'm writing this book, Congress is about to pass H. R. 1., the federalization of elections.

An Act To expand Americans' access to the ballot box, reduce the influence of big money in politics, strengthen ethics rules for public servants, and implement other anti-corruption measures to fortify our democracy and for other nefarious purposes.

What can be wrong with having a better, more democratic election making sure that all people can vote? First, the elections laws are to be governed by each states' constitution and laws. But aside from this inconvenient detail, why do they want to change the voting methods? In 2020 some states took a shotgun approach and send mail-in ballots to all state residents, legal, illegal, from out of state, dead or alive, or as long as their names appeared somewhere on some State record.

Ballot harvesting in the future will become the mainstay of the Democrats to stay in power.

Mandatory voting by all will be another law they'll pass in the future to ensure that no one is disfranchised, and to make it easier for everyone to cast their votes, mail voting or even online voting could become the new normal.

Another way for the Democrats to get a supermajority is to add more states to the Union. California is a big state, but they could divide it into two or even three states. So, it would be for Massachusetts, East, and West. Or Long Island could become a state. Or create new states, like Washington, D.C., or Puerto Rico, or American Samoa. The newly added states would be Democrat, ensuring additional votes for them and a permanent majority.

B-Abolish Electoral College.

The obstacle to perpetual election to the Executive Branch, the Presidency, is the Electoral College, which has been the equalizer of the States' rights but works against the popular vote. Why should we elect the President indirectly by the Electoral College when we elect Congress representatives by popular vote? One voting rule for all, and eliminate the Electoral College.

The only true federal election we have is for the Presidency. The Congress is elected from each state, and the seats approportionated based on state population, the more populous state the more representatives they have in Congress. If the Electoral College is eliminated, the populous states, like California, will always dictate what party and who will be the President.

To eliminate the Electoral College, the Constitution must be changed, and that will take two-thirds of the votes in Senate and House. Will they be able to do it? This change is a must for the Democrat-Socialist party as we can vote them out of executive power, fraudulent elections or not. If they abolish the Electoral College, the United States of America will become a one-party totalitarian country.

Without a supermajority the Democrat Socialist party will not succeed. But a halfway there is to expand the number of representatives and senators in Congress by adding more states to the Union, which is just a matter of passing a new Federal law.

C-Legislation.

Eliminate the filibuster in the Senate. A filibuster is a tool used by a minority party to block proposed legislation by running out the clock. Once eliminated, the simple vote of 51 to 49 will pass any law. As it is today, a 50-50 vote will still pass with the Democrat VP breaking the tie.

The majority party has the power to change the rules in the House and Senate, and they will change the rules in favor of the Democrat Socialist Party.

D-Judicial.

The supreme court and all other federal courts will need to be transformed to align with the Democrat Socialist Party ideology. President Trump has packed the courts with conservative Judges. To remedy that the Supreme court must be enlarged, double it and assign only Liberal-Socialist judges. With the additional States, the US Court of Appeals will need to be expanded by creating more justices and so on for all Appellate courts.

Without a balanced court the political crimes will increase against the opposition party, bringing the dissidents to trial on fabricated charges. Sympathetic judges are essential to sustain the verdicts against them.

E-Amnesty of all illegal aliens.

All illegal aliens that have lived for more (or less) than five years in this country will be allowed to vote, regardless of their citizen status. They will send a vote by mail ballot to anyone with an ID or DMV license. Thus, the illegal immigrants will become de facto undocumented Democrat voters. But, if they're allowed to vote, will the non-citizens vote while residing in their home country by mail-in ballots? Ballot harvesting will increase.

F-Reduce voting age to 16 years old.

Voting will be allowed on the school premises and during classes. What does a 16-year-old know about politics, or what's good for our country, except what the teachers tell them? The Democrat Socialist Party will reign supreme with these voters.

G-Inmates to vote.

The incarcerated people are not allowed to vote. They forfeited their liberty by committing crimes. But they should have the right to vote from behind bars. Why shouldn't they? For one, they could vote their way out of prison. If the incarcerated inmates will be allowed to vote from prison, who will they vote for? Those demagogues who promise them early release or immediate release from prison and other social benefits. They'll vote for the Democrat Socialists.

Chapter 6.2. Immigration

There has never been a country in the world's history that willingly allows open borders and illegal immigration. Unless one party, in particular, wants to increase the party's membership. Unfortunately, the Democrat Socialist Party is doing exactly that. To get complete power, the Democrat Socialist Party is destroying what once America was into a nation of Babel. California of old is no longer, because immigration from south of the border has transformed California into Cali-Mexico. And as California goes, so goes the nation.

I am an immigrant. I came to this country in 1972. My wife is an immigrant, she's a Latina from Nicaragua. So, what do I have to say about this issue? Am I for it, against it because I'm already here, or I don't care? As an American citizen, I care; I have to care otherwise, why call myself a citizen.

The simplest way to explain how I feel about immigration and immigrants is through the words from the Declaration of Independence regarding every person on Earth:

> *...with certain unalienable Rights, that among these are Life, Liberty and the* Pursuit of Happiness.

Just like I didn't know about these words when I was in Socialist Romania, billions of people in the world have not read or heard them either. But instinctively, we all know them. Every human wants to live free and happy. All immigrants, legal or illegal, want a better economic life for themselves and their kids and the *Pursuit of Happiness*.

Since these words are universal, they apply to us, we the citizens of the United States of America, who own this country. We want to maintain our *Life, Liberty, and the Pursuit of Happiness*. I know that sounds selfish, but that's how it is as long as there will be nations. Suppose we would allow everyone who wants to come to America. What would happen to our country and the American population? Simple, our streets would resemble the streets of India, Bangladesh or Mexico-Tijuana, crowded and impoverished. Wealth will decrease and poverty will follow with more people from different cultures, religions, skills, and languages. Balkanization will be inevitable.

People immigrating to the US fall into three categories: want to become American citizens, make money to support their families and then go back to their country, or have no choice like the kids brought here illegally.

I ran away from socialist slavery to be free, and I wanted to become an American. I wear my American citizenship as a badge of honor. For me, there is no greater country in the world. There is also no country to go back to. When I came to America, I burned my "ship" on the shore. There was only to go ahead, no way back.

America is a country of immigrants. My view on legal immigration is that immigrants should be allowed in our country based on what they bring with them to benefit us, the rest of our country, and themselves. What do we need in America? Educated people or goat herders, skilled people or manual laborers? This common-sense question is so obvious that it eludes the Democrats, or their ulterior motives of total power trump the nation's needs. In Ann Coulter's book "Adios America" [23 pg 15] it's stated that 18% of the immigrants are on welfare. None should be on welfare. When I brought my mom and dad to this country, they went to work, paid taxes and social security, and eventually retired. They were shocked to learn that newly arrived immigrants could collect welfare and Social Security without paying a dime in the system, if they were older than 62 years.

In "Adios America," Ann Coulter writes:

> It was Teddy Kennedy's 1965 immigration act that snuffed out the generous quotas for immigrants from countries that had traditionally populated America – England, Ireland, Germany– and added "family reunification" policies, allowing recent immigrants to bring their relatives and those relatives their relatives until entire Somali villages have moved to Minneapolis. [23 pg 17]

And what did we get from our generosity? Ilhan Abdullah Omar, the congresswoman from Minnesota, who hates our country. Just like Lyndon Johnson passed the War on Poverty to gain all the Black people's votes for the Democrat Party, Ted Kennedy, the one who killed Mary Jo Kopechne by abandoning her in his submerged car, figured out that non-whites vote more for the Democrat Party. So, open the gates to paradise to families with nine children and no modern skills to support themselves, after all this is the land of the plenty. But it will not be for long.

As for Ted Kennedy, in the early 1990s, Ted Kennedy wrote a letter to Yuri Andropov, who was the General Secretary of the Soviet Union, asking him for help to neutralize Ronald Reagan who was our President, and prevent him from being reelected. I call that an act of treason.

They have twisted the entire immigration issue to where, if you say anything against it, you are an Islamophobic, Brownphobic, Latinophobic, Xenophobic, you-name-it-phobic, and definitely a Racist and White Supremacist.

Take, for example, the revision in the Immigration policy in 1990 as reported by the Center of Immigration Studies saying:

> The law also provided for the admission of immigrants from "underrepresented" countries to increase the diversity of the immigrant flow by creating a lottery system.

I thought we were a country, not the United Nations. Does the United States of America have to mimic the population distribution throughout the world? Allow immigration through a lottery system, not skills? Incredible, but true.

Ted Kennedy single handedly destroyed America as it was once. Just by the new immigration rules, he made sure that America changed from a White European culture, Christian, and English-speaking country to a Third World Ghetto.

Since I said that immigration should be allowed on merit and the needs of our country, my son-in-law, a lawyer, asked me why I was allowed to immigrate to the US? Considering that I was 18 years old, spoke little English, was a high school dropout, and had no skills, why did the US Immigration accept me? A fair question.

I was a political refugee for one, but that is not the complete reason. What I brought with me was the anti-communist sentiment, which was valuable in the 1970s. I was another nail in the socialism's casket. I had family and friends back there, and what do you think they thought about capitalism when after one year in the US, I bought a car. Sure, it was a jalopy, but a year later I bought a new car. In a socialist country, a family had to save for 20 years to buy a car. My dad couldn't afford one. And then the pictures I sent back, showing the markets loaded with food of any kind, proved to everyone back there what a hell hole Socialism was. Better yet, in 1977, five years after I landed in New York with the shirt on my back, no skills, and no English, I bought my first house. And I did all that with no *white privilege* help. There is no such thing as white privilege. Hard work and education are the only privileges.

Buying your own house was beyond belief back in Socialist Romania. A house! People back there had to wait for many years to get a two-bedroom apartment in the Stalinist *projects*. I am glad I was a nail in the socialism's coffin, and I did my best.

I began this chapter by saying: There has never been a country in the world's history that willingly allows open borders and illegal immigration like our nation. To the Democrat Socialist Party, political supremacy is more important than our nation, and allowing undocumented Democrat voters is for their political benefit.

Once upon a time, there was a great empire in the world, the Roman Empire. Today, after centuries of national reformation, it is Italy. Not bad, but not an empire and the population are not Roman. That's what immigration did to the Roman Empire.

Chapter 6.3. Control the Media

After his election, Hitler and his party moved quickly to shut down many opposition newspapers. The largest newspapers were allowed to continue, but only with strict censorship by the Minister of Propaganda Joseph Goebbels.

The Democrat Socialist party is in complete control of all the major media outlets. And all these "bastions of freedom" voluntarily obey or collude with the party. Even the mighty Fox News is buckling and softening its conservative stand. The time when the media was impartial and kept the politicians honest died decades ago, as far back as the Reagan presidency. We hear and see only what the "Socialist Politburo" wants us to know. They forbid opposing points of view.

The CNN, MSNBC, MBC, CBS, ABC, Washington Post, New York Times, and many others are the mouthpieces of the Democrat Socialist Party and keep up the indoctrination that we are in peril from the White supremacists. Sure, there are White supremacists in our country, but hardly a political force to reckon with. Instead, the American Freedom Loving patriots are called *White supremacists*. And they must be destroyed as far as the Democrat Party is concerned.

Having most of the Media on their side is not enough. Dissent is not allowed. At first, they will de-platform the conservative TV stations like Fox News, Newsmax TV, OANN TV, and conservative radio stations. It will culminate with the shutdown of those media outlets, to eliminate any opposition voices. Just like Hitler did.

The Digital Communist Platforms united and acted against all these "dangerous" people. They canceled Donald Trump from using their platforms. Mark Zuckerberg of Facebook, Jack Dorsey of Twitter, Susan Wojcicki of YouTube, Jeff Bezos of Amazon, Tim Cook of Apple, Larry Page, Sergey Brin, and Sundar Pichai of Google, just to name a few of them, banded together and became the de facto political power in our country. If you use their platforms, they will brainwash you, spy upon you, report you to the FBI if needed, or cancel you. For life. The Communist Digital Platforms are a dream come true for the old Communists. It is not in "1984" England or 1984 Soviet Union, but 2021 America.

Best to stay off those Communist platforms if you can. Use e-mails instead.

Chapter 6.4. Control the Police

In 1933 when Chancellor Hitler formed a coalition government, he wanted only two cabinet positions: the Interior Ministry and the Police of Prussia. His coalition parties got all the rest of the Cabinet ministry positions. They were happy and thought that they could control Hitler, while Hitler had the police in his hands?

The American police differ from other countries' police. In other countries, the police are the government's police, while here the police are the people's police. Their function is to keep peace and protect property, not protect the government from the people, as in socialist countries. Moreover, the police are local, and they will not shoot against their families, neighbors, and friends in case of an uprising.

In Socialist Romania, the militia (police) were to be avoided at all costs. You change direction if you saw one coming your way. The Communist militia could stop you for no reason, ask for your ID, question you what you were doing at that moment, where were you going, and could search you. That's right, search you. And they never addressed you as *sir*, or *ma'am*. How violated would you be if that would happen to you? After the officer was satisfied that everything was in order, he gave you a stern look and told you to watch yourself, comrade. After that encounter, you needed a shower and clean underwear. This was a good outcome. If the cop suspected anything, he called for the Militia-van and took you to the station for further interrogation. You'd better start praying.

In the view of the socialists, the American police will have to change. The police are defunded and re-imaged to convert the people's police into the government's police. President Biden has begun that effort to convert the local police to federal police. The liars on MSM and Biden's spokesperson, accuse the Republicans for defunding the police. Scuse me? I didn't know that mayors, De Blasio and Eric Garcetti of LA, were Republicans. They'll give the police tools to spy and monitor the population just the way is done in China. The Digital Communist Platforms and their Leftist employees will cooperate eagerly and offer their databases to eliminate the "domestic terrorists." All citizens will be suspected, especially if you match a certain profile. The new government police will have the power to prevent you from flying anywhere, keeping you under city arrest. Your home will be bugged, and they'll know even when you go to the bathroom. But they may not have to do that if you have a smartphone, a wrist gizmo, a laptop, or Amazon's Alexa. You may want to tape the lens on your laptop/PC camera lens and place a metal bucket over Alexa when not in use. Who knows, even our flat-screen TVs will be able to spy on us, just like in "1984." Many citizens, without knowing, will have a dossier opened to monitor them. I had such a dossier on me back in Romania.

Freedom will be dead.

Warning: Do not use any public communications if you object to the Democrat Socialist Party. The FBI has declared a political war against the Free American citizens, and who knows how many other spy agencies, including IRS, are at work to instill fear in our souls and control us.

It will not be necessary to revamp the police everywhere at once. At first, it will take place in the large, Democrat governed cities like Los

Angeles, San Francisco, New York, Chicago, Portland, Seattle, and other big Democrat Socialist cities.

They will Federally fund the police to ensure the Democrat Socialist Party's control. They will purge the police of unwanted, "impure" officers, and the remaining officers will undergo vigorous pro-government training or indoctrination in Critical Race Theory and Equity. All the higher ranks of the police will have to be Democrat Socialist Party members, without exception. As time passes, the police's sole role will be to protect the Democrat Socialist Party government. America will become a police state. The f*ear* I mentioned at the beginning of the book will permeate even deeper through society and everyone else's soul.

However, until the re-imaging of the police takes place, there is another way to influence the Law Enforcements. That is by electing pro-liberal District Attorneys. This is the new way about changing our political structure by George Soros and his Open Society Foundations by supporting and donating to liberal candidates to be elected as DAs.

Case in point, Kim Foxx is serving as the State's Attorney for Cook County, Illinois. She was elected with funds from Soros. Remember Jussie Smollett, the black, gay actor who staged a white, hate crime against himself by hiring two Nigerian brothers to attack him under the pretext of "this is MAGA country?" Kim Foxx did not charge him with the crime of staging a Fake Hate Crime or for thousands of dollars spent by the Chicago police to investigate the alleged crime. After they defunded Chicago Police, lenient charges by Kim Foxx and other Democrat Leftists DA's like her, the crime, shootings, and murders were up by over 105% in 2020.

Remember the couple in St Louis, Mark and Patricia McCloskey, wielding their guns, trying to protect their property from the mob crossing their yard? Kim Gardner, the Circuit Attorney for the City of St. Louis, elected with funds from Soros, charged the McCloskey's with unlawful use of weapons. In other words, in the United States of America, under the Second Amendment, the citizens with registered guns cannot protect their property against trespassers merely by showing their guns to warn the trespassers not to escalate their crimes.

The bizarre situation of Los Angeles DA George Gascón, preventing his prosecutors from charging certain criminals for their crimes, or dismantling the LAPD Gang Investigating unit, is another example. Los Angeles is only second to Chicago as far as gang activities. George Gascón released thousands of criminals from prison. He believes in re-habilitation by releasing them in the streets without punishment. And yes, Gascón is a Democrat like the others, elected with funds from George Soros. In Los Angeles after Mayor Eric Garcetti, a Democrat, slashed the budget of LAPD by $150 million, and took a knee in a moment of solidarity with BLM, homicides increased by 36%, and victims shot increased by 41%. Is George Floyd's death worth the death of so many Angelinos?

And while we're talking about an increase in crime since the Police Dept's budgets were cut, we cannot ignore the Big Apple, New York, under the Communist Mayor Bill de Blasio. In 2020, the shootings were up by 97%, 1,531, and murders by 44%, 462 people dead.

It will come a time when people will demand an increase in police funding, and the Democrat Socialist Party will be there with federal money and strings attached to do their bidding.

Chapter 6.5. Control the Military

Hitler did not control the Wehrmacht, German Army, at first, but he changed their minds about the NAZI-Socialist party by arming Germany. What military officer would refuse a new, shining weapon, and Hitler fulfilled their wishes, and in the end, the officer corps had to swear fealty to him. In Germany, they took their oaths seriously.

The United States Military is a good example of serving the country's civilian government and not being involved in domestic, political affairs. The military has all the big guns and could be the ultimate arbiter of our political outcome. In the future, if the country erupts in civil war, they will have to intervene to restore peace. That is not acceptable to the Democrat Socialist Party, as the military might act against them. Therefore, they must be aligned and re-programed to their Socialist political views.

The Military consists of officers and regular soldiers. The officers graduate from military academies. The regular soldiers only need high school or GED. By not having college degrees, the regular soldiers escaped the Marxist indoctrination. The officers may have escaped the Marxist indoctrination, although they have higher educational degrees in cadet academies. That may not be for long as Marxism and Critical Race Theory will soon be taught in military academies, if it hasn't happened already.

However, the devil never sleeps, and under President Biden, his Secretary of Defense, whose name he cannot remember at times, Lloyd J. Austin III, has been ordered to conduct Critical Race Theory indoctrination and to purge all the "White Supremacists" from the officer ranks. In short, the Secretary of Defense, Lloyd J. Austin III, has become a de facto *Political Commissar*. Indoctrinating the US Armed Forces into Marxism under the pretext of Critical Race Theory and eliminating the White supremacists will ensure that the US Armed forces will take the Democrat Socialist Party's side in case of civilian armed rebellions.

Secretary of Defense, Austin, is not alone in his zeal to re-image our military, we have Gen Mark Milley who wants to understand *white rage* and Adm. Michael Gilday who is Woke. Let's hope these two may be the exception and Marxism and Critical Race Theory have not influenced all our military brass. God help us if we get in a war with non-white nations and our troops are race sensitive and restrain their *white rage*.

The Russians and the Chinese must be incredulous of their good fortunes to see the US Military self-destroy. Welcome to the Socialist America.

Chapter 6.6. Take Over the Unions

The Trade Unions were the stronghold of Communists and Democratic-Socialists in Germany. The NAZI-Socialists tried to infiltrate the unions but with lukewarm success. To consolidate his power, Hitler had to control the unions, as they could organize general strikes and cripple his rearmament of Germany. So, Hitler, like a good socialist, adopted May Day as a national holiday, renamed it the *Day of National Labor*, held a grand celebration, and invited all trade union representatives to attend. The next day, on May 2, 1933, the SS occupied all union headquarters. They dissolved the unions, their leaders thrown in prison, and union funds confiscated. The Nazi-Socialists formed a new, all-encompassing union, the German Labor Front. From the "Hitler Was a Socialist: the following was said about the unions:

> Similarly, in the Soviet Union, and later in all the European Communist-Socialist countries, the independent unions were incorporated under one state union, and the communist party controlled the unions. Under Communism-Socialism, the unions became company unions and were organized by factory rather than by trade. Every factory had a union under the umbrella of the All-Union Central Council, and its members did not communicate with members from other factories, preventing them from uniting. The union gave the workers a place to voice their opinions or grievances, be indoctrinated in the Marxist-Leninist cause, and keep an eye out for troublemakers. [10; pg 125]

The Unions in the United States favor the Democrat party, and it seems irrelevant for the Democrat Socialist Party to take over their control. But the Unions have their own leadership and could change their minds on a dime. Under socialism, there shall not be any dissenting voice. The Unions have hundreds of thousands of members, a political force to be reckoned with in times of crisis, and must be controlled. Unlike Hitler, who took over the German unions in one swift move, the Democrat Socialist Party will not be able or even be advisable to do so. But they'll take control of the Unions through infiltration, indoctrination, cajoling, or giving the impression of sharing political and economic power with them until one day the entire Unions' leadership will be the Democrat Socialist Party members. The Teachers Union belongs to the Democrat Socialist Party. There will be no organized group of people operating without the Democrat Socialist Party control.

Chapter 6.7. The Leader's Image

Hitler, just like Stalin and Mao, were the leaders of their parties and government. One individual, all-powerful and wise, to guide the nation on the "right path." This is why we have saints. It is easier to love a saint in the human form than an ideology. Tyrants make such "lovable" images. Stalin's firing squad executed one of Stalin minions, as he was dying he whispered Stalin's name.

Only under a totalitarian, non-democratic government the rise of an absolute leader is inevitable, and so will be under the rule of the Democrat Socialist Party. Our political system has made sure that no one individual becomes a dictator, a tyrant. We limit the Presidency to two terms, and after that, the ex-President becomes a private citizen with no government power, as it should be.

Who today is the most popular politician or ex-President? Barack Obama. He is young, born in 1961, and could have a "bright" future at the helm of Socialism. But he cannot run again for President. Says who? The Democrat Socialist Congress will amend that restriction. Even without him being elected again, currently, he is a shadow President. His people surround President Biden, and how many of them call Obama for advice and input? Perhaps all. He can also play the king-maker role.

Even if he's not that future leader, it will be inevitable that one such individual will arise. Nancy Pelosi is too old, luckily for us, but she's smart, shrewd, and evil, the necessary ingredients to be a dictator. Just look how she's handling her party in the House, with a firm hand, using fear.

Chapter 6.8. Disarm the Population

At first, Hitler encouraged the German people to keep their guns until he became the Fuhrer. Afterward, he began disarming the population, declaring himself the protector and father of all Germans. After the war started, and it was a moot point to disarm the population when the soldiers and the nation were rearmed.

The US Constitution, Second Amendment states:

> A well-regulated Militia, being necessary to the security of a free State, the right of the people to keep and bear Arms, shall not be infringed.

Politicians don't like an armed population. In a time of crisis, they can rise and overthrow the government. Why our Founding Fathers allow the US citizens to bear arms? One and only one reason: prevent *tyranny*. The colonists revolted against the English crown. That many people were armed already made it easier for a revolution to start and be successful. What our Founding Fathers did not want was to exchange one tyranny for another. They went to great lengths to establish democracy and prevent it from being destroyed. Only an armed population can maintain democracy.

But if they're not armed, they'll be able to do nothing about tyranny, just like the Soviets, Chinese, Hungarians, Romanians, Polish, Cubans, Venezuelans, North Koreans, and others, among many other Socialist countries, couldn't or cannot. Everything the Left says against the right to bear arms is a lie or an excuse or placate the actual issue.

Weapons mean Freedom. Please don't give them up.

The Democrat Socialist Party's goal is to abolish the Second Amendment. Before that happens, they'll make use of different laws to criminalize the possession of guns. In California, Gavin Newsom as the Lieutenant Governor, before becoming the governor, has pushed through an ammunition law. When you buy your gun ammunition now, you must give your driver's license. Imagine if they will stop gun ammunition from being sold or even produced? What good is a gun without bullets?

The Left will be relentless to disarm the population. It is up to us to fight them.

Chapter 6.9. Religion

Hitler didn't oppose religion in his early years. But once in power, despite being a Roman Catholic, he had no problem arresting any dissenting priest and throwing him in jail for future reprisal. Hitler recognized that religion would be competition and an adversary to the NAZI-Socialist party. He planned in the future to abolish all religions in the Third Reich, and institute a NAZI religion with his book Mein Kamp as the bible.

There was no religion in the Socialist countries, as far as the governments were concerned. You can have loyalty only to the Communist Party and no other invented god or ideology. Did the communists erase religion from the former Socialist countries? No. But religious education was not practiced in schools, and the people became nonreligious, which is what they wanted. Although most people were not religious, they didn't stop believing in God.

The Democrat Socialist Party will not have to dissuade people from being religious or even believing in God. Our atheist school system accomplished exactly what the Communists did in the Socialist countries. But religion and belief in God will continue to be under assault to be eliminated.

Chapter 6.10. Indoctrination and Education

Once Adolph Hitler became the Chancellor of Germany, he moved swiftly to change the curriculum of the German schools. They burned the books that were dimmed bad for "healthy thinking," and many such bonfires took place in German cities. Hitler instituted the Hitler Youth schools, and before the war began, all private or religious sponsored education were closed, and only the NAZI State schools were allowed.

Who decides what they teach to our children in schools? In Socialist Romania, the Communist Party and the State decided. The Romanian kids learned what the Communist Party wanted them to learn. Who is responsible for the American kids' education? We the parents or the government? The National Education Association, School Boards? And who are these educator bureaucrats? They are the Marxists indoctrinated teachers representing the State, not the parents. They decide what to teach and not to teach our kids, what kind of ideological poison to feed our kids to transform the society from a Free society to a Marxist Socialist society. But the School Boards hold meetings with the parents to share their latest decisions in education. Sure, and are the parents able to change any decision or curriculum they shove down our throats? Not likely, since many of the new curriculum has been voted in law by the State legislators.

They planned the current situation in our schools a long time ago. As mentioned in "The 45 Communist Goals" published in 1963, the following points need repeating:

17. Get control of the schools. Use them as transmission belts for socialism and current Communist propaganda. Soften the curriculum. Get control of teachers' associations. Put the party line in textbooks.

25. Break down cultural standards of morality by promoting pornography and obscenity in books, magazines, motion pictures, radio, and TV.

26. Present homosexuality, degeneracy and promiscuity as "normal, natural, healthy."

I recently watched a video of an irate mother confronting her local School Board about what they were teaching her 10-year-old kid in a book, "It's Perfectly Normal."

https://rumble.com/vietef-mother-unloads-on-school-when-she-finds-out-what-they-are-teaching-5-year-o.html

In short, the book is pure porn, teaching the kids about the sexual organs with pictures, about oral and anal sex, masturbation, and of course that LGBTQ is normal. We, the parents, have lost control over our kids' education.

Indoctrination and education go hand in hand. We can teach our young to become productive members of our society believing in the Constitution, God, our country, freedom, and the sanctity of private property, or teach them about Marxism-Leninism, Critical Race Theory, hatred against God and religion, and the most productive members of our society.

Although the Democrat Socialist Party has marginal control in 2021/22 Congress over the Federal Government, the educator minions have begun the indoctrination long ago, and now they are teaching their ideology, the Critical Race Theory, to our kids.

Critical Race Theory is the new belief, which is a Trojan Horse to introduce Marxism-Socialism in our country. According to Wikipedia, they say the following about Critical Race Theory:

> CRT is loosely unified by two common themes:
>
> First, that white supremacy (societal racism) exists and maintains power through the law.
>
> Second, that transforming the relationship between law and racial power, and also achieving racial emancipation and anti-subordination more broadly, are possible.
>
> Critics of CRT argue that it relies on social constructionism, elevates storytelling over evidence and reason, rejects the concepts of truth and merit, and opposes liberalism.

And I thought we changed the laws to prohibit racism, but CRT is a reversed form of racism against white people.

But the indoctrination doesn't stop in our schools, the indoctrination of the entire population must continue as well, just as the Socialists countries conducted weekly communist propaganda meetings at the place of employment. I found out what Disney company is doing to their employees.

Disney Employees Undergo Critical Race Theory Training:

https://www.newsmax.com/newsfront/disney-critical-race-theory-woke-liberal/2021/05/08/id/1020630/?ns_mail_uid=9f1aa507-a790-4185-afdd-6367d4614e27&ns_mail_job=DM217061_05082021&s=acs&dkt_nbr=010502ft3w4l

Pictures of a handbook titled "Reimagine Tomorrow" appear on one of Rufo's Twitter posts with the accompanying message:

> "According to a trove of whistleblower materials, Disney has launched a 'diversity and inclusion' program, called 'Reimagine Tomorrow,' which includes trainings on 'systemic racism,' 'white privilege,' 'white fragility,' 'white saviors,' 'microaggressions,' and 'antiracism.'"

Disney suggests its employees should read into "75 Things White People Can Do for Racial Justice," which lists groups or activities such as "defund the police," "participate in reparations," "decolonize your bookshelf," and "find and join a local 'white space.'"

Does this mean that Disney will burn all their cartoons and movies? I see a lot of "racism" in all their past movies. I'll keep my collection of Disney DVD before they burn their own library of movies.

Indoctrination at work is no joke. If you work, your employer, by the power of employing you, will herd you in a conference room and give a presentation on how *evil* you are by being a white person. Don't you feel guilty because you prospered while other races stayed poor? You benefited from White Privileges and are a racist. You live in a *bubble*. Do you feel you are a racist? You may not have known that until some Woke Zombie told you that. The only racists I know are all the people in the education, MSM, CDP, and government saying we are racists.

Imagine you are attending such an indoctrination seminar and are giving a questionnaire called *Reimagine Tomorrow* and asked to self-assess yourself, identify your white privileges, how you discriminate against the black people, that you are inferior, and made it in your life on the back of the blacks and so forth. That's what Socialism does, and what I experienced in my early years under Socialism. Brainwashing.

This undertaking at Disney Co. and other companies is unconstitutional. Why? Just as they don't have the right to discriminate against your religion or lack of religion, they don't have the right to infringe on your constitutional rights of what you believe in. Critical Race Theory is a new, man-made religion. And they shove it down our throats the old Communist way, through *intimidation, force, and fear*.

However, the indoctrination doesn't stop in schools and employment; it expands now to every other institution that you and I may contact. For example, my wife, Sofia, donated to the City of Hope, a Comprehensive Cancer Medical Center, on behalf of a good friend who passed away from leukemia. She received an e-mail from the City of Hope representative highlighting all the injustices done against people of color's health and medical attention, saying:

> Sofia, that is why I urge you to invite your family and friends to gather around the table for a conversation about health disparities, what we can do as individuals

and ways to support City of Hope's health equities programs.

The message: Gather around folks, friends and family and learn about Critical Race Theory and Equity. If you are white you are evil, but you can redeem yourself by accepting your faults. If this is not a new religion, I don't know what it is?

Chapter 6.11. History

Who are we, how we got here is *history*. We place our pride on what our forefathers have done, the sacrifices they made, and we want to make them proud as the custodians of our country. We also want to make the future generations as proud of us, as we are of past generations.

History must be written to be remembered. Who writes our country's history? We do, through the actions and writing we do every day. Whatever we do it is within the context of our times and culture. However, historians in the future will interpret our actions based on their times and cultural norms, just as we revise our history today to portray it through our modern lenses. In my opinion it is wrong to reinterpret the history through our modern believes. Our entire human civilization is based on wars, killing and crimes. Should we despise our ancestors, including ourselves, for what they did? Should we despise our parents and grandparents for what they did in their life times? All our ancestors lived their life based on the laws and morals of their time. And whatever was done is done. We can learn from it and do better, if there is such thing as better, based on our laws and morals of today.

Rewriting history has been underway for some time, and it is intensifying now. Besides, the entire philosophy of Marxism is that history provides a distorted view of reality. The Socialists claim that the history of the country was written for and by the White people, men in power, who ignored their wrongdoings, such as owning black slaves to enrich themselves, keeping the black people in poverty, and depriving them of any rights after they were liberated. The evil White men kept the women oppressed and without rights. Not to mention keeping the majority of the people in poverty while they lived an enviable life. Most of the White people are the oppressors, the "Fascists."

Rewriting history can be used as a propaganda tool, a perfect tool to "enlighten" the people of the wrongdoing of the past, and the correction that only the Marxist-Socialists can undertake. And so, the founders of our nation, the movers and shakers, who have made America the greatest country in the world will be condemned for their past sins and banished from history, or if they remain on the pages of history, we will be reminded how evil they were. George Washington, Thomas Jefferson, and many others were slave owners, evil to the core. Benjamin Franklin and John Adams did not own slaves, but they fraternized with the slave owners; therefore, they are evil. They will rewrite history to expose the unfairness and injustice against the black, colored, and poor people. Our history already reflects those facts, but the new narrative will triple down on the evil of the Western Civilization and the white men. This will be in line with the hateful socialist teaching.

Are you surprised that the statues of George Washington, Abraham Lincoln, and Teddy Roosevelt were toppled or removed? Their names of high schools taken down? They will remove many other such statues as they are already doing. Politically incorrect old paintings will be hidden in warehouses.

Nothing must remain of the past, but only what represented the injustice of the white men.

Marxism-Socialism is the ideology of antagonism and hatred. The history is a good source of causing hatred in the mind of the young people. Our forefathers were white men, and some were slave owners. Bad, bad, bad.

In the book "1984" by George Orwell there is a passage that must be mentioned about how history is viewed in that world:

> "Who controls the past controls the future: who controls the present controls the past," repeated Winston obediently.

> "Who controls the present controls the past," said O'Brien, nodding his head with slow approval. 'Is it your opinion, Winston, that the past has real existence?'
>
> Again the feeling of helplessness descended upon Winston. His eyes flitted towards the dial. He not only did not know whether 'yes' or 'no' was the answer that would save him from pain; he did not even know which answer he believed to be the true one.
>
> O'Brien smiled faintly. 'You are no metaphysician, Winston,' he said. 'Until this moment you had never considered what is meant by existence. I will put it more precisely. Does the past exist concretely, in space? Is there somewhere or other a place, a world of solid objects, where the past is still happening?'
>
> 'No.'
>
> 'Then where does the past exist, if at all?'
>
> 'In records. It is written down.'
>
> 'In records. And- ?'
>
> 'In the mind. In human memories.
>
> 'In memory. Very well, then. We, the Party, control all records, and we control all memories. Then we control the past, do we not?'
>
> 'But how can you stop people remembering things?' cried Winston again momentarily forgetting the dial. 'It is involuntary. It is outside oneself. How can you control memory? You have not controlled mine!'

Frightening, but this is Socialist reality. *"Who controls the past controls the future: who controls the present controls the past."* That's why history is revised to favor the neo-Marxists actions today, which will determine our future. And what is the past? If it is not written or remembered it does not exist, and if it does not exist, it can be reinvented.

Under Socialism, the history of the country is re-written. The United States of America's birth is not in 1776 and the Revolution of Independence, but in 1619 when the first African slaves were brought to the colonies. The Founding Fathers of our country were evil, slave white owners. Our heroes who fought and died for our country are ignored, and a few unknown, underground anti-slavery people are the heroes now. The entire Western Civilization, white civilization, that has brought our unimaginable and improved standard of living is discredited and abandoned. Western Literature and Shakespeare are white and bad. Mathematics and grammar are racist. Old history must not to be taught in classes. Even Musical notation and writing is to be abolished because the white men created them during colonialism.

At the New York Times they invented both *Project 1619*, which states that when the first slave ship, with 20 enslaved Africans, landed in Virginia, America began as we know it, and everything that America is, was built from the labor of the Blacks. In 1620 there were 2,302 white people in the colonies and 20 new black arrivals. And there were none before that.

(https://courses.lumenlearning.com/suny-ushistory2os2xmaster/chapter/united-states-population-chart/)

Twenty African slaves represented less than one percent of the population of future America, and *they* created the United States of America?

As for the *Critical Race Theory* that is pushed in our schools, according to our Socialist flag newspaper, the New York Times:

> Our democracy's founding ideals were false when they were written. Black Americans have fought to make them true. *Nicole Hannah-Jones*

There you have it, folks, our History and Constitution are false, and it needs to be overhauled. What did the Black Americans fight for? Read BLM demands again, and you understand this enormous lie that is inflicted upon our schools by the Democrat Socialist Party.

Who is Nikole Hannah-Jones? A Pulitzer Prize-winning, nevertheless, black reporter working for NY Times. The "luminary" reporter, working for a socialist newspaper, proved the historians wrong about the founding of America, they want us to believe.

But wait, they must replace the banished heroes with "righteous" ones. Who are those men and women? Anyone that has taken some acts of rebellion, criminals, prisoners, and if they were not white men, the better. The insignificant people of the past or present, many criminals, will take center stage, not the builders, inventors, and entrepreneurs who made America great. Drug heads, like George Floyd, will be declared martyrs, and their statues will replace George Washington. We already experienced the BLM sign posted at the American Embassies in foreign countries. Our American ambassador at the UN declared the United States racist. Our history is rewritten in real time.

Chapter 6.12. Freedom

The Nazi-Socialist party curtailed freedom immediately in Germany after Adolph Hitler became a dictator. Even before the Germans elected the NAZI-Socialist party in Reichstag, the Brown Shirts intimidated the population, just as the BLM and Antifa, with the full support of Main Stream Media, are doing in America. Let's understand that there was "freedom" in Nazi-Germany, except it was the NAZI-Socialist freedom. All newspapers, radio, and cinema were censored by the Minister of Propaganda under Joseph Goebbels, and only the truth as dictated by the NAZI-Socialist Party was allowed.

The same thing was true in Socialist Romania; there was "freedom," the Communist Party type of freedom.

Freedom is the mortal enemy of Totalitarianism.

The Democrat Socialist party, once in full control, will censor our freedom. More so than they already do. At first, they'll tell us we have the freedom to say what we want, as long as it is not *hateful*. But who's to say what hateful speech is? Who is the ~~Czar~~ Commissar of Truth, who can guide us and prevent us from politically sinful speech? The truth is in the eyes of the beholder. That's why freedom guarantees Free Speech, regardless if it's hateful or not. Everything said on the Mainstream Socialist Media is hateful to me. Should we ban it? Not if I believe in freedom.

The books "Escape from Communism," "Hitler was a Socialist," and this book "Freedom Trumps Socialism" might be hurtful to some people, but never for those who lived under Socialist tyranny. Should they ban my books and others like them? Yes, according to some zealots at Amazon.

The people who live in *Freedom* do not understand freedom. Does a fish understand water? It does when it flops on the beach, gasping for ... water. And so, it is with freedom, when you don't have it, you'll know it, but it may be too late.

The saddest part of all is the people don't care about Freedom, even if they don't have it, as long as our lives are fulfilled materially. The Chinese people are living far, much better today than when they lived under Mao. In Tiananmen Square in 1989, the people demonstrated for freedom when Communism-economy was hurting them. But they won't do it soon, for as long as Communist-Fascist China will keep taking Western jobs to give them to their people, while keeping a tight rein on the dissenters.

Does this mean that the fight for Freedom will die in America? No. But lack of freedom will hurt us, as our standard of living will decline. For the Chinese people, everyday life is up and up. Many Chinese remember the bicycles were the mode of transportation until the 1980s. But today their streets are clogged with cars. For the Americans, if Socialism wins, everyday life will deteriorate, and we will remember when the American roads were clogged with cars instead of bicycles, as the Green New Deal will shove down our throats.

Only when we, the Americans, feel the Socialism poverty pains will we wonder what happened? How come we had plenty before? We had Freedom before.

Chapter 6.13. Population's Standard of Living

Hitler and the NAZI-Socialist Party came to power because of the Great Depression. The Standard of Living for the German population, although already low after the war, became abysmal during the Depression. The German people wanted and demanded change, and Hitler promised a better life. What's even more amazing is that Hitler delivered. The economy, the employment improved because Hitler embarked on rearming Germany. The people were content, and Hitler continued tightening his control.

Until the Democrat Socialist Party is in full control, the population's Standard of Living must be maintained. Even if the population's Standard of Living will not improve, propaganda will tell us otherwise, with full compliance by MSM. The United States of America is a wealthy country, but Socialism will diminish the population's Standard of Living. After President Biden took office the gasoline prices went up by more than a dollar per gallon, at least in California, and the inflation is climbing. What will the Democrat Socialist Party do to give the illusion of prosperity?

Not as Hitler did, arming the United States is out of the question, but disarming our military is the alternative. The United States spends over $900 billion on military spending, which is 15% of the annual budget. Considering how many people hate our country and agree with Barack Obama that America is one among equals, not superior, why spend on military? China will dominate the Pacific, Europe should take care of the Atlantic and Mediterranean, and NATO will shrink or be abandoned to save money. They could make lots of money from shrinking the Military and transfer the money to social programs.

President Biden is giving away trillions to boost his popularity and make sure people will re-elect him and the Democrat Socialist Party in the future. The Covid-19 Stimulus plan, $1.9 trillion, could be justifiable, but $4 trillion more to stimulate the economy is nothing else but a welfare program. Remove the artificial Covid restrictions, and the economy will grow again. But that's not their plan.

The Democrat Socialist party should remember Bill Clinton's saying: "Is the economy stupid." Exactly, but Socialism will destroy the economy.

Chapter 6.14. Central Planning

Hitler did not nationalize the economy. Unlike the Soviet Union that nationalized it and adhered to it until it collapsed. However, that didn't mean Hitler and the NAZI-Socialists allowed the industrialists to do as they pleased. The Nazi-Socialists controlled the economy, every aspect of it, just as it was in Fascist Italy.

Marxism-Socialism relies on central, authoritarian power. It cannot exist with independent and wealthy capitalists interfering with their plans. And just like Hitler's Germany and China today, the Democrat Socialist Party will need to tighten its control and impose central planning on the economy in the near future, with the help of the Corporate Bureaucrats, who will gladly do what the Party orders.

Controlling the economy will not be difficult. Because of the unknown number of laws, rules, and regulations that affect the economy, the US Government already controls it. The US Treasury, by controlling the money supply, is controlling the economy. Taxation laws control the economy. But the businesses decide how to run their companies based on Free Market Capitalism, right? That's true at this time. We don't have pure capitalism in the USA, as we did in the 19th century. We have a mixed Capitalist economy, evolving toward crony-Capitalism.

We have Institutionalized Corporatism. Most of the large companies are owned by the public and managed by business managers. In reality the businesses are managed by Financial Bureaucrats or Corporate Bureaucrats. Although the Corporate Bureaucrats own some stock in the companies they work for, they are no different from any salaried employee. Their position and salaries are their principal source of wealth. In a typical capitalist-company, the owner-entrepreneurs built their companies from the ground up, and their number one priority was to grow and expand their businesses. Look at Jeff Bezos of Amazon. Sure, he is the richest man, but his wealth is derived from the ownership of Amazon. In 2019, Amazon paid Bezos a base salary of $81,840. That's far less than what I was paid when I was employed in 2012. Of course, he had bonuses over his base salary, but only if Amazon prospered, which it did. This denotes the goals and rewards of a Capitalist-Entrepreneur versus the Corporate Bureaucrat. The Capitalist-Entrepreneur wants his business to grow and succeed. The Corporate Bureaucrat wants his pay and bonuses to grow, just like any other employee would.

Compare Bezos' salary with other typical Corporate Bureaucrats, like Tim Cook, the CEO of Apple. His compensation is $133 million, salary, bonus, stock awards. Or Joseph Ianniello, former acting CEO of CBS, $125 million salary, stock awards, and perks. Or Tom

Rutledge, CEO of Charter Communications, $116 million, salary, bonus, stock, and option awards. How about Sundar Pichai, CEO of Alphabet/Google, $86 million, salary, and stock awards. None of these people created the companies they work for. These people make astronomical incomes being *employees*, not entrepreneurs. I'm not picking on these guys for making so much money compared to the grunt employees in their companies. All I'm saying is that their *gold mine* is their employment. That's why the huge discrepancy between the average employee and them. While in charge, "steal" all you can.

Do those Corporate Bureaucrats have ownership interest? Aside from owning some stock that was *awarded* to them as part of their compensation, they are employees, not owners. Tim Cook doesn't care that he employs Chinese workers rather than Americans. But that's the reality of business today. You cannot be competitive today if you don't go offshore. Then what's Elon Musk doing wrong by manufacturing electric cars, Tesla, in the US? Maybe that's because he's an engineer and not a bean counter. Wait until Corporate Bureaucrats manage Tesla.

What's the point I'm trying to make. For one, all these highly paid corporate executives are compensated by how much the company's stock grows. None will shed a tear if they have to move the production to China, as long as the stock prices increase and their compensation increases. Their job is not to grow the enterprise but to grow the valuation of the enterprise, whichever way they need to do that. The second thing is that today's corporations have become so large and government-regulated that all executives must be first politicians to survive. They are running politically influenced enterprises. When the State says jump, they will jump.

Part of the Central Planning is Free National Health. No more premiums and high deductible, or not having any health coverage. That sounds great, or is it?

Free National Health coverage for all, legal and illegals alike. In 2019, 92% of the people had health insurance. But 28 million did not, although they'll be treated, legal or illegals, if they have a medical emergency. In my opinion, we have more than 11 million illegals, more like 30 million and more to come with a free pass from Biden Administration. If our healthcare is nationalized, overnight the government will add 28 million uninsured plus 30 million illegals for a total of 58 million people to the national health system. Private health insurance is for profit. The Left claims it is more expensive, and the State should take over and manage the National Health System for less and for everyone. Remember what happened with the V.A. Health program, where people were dying before seeing a doctor? That will happen to all of us under a National Health System.

When it comes to health care, there will never be enough money to cover everyone's health care needs. Rationing, long lines, and death will follow, especially for the oldest citizens. You may say that doesn't happen in Canada. Yes, it does, that's why many Canadians come to the US for procedures that the Canadian health system may never cover, or it takes too long to be attended to before a Canadian will die. In the UK, they quarter the hospitalized patients in the hallways because the budget cannot cover all the sick people in UK.

Any organization ran by the government becomes bureaucratic and inefficient. Unlike the competitive Health Care under Free-Market, the National Health System will be bloated with employees, mostly non-medical, who don't have to fear being fired. There will be no more lawsuits against malpractice; the Socialist government will outlaw them. If you suffer or die because of incompetent or negligent doctors, so be it.

But why would the State want to control or plan the economy? The politicians don't want the business people to make random decisions as dictated by the market and affect their jobs. They want to control, plan and steer the economy as they see fit for the glory of Socialism. Call that the Green New Deal?

Chapter 6.15. The Green New Deal

Point 7 of Communist Manifesto, "*Extension of factories and instruments of production owned by the State; the bringing into cultivation of wastelands, and the improvement of soil generally in accordance with a common plan,*" requires Central Planning. This will ensure the *party* controls our economic destiny and not the profit-minded individuals operating in a Free Market. The Green New Deal is such an example of *central planning*. Through this Government sponsored and paid program, they'll create employment and potential prosperity under the disguise of *Global Climate change*.

In modern times, we base our entire economy and prosperity on energy. At first, it was the muscle power of man or beast, then water from river and wind to create the energy needed. Steam and then combustion engines increased our power supply geometrically. Electrical motors are superior to combustion engines, just as combustion engines are superior to steam engines. Electricity is clean energy, providing that another *clean* energy produces it. Chemical reactions (solar panels) can produce electricity, however for our industrial needs, spinning generators are needed to produce massive electrical power, and that requires fossil or nuclear fuels.

In 1760, when the Industrial Revolution started, the Earth's population was 760 million people. Today the population is 7.8 billion. It is the "evil" Western Civilization with its Free Market Capitalism starting with the Industrial Revolution followed by mass production, all along with new scientific discoveries that are responsible for the increase in population. There is more food and better medicine, resulting in a 10-fold population expansion in 280 years. As it happens, all these people need more pots and pans, shelter, AC's and cars, which use more energy, which causes more pollution. So, we need to rectify our behavior to save the planet.

President Franklin D. Roosevelt drafted the New Deal in 1933 to solve the economic crises caused by the Great Depression of 1929. In the end, World War II solved the financial crisis and not the New Deal. It was a fair effort to solve unemployment, but at the same time, it opened the gates for big government and socialism.

Our planet is in peril because of us, says Alexandra Ocasio Cortez. We must take drastic government interventions in our economy in the next ten years to solve all that ails our planet caused by Capitalism, or we'll go *extinct*. We have until 2028, seven more years now, Alexandra "wisely" predicts, and then lights will go out on Earth.

Along with like-minded Democrat Socialists, she drafted “The Green New Deal,” and they hope to pass it into law to save our planet. Unlike in the past when the Private Enterprises took care of business, this time the Big Government will take the initiative on the same grand scale as it did in the former Communist Bloc nations, which they failed miserably.

The Green New Deal has as much to do with *Green* as Black Lives Matter has to do with *Black Lives*.

The following is the HR 109 as proposed, and my comments about each point. I grew up in Communism-Socialism, and this Green New Deal sounds just as the Communist Central Planning Committee would have written it.

IN THE HOUSE OF REPRESENTATIVES
RESOLUTION H. RES. 109
Recognizing the duty of the Federal Government to create
a Green New Deal.
Whereas the October 2018 report entitled ‘‘Special Report on
Global Warming of 1.50 C” by the Intergovernmental
Panel on Climate Change and the November 2018
Items not related to *Global Warming* will be tagged with *.
Fourth National Climate Assessment report found that—
(1) human activity is the dominant cause of observed
climate change over the past century;

- Absolutely: almost 8 billion people and growing will affect any planet.

(2) a changing climate is causing sea levels to rise
and an increase in wildfires, severe storms, droughts, and
other extreme weather events that threaten human life,
healthy communities, and critical infrastructure;

- Possibly, but doubtful: Sea levels have not risen. Most of the melting ice is at the North Pole, not affecting the sea level. Polar bears don’t go starving. Government forest mismanagement causes most wildfires and expanding population. Deforestation causes droughts and grazing animals to supply food for a growing population.

(3) global warming at or above 2 degrees Celsius beyond pre-industrialized levels will cause—

- The temperature since 1880 has increased by 1.10 C (2.98 F.) Why would another 0.90 C (1.62 F) be so disastrous?

(A) mass migration from the regions most affected by climate change;

- Speculation. Economic pressures, because of increased population, cause migrations.

(B) more than $500,000,000,000 in lost annual economic output in the United States by the year 2100;

- Speculation.

(C) wildfires that, by 2050, will annually burn at least twice as much forest area in the western United States than was typically burned by wildfires in the years preceding 2019;

- Speculation. Europe does not have wildfire problems like California has because they manage their forests.

(D) a loss of more than 99 percent of all coral reefs on Earth;

- The coral reefs suffered, but not the same way in all the oceans. Work is underway to improve the situation by creating higher temperature-resistant corals.

(E) more than 350,000,000 more people to be exposed globally to deadly heat stress by 2050;

- Speculation. However, if the AC's, energy users, will be banned, what would happen in the future?

(F) a risk of damage to $1,000,000,000,000 of public infrastructure and coastal real estate in the United States;

- Spend more money to fix imaginary threats.

(4) global temperatures must be kept below 1.5 degrees Celsius above pre-industrialized levels to avoid the most severe impacts of a changing climate, which will require—

- Our level today is 1.1 C. Does this mean that we can continue to pollute by 0.4 C up to the 1.5 C target?

(A) global reductions in greenhouse gas emissions from human sources of 40 to 60 percent from 2010 levels by 2030;

- This would be good, but impossible. Will China comply? Every month they are firing a new coal power plant.

(B) net-zero global emissions by 2050; Whereas, because the United States has historically been responsible for a disproportionate

amount of greenhouse gas emissions, having emitted 20 percent of global greenhouse gas emissions through 2014, and has a high technological capacity, the United States must take a leading role in reducing emissions through economic transformation;

- Punish the American people. China is the biggest polluter, amounting to 1/3 of global pollution, twice as much as the US.

Whereas the United States is currently experiencing several related crises, with—

(1) life expectancy declining while basic needs, such as clean air, clean water, healthy food, and adequate health care, housing, transportation, and education, are inaccessible to a significant portion of the United States population;

- Have you observed a decline in our basic needs? This is a Socialist Lie.

(2) a 4-decade trend of wage stagnation, deindustrialization, and antilabor policies that has led to—

- This results from exporting our industrial jobs to China. Bring them back, and it will solve the problem, as President Trump's policies have shown. *

(A) hourly wages overall stagnating since the 1970s despite increased worker productivity;

- The result of automation to stay competitive with China, and job losses to China as well. *

(B) the third-worst level of socioeconomic mobility in the developed world before the Great Recession;

- Under President Trump, we had the highest employment levels and rising wages. President Biden will reverse that, and the Green New Deal will make it worse.

(C) the erosion of the earning and bargaining power of workers in the United States;

- We shipped Industrial jobs to China, what is to be expected? *

(D) inadequate resources for public sector workers to confront the challenges of climate change at local, State, and Federal levels;

- More Bureaucracy will solve the Climate Change?

(3) the greatest income inequality since the 1920s, with—

- Because we shipped Industrial jobs to China. They brought high-Tech skill employees from India under the H-1B visa, because they are cheaper, while our High-Tech employees were fired. *

(A) the top 1 percent of earners accruing 91percent of gains in the first few years of economic recovery after the Great Recession;

- The government bailed the financial institutions out while foreclosing on the homeowners, being barred for 7 years from buying another house. Who is at fault here but the government applying socialist policies? *

(B) a large racial wealth divide amounting to a difference of 20 times more wealth between the average white family and the average black family;

- The facts are correct, however, the reasons given are Socialist lies. Learning and working hard is the key to success, not government subsidies as we have done so far. *

(C) a gender earnings gap that results in women earning approximately 80 percent as much as men, at the median; Whereas climate change, pollution, and environmental destruction have exacerbated systemic racial, regional, social, environmental, and economic injustices (referred to in this preamble as ''systemic injustices'') by disproportionately affecting indigenous peoples, communities of color, migrant communities, deindustrialized communities, depopulated rural communities, the poor, low-income workers, women, the elderly, the unhoused, people with disabilities, and youth (referred to in this preamble as ''frontline and vulnerable communities'');

- Mostly incorrect. We pay men and women the same for same jobs and qualifications, however, because women take time from work for motherhood, their choices, their total compensation seems to be smaller than that of men.
- They fabricated Systemic injustices. Lies to be used by the Socialists for political power.

Whereas, climate change constitutes a direct threat to the national security of the United States—

- China is a direct threat to the national security of the United States, not climate change.

(1) by impacting the economic, environmental, and social stability of countries and communities around the world;

- The United States is responsible for the entire world now? *

(2) by acting as a threat multiplier; Whereas the Federal Government-led mobilizations during World War II and the New Deal created the greatest middle class that the United States has ever seen, but many members of frontline and vulnerable communities were excluded from many of the economic and societal benefits of those mobilizations; and Whereas the House of Representatives recognizes that a new national, social, industrial, and economic mobilization on a scale not seen since World War II and the New Deal era is a historic opportunity—

- It was *not* the New Deal that helped the middle class, but the world reconstruction after WWII. The Green New Deal is a historic opportunity to screw up and become a Socialist destitute country.

(1) to create millions of good, high-wage jobs in the United States;

- Pie in the sky. Renewable energy sources are job killers, a study from Germany showed. Employment in the US will be only for installations. China will build the hardware.

(2) to provide unprecedented levels of prosperity and economic security for all people of the United States;

- Poverty and misery will happen with a government command-and-control economy. *

(3) to counteract systemic injustices: Now, therefore, be it Resolved, that it is the sense of the House of Representatives that—

- The Critical Race Theory invented the Systemic Injustice lies. *

(1) it is the duty of the Federal Government to create a Green New Deal—

- No, it is not the duty of the Federal Government to create a Green New Deal. This is a fake crisis to allow a Socialist government to takeover.

(A) to achieve net-zero greenhouse gas emissions through a fair and just transition for all communities and workers;

- Communist-Socialist Speak, comrades.

(B) to create millions of good, high-wage jobs and ensure prosperity and economic security for all people of the United States;

- Speculation. The reality will be exactly the opposite. *

(C) to invest in the infrastructure and industry of the United States to sustainably meet the challenges of the 21st century;

- Infrastructure: yes. The industry is not the Government's responsibility. *

(D) to secure for all people of the United States for generations to come—

(i) clean air and water;

(ii) climate and community resiliency;

(iii) healthy food;

(iv) access to nature; and

(v) a sustainable environment; and

- This sounds as if the US is a third-world country, and we need AOC and the Democrat Socialists to save us. Propaganda, Communist-Socialist Speak, comrades.

(E) to promote justice and equity by stopping current, preventing future, and repairing historic oppression of indigenous peoples, communities of color, migrant communities, deindustrialized communities, depopulated rural communities, the poor, low-income workers, women, the elderly, the unhoused, people with disabilities, and youth (referred to in this resolution as "frontline and vulnerable communities");

- Critical Race Theory, Black Lives Matter, Communist-Socialist Speak comrades. *

(2) the goals described in subparagraphs (A)through (E) of paragraph (1) (referred to in this

resolution as the "Green New Deal goals") should be accomplished through a 10-year national mobilization (referred to in this resolution as the "Green New Deal mobilization") that will require the following goals and projects—

- Here is your Communist Party 10-year plan, comrades.

(A) building resiliency against climate change-related disasters, such as extreme weather, including by leveraging funding and providing investments for community-defined projects and strategies;

- Don't we have FEMA for this?

(B) repairing and upgrading the infrastructure in the United States, including—

- Every President has been talking about this, President Biden is finally implementing it. Maybe. Except out of $1.9 trillion, only 621 billion are for infrastructure. That's the government in action for us. *

(i) by eliminating pollution and greenhouse gas emissions as much as technologically feasible;

- Aren't we doing this already? Cars, refrigerators, AC's are more efficient. The government is telling us even how much water to use.

(ii) by guaranteeing universal access to clean water;

- Nobody gets Montezuma's revenge by drinking tap water. The US has the cleanest water in the world.

(iii) by reducing the risks posed by climate impacts; and

- How? By destroying our economy?

(iv) by ensuring that any infrastructure bill considered by Congress addresses climate change;

- This must be the excuse to use the money for infrastructure but for other purposes.

(C) meeting 100 percent of the power demand in the United States through clean, renewable, and zero-emission energy sources, including—

(i) by dramatically expanding and upgrading renewable power sources; and

- At this time, there are no renewable, non-polluting large enough sources to satisfy the nation's power needs.

(ii) by deploying new capacity;

- Capacity of what? Transmission lines that destroy the environment, storage batteries? Lithium batteries are highly toxic.

(D) building or upgrading to energy-efficient, distributed, and ''smart'' power grids, and ensuring affordable access to electricity;

- I didn't know that our power grids were of the "stupid" kind. The power grids are as "smart" as we can make them. How can we have affordable electricity when "green" electricity is much more expensive? *

(E) upgrading all existing buildings in the United States and building new buildings to achieve maximum energy efficiency, water

efficiency, safety, affordability, comfort, and durability, including through electrification;

- All new constructions in the US are per the latest codes, and it has been that way for decades. As the electricity will become more expensive, the building owners will upgrade their buildings, and for electricity, the Utility Companies have been helping the electrical "Rate Payers" (that's what utilities call their customers) to lower their electric consumption.

(F) spurring massive growth in clean manufacturing in the United States and removing pollution and greenhouse gas emissions from manufacturing and industry as much as is technologically feasible, including by expanding renewable energy manufacturing and investing in existing manufacturing and industry;

- This is what happens when Liberal Arts grad people write this crap. All manufacturing is as clean or dirty as it can be. Improvements can be made, but the cost will go up. To satisfy this requirement is to send all manufacturing to China or return to the pre-industrial world. No high wages there.

(G) working collaboratively with farmers and ranchers in the United States to remove pollution and greenhouse gas emissions from the agricultural sector as much as is technologically feasible, including—

- Cultivating crops produces oxygen, not pollution. Decaying vegetation happens all over the world. It's natural. Should we regulate the wild flora too?

(i) by supporting family farming;

- Inefficient, reduced production, mass starvation will follow. But maybe that's their hidden plan of reducing world population through starvation. Famine is the favorite method of killing the population by the Communist-Socialists.

(ii) by investing in sustainable farming and land use practices that increases soil health; and

- Yes, minerals in the soil degrade, as the land is cultivated continuously. But aren't farmers aware of that and condition the soil or rotate the crops? Farmers don't need help from government bureaucracy. This sounds like USSR and how they ruined their agriculture.

(iii) by building a more sustainable food system that ensures universal access to healthy food;

- Unhealthy food in the US? Since when have we become a third-world country? Don't we have the USDA and FDA that monitor the foods we eat?

(H) overhauling transportation systems in the United States to remove pollution and greenhouse gas emissions from the transportation sector as much as is technologically feasible, including through investment in—

- All transportation will be electrified. But how will the electricity be produced, and won't solar panels and batteries disposal pollute? That is the dirty truth they don't talk about.

(i) zero-emission vehicle infrastructure and manufacturing;

- We can make Transportation zero-emission, but it will be more expensive. Aviation will be impossible to go electric. For some manufacturing is impossible to have zero emissions.

(ii) clean, affordable, and accessible public transit;

- This intends to remove personal transportation. You will not own a car and will be forced to live in crowded cities. But you can own a bicycle, the way it used to be in China.

(iii) high-speed rail;

- This will replace the Freeways and personal automobile transportation. High-speed rail costs as much as traveling by airplane. But I forgot, airplanes pollute, get everyone on the ground. Shall we build a high-speed rail to Hawaii?

(I) mitigating and managing the long-term adverse health, economic, and other effects of pollution and climate change, including by providing funding for community-defined projects and strategies;

- I am all for eliminating pollution. But what is the meaning of providing funding for community-defined projects and strategies? More money to waste for what reason?

(J) removing greenhouse gases from the atmosphere and reducing pollution by restoring natural ecosystems through proven low-tech solutions that increase soil carbon storage, such as land preservation and afforestation;

- Removing greenhouse gases from the atmosphere is prohibitable expensive. However, banning greenhouse gases, we already do.
- Afforestation means reclaiming the agricultural lands and foresting them, which will capture the CO2 from the atmosphere. I agree, but how will we feed the billions of mouths in this world, and do we have hundreds of years for the forests to remove enough carbon?

(K) restoring and protecting threatened, endangered, and fragile ecosystems through locally appropriate and science-based projects that enhance biodiversity and support climate resiliency;

- This means more money and bureaucracy.

(L) cleaning up existing hazardous waste and abandoned sites, ensuring economic development and sustainability on those sites;

- I agree, but don't we have the EPA for this? Besides, where are we going to place the hazardous waste?

(M) identifying other emission and pollution sources and creating solutions to remove them;

- Don't we have the EPA for this?

(N) promoting the international exchange of technology, expertise, products, funding, and services, with the aim of making the United States the international leader on climate action, and to help other countries achieve a Green New Deal;

- These people are delusional, thinking that the Green New Deal will be the answer to all our ills and will increase prosperity. It will bankrupt us, and our standard of living will decline. Apart from China stealing all our technology, expertise, and products, we should give them whatever is left or will be invented at our cost for their benefit. This is an example of Communism and Globalism.

(3) a Green New Deal must be developed through transparent and inclusive consultation, collaboration, and partnership with frontline and vulnerable communities, labor unions, worker cooperatives, civil society groups, academia, and businesses;

- Excellent *Cover Your Ass* proposal. The more people are involved in making decisions, the harder it is to come up with solutions and discover those who screwed up.

(4) to achieve the Green New Deal goals and mobilization, a Green New Deal will require the following goals and projects—

(A) providing and leveraging, in a way that ensures that the public receives appropriate ownership stakes and returns on investment, adequate capital (including through community grants, public banks, and other public financing), technical expertise, supporting policies, and other forms of assistance to communities, organizations, Federal, State, and local government agencies, and businesses working on the Green New Deal mobilization;

- WTF is this? More Communist-Socialist speak, comrades. *

(B) ensuring that the Federal Government takes into account the complete environmental and social costs and impacts of emissions through—

- How about the economic costs?

(i) existing laws;

(ii) new policies and programs; and

(iii) ensuring that frontline and vulnerable communities shall not be adversely affected;

- Try to do good but don't destroy what works.

(C) providing resources, training, and high-quality education, including higher education, to all people of the United States, with a focus on frontline and vulnerable communities, so that all people of the United States may be full and equal participants in the Green New Deal mobilization;

- I'm scratching my head about what this means. I think it is Communist Manifesto, Critical Race Theory, and BLM Speak. *

(D) making public investments in the research and development of new clean and renewable energy technologies and industries;

- I agree with this, but how would we ensure the US benefits from our investments and not be stolen or given to others, like China? Wait, I forgot, we must share new technologies for free with the rest of the world.

(E) directing investments to spur economic development, deepen and diversify industry and business in local and regional economies, and build wealth and community ownership, while prioritizing high-quality job creation and economic, social, and environmental benefits in frontline and vulnerable communities, and deindustrialized

communities, that may otherwise struggle with the transition away from greenhouse gas intensive industries

- The Communist-Socialist Romanian government tried to do this. It failed miserably. And how would this be achieved, retraining? Joe Biden said that if a miner can go in a shaft 2,000 feet down, he can learn how to program. Try to learn to program if you're over 50 and worked with your hands all your life. We all due respect for the office of the Presidency, Joe Biden is an idiot.

(F) ensuring the use of democratic and participatory processes that are inclusive of and led by frontline and vulnerable communities and workers to plan, implement, and administer the Green New Deal mobilization at the local level;

- The often-mentioned vulnerable communities cannot get their act together now; what magic will the Green New Deal bring?

(G) ensuring that the Green New Deal mobilization creates high-quality union jobs that pay prevailing wages, hires local workers, offers training and advancement opportunities, and

guarantees wage and benefit parity for workers affected by the transition;

- This is lip-service to all the unionized workers. Don't worry, they'll take care of you with high-quality union jobs, which they're not sure how or if they will be created.

(H) guaranteeing a job with a family-sustaining wage, adequate family and medical leave, paid vacations, and retirement security to all people of the United States;

- They forgot to mention Equity. This is like what the USSR constitution says: You have a right to employment. Great, but who will fulfill that, right? The government of the USSR did that, and look at what happened to them.

(I) strengthening and protecting the right of all workers to organize, unionize, and collectively bargain free of coercion, intimidation, and harassment;

- Isn't this part of the law today? *

(J) strengthening and enforcing labor, workplace health and safety, antidiscrimination, and wage and hour standards across all employers, industries, and sectors;

- We have OSHA and other laws doing this already. *

(K) enacting and enforcing trade rules, procurement standards, and border adjustments with strong labor and environmental protections—

- Don't we do this already?

(i) to stop the transfer of jobs and pollution overseas;

- Something positive for a change.

(ii) to grow domestic manufacturing in the United States;

- Only by stopping the jobs from going to other nations. But if we do that, what would our Communist Chinese Comrades do?

(L) ensuring that public lands, waters, and oceans are protected and that eminent domain is not abused;

(M) obtaining the free, prior, and informed consent of indigenous peoples for all decisions that affect indigenous peoples and their traditional territories, honoring all treaties and agreements with indigenous peoples, and protecting and enforcing the sovereignty and land rights of indigenous peoples;

- We have laws for these.

(N) ensuring a commercial environment where every businessperson is free from unfair competition and domination by domestic or international monopolies;

- I'm all for preventing monopolies like Amazon, Facebook, Twitter, Google, and all others like them.

(O) providing all people of the United States with—

(i) high-quality health care;

- The Untired States' people have the highest quality health care in the world. Socialized government managed health care will destroy our highest quality health care and reduce our longevity. *

(ii) affordable, safe, and adequate housing;

- This would be doable, but the environmental and city codes slow housing development. Would the Green New Deal eliminate these things? Not from what they said so far.

(iii) economic security;

- This is an individual responsibility. But they want Socialism and the government to provide for us from the cradle to grave. The individual needs to do nothing, so we are completely dependent on the Socialist government, just like slaves on plantations. *

(iv) clean water, clean air, healthy and affordable food, and access to nature.

- Are we talking about the United States or Haiti here?

* Not related to *Global Warming*.

If you had the patience to read through the Green New Deal, at first, it might appear, despite my comments, that it is nothing wrong with it. Well, the United States of America did not become the most prosperous nation on Earth because the government came out with an economic plan, but because the government stayed out of the way and let the entrepreneurs do what they do best.

However, there are enormous consequences to everything proposed in the New Green Deal. Take for one housing. A smaller house uses less energy, and an apartment even less. Large houses with swimming pools sprawled on large parcels are using more energy and water and land that could be used for agriculture or forestation. So, expect single residence housing to be taxed or outlawed in favor of Stalinist block apartments with bedrooms not much larger than a king-size bed.

In the old days, American cars were large and luxurious—gas guzzlers. The cars have shrunk in size to be more fuel-efficient. But the preferred personal transportation are the SUVs. That's bad, they say. Expect for the SUVs to be taxed more or outlawed. Cars, before disappearing to favor mass transportation, will shrink in size to a three-wheeled vehicle.

Many foods we eat today will become more expensive or outlawed altogether. Meats will be the number one target, being replaced by protein-based vegetables and beans. Meat will be sparsely available, just like in Cuba. Over there Steaks are referred by the name of "Jesus." Everyone knows he exists, but no one have seen him. Water-intensive crops may be eliminated from arid areas. Expect neighborhoods to raise crops in the streets and on the roofs of the buildings.

The Green New Deal is nothing else but the *New Green Communist Manifesto*.

Book 3. Present and Future

We are in a Civil and Cultural War. God help us not to escalate into a bloody Civil War. We are polarized, hating each other's guts, even among family members. Normal is abnormal, and we are constantly reminded about "New Normal(s)." Who polarized us, the Left, the Marxists, the anarchists? The Leftist Intellectuals carried out the brainwashing, and the Marxist-Socialists infiltrated the Democrat Party.

History does not repeat exactly; with every generation we are different people, different circumstances, changing culture. Predicting the future is difficult because of the dynamics involved. The actions and reactions among us will determine the outcome for the best or worst for all of us. But so far, the American Democrat Socialist Party followed closely Hitler's playbook for their political gains.

Unlike Russia in 1917, which was poor and ignorant, the United States is prosperous and oblivious. Right there, the dynamics are different. Neo-Marxism has accomplished an incredible achievement, equal only to Nazi-Germany and Fascist Italy. The transformation to Socialism will continue if we don't stop it. In Russia it was the struggle of the proletariat, in Germany it was the struggle of the German workers. Ideologies adapt to the current social situations. In the United States, it is the battle of the counterculture and races. Replace German workers struggle with American race struggle, and that's our situation now.

In 2022 the American People will have an opportunity to reverse the slide into Socialism by depriving the Democrat Socialists Party of a majority in Congress, preferably in both Houses. Of course, just having the Republican Party in the majority is not a finished job. The Republicans, unlike the Democrats, are more independent and are not corralled in place through fear as Nancy Pelosi does to the Democrats. Another problem with the Republicans is that they, too, succumb to Woke-ness. As Tim Groseclose said in the book "Left Turn," the entire population has been influenced to the Left by the Mainstream

Socialist Media, including the Republicans. The Republicans still live in senator Bob Dole's time when *the gentlemen reached across the aisle to settle their differences and do best for the United States.* Wrong. The Democrat Socialists are not gentlemen/women anymore. They are tyrants thirsty for power at any cost. The Republicans are naive sheep, easy prey for the Democrat Socialist wolves.

As long as we have the turncoats Romney, Murkowski, Burr, Cassidy, Collins, Sasse, and Toomey in the Republican Party, the Democrat Socialists will divide and conquer. Unfortunately, only Murkowski is up for reelection in 2022, and until we clean house of those traitors and not elect others like them, the Republican Party will be weak, while Socialism will march on. The seven senators mentioned above did not comprehend that the Democrats attempted a coup d'état against President Trump by impeaching him twice. As far as the House Representatives, Liz Chaney, Tom Rice, Dan Newhouse, Adam Kinzinger, Anthony Gonzalez, Fred Upton, Jaime Herrera Beutler, Peter Meijer, John Katko, and David Valadao will face reelection in 2022. Let's see if the voters will wise up and kick them out. If the Republican voters don't show solidarity for freedom, the Democrat Socialists' tyranny will prevail.

There will be a new Presidential election in 2024. Our chance to get rid of President Biden, if he can function until then. Who should be the Republican candidate? Donald Trump carries the most weight among the Republicans. But he is very polarizing, and he will be 78 years old by that time, just as old as Joe Biden was when he became the President. Will Donald Trump be as sharp as he was at 74? Will he become less antagonistic and appeal to a larger population segment and deliver us from evil? But it doesn't matter, anyone who is determined to destroy socialism will be fought against with fanatical fervor. So, yes let's hope Donald Trump will run and win in 2024. I don't see any other promising candidate who wants to destroy socialism. This is a matter of life and death, freedom and slavery.

Will the Democrats cheat again during elections? For sure, the current Democrat Socialist Congress will do everything it can to ensure continuous voter fraud. By insisting that voters must present IDs to vote, President Biden considers that the biggest challenge to our country since the Civil War. The only challenge the Democrats face is not winning if they're not allowed to cheat. The best-case scenario is that the Joe Biden-Harris administration, their anti-white racism and socialist agenda, Systemic Racism, Project 1619, Critical Race Theory, BLM, and Antifa will make the people aware of how destructive the Democrats are.

If not, the worst is yet to come.

Chapter 1. What to Expect from the Democrat-Socialist Tyranny

What if the Democrat Socialist Party achieves total power? I hope not, but it may happen. We, collectively, are responsible for our future.

The Democrat-Socialist Party will not rest until they acquire total and absolute power in our country. Socialism cannot thrive in democracy, although they will pretend that the Democrats are for *democracy*.

Suppose the Democrat-Socialist Party increases its majority in Congress in 2022. In that case, they will not be voted out of power, ever. Thus, voting fraud will be a permanent staple of our politics until elections are abolished, which will be the ultimate goal of the neo-Socialists—the dictatorship of the Elites.

To consolidate their power, the Democrat Socialist Party will take the following steps, not necessarily in the order listed below:

Priority 1. Increase Taxation.

The taxation enriches no country. People will work less and earn less when the taxes increase over a certain point. Enterprises will replace people with machines, reducing employment, while the prices of goods will rise. The average person understands that the consumers pay the corporate taxes in the form of higher retail prices. That must be shocking news to President Biden, Bernie Sanders, Elizabeth Warren, and Alexandria Ocasio Cortez, who keep pushing for higher corporate taxes. But maybe they know that demanding higher corporate taxes placates public opinion about fair taxation while keeping the personal income tax a bit lower. In the end, the consumer pays for all the taxes collected by the government.

I remember a story my dad told me about taxes. Long ago, in the hills of western Transylvania, the sheepherders used the government land for pasture. It was for a fee. From time to time, the government increased the fees. The sheepherders never got upset, but some of the asset-less citizens were. What did they care? Simple, the herders were going to pass on the cost to the consumer, while the irate citizens were going to pay more for cheese because they knew they were at the end of the line, holding the bag.

Another story, a peasant may have an ox to help him plow a few acres of land to feed his family and prosper. The ox was property, and it was taxed, and when it became impossible for that peasant to pay the higher taxes, he either sold his ox or butchered it and sold the meat. Afterward, the peasant worked smaller parts of his land. He became poorer; the government did not collect taxes on the ox, and the country and the population became poorer as well.

Excessive taxation kills the Goose that Lays the Golden Eggs.

Increase Taxes. Socialism and Taxes are synonyms. Socialism is money-hungry to satisfy the social promises they make. Rule 2 of the Communist manifesto: *A heavy progressive or graduated income tax*. Taxation will be the tool by which the Socialists will transfer wealth from the rich to the Socialist government. President Biden proposed to raise the personal taxes from 37% to 39.6% and corporate taxes from 21% to 28%. A Socialist America needs lots of money. They will increase taxation on Capital Gain from max 20% to a higher percentage equal to all the other tax rates.

Asset Taxation. Eventually, the net worth of wealth will be taxed, like an estate tax. After paying your taxes on the income and profit you made from other investments, they will tax you again on the total assessed value of your possessions, real and liquid. Even though investors with large Real Estate holdings are already taxed by their County Assessors, the Federal Socialist Government will tax them again as wealth taxes. As promised by Elizabeth Warren, the assets of the rich will be imposed on people with assets in the millions, including Real Estate and equity holdings. This will be a rich source of revenue. But just as they implemented the income tax in 1909 only on the rich people, shortly after, the taxes crept up and included all of us. Asset taxation will be the norm for all of us. That's one way to make sure that the people will own nothing eventually, as in Communism Manifesto Rule 1.

Inheritance taxes. Another easy source of revenue would be taxing on a gradual scale the inheritances. It will not happen for every individual all at once. It will be easy to increase the taxes over time to the point that there will be no inheritance whatsoever. California already increased the inheritance tax.

Increase Petroleum Taxes. Federal Gasoline Tax is 18.4 cents per gallon and 24.4 for diesel. California charges 50.5 cents per gallon, and more taxes are proposed. Do you want to live in the Socialist Republic of California? For *green* reasons and to save the planet the fuel taxes must be increased. It reduces pollution and brings additional revenue to the Socialist government. But that's not fair to the poor. The Green New Deal wants to put us on mass transportation, which will solve the issue, they say.

National Health Care Taxes. Health care is not free or cheap. Someone must pay for it. National Health Care managed by the government will be at best half as good as it is now. But other countries like UK and Canada spend less than we do on Health Care. Yes, the US spends 17.5% of the GDP, and even if we continue to spend the same, there will be more people to care for. And the people who pay into the system will have to pay for those who do not. We will see immediately after the National Health Care is instituted, an increase in health taxes, and the waiting to see a doctor will increase. The "Don't call us, we'll call you" syndrome will take place. The queue will become longer, and older people will die sooner.

Black Population Reparation Taxes. If this comes to pass, expect an additional tax for reparations to all black people in the USA, legal or otherwise.

Note: The chances are that this will not happen, or if it does, will be a token of what black people expect. It is an expense that even the United States of America cannot afford. Lip service will be abundant and committees will be set up to explore the possibility. Considering other benefits that black people receive, like health care and education and guaranteed jobs (soon to come), that will suffice and there will be no reparations paid.

Free Education Taxes. We already pay for free education for K12. This tax will be for paying off the student loans and educating everyone through college and beyond. Sending more people for free to colleges will expand the brainwashing.

Social Security Benefits. It is unfortunate that the average person either makes too little money or spends too much to save for old age. The government has to help us out, or so we demand. Social Security fulfills that need. Although not designed as a retirement program, it is viewed as such by the majority of people. Unfortunately, the SS is based on a pyramid scheme. The grandest of all, ran by the government. The younger workers pay for the retirement of older people. With more and more retirees and fewer and fewer workers, Social Security will be bankrupt soon. What should we do as the SS is becoming the most significant expense for our country? Sure, they'll increase the deduction each of us and the employers have to make, but that won't be enough. Immigration is an alternative, expanding the workforce. But immigration won't solve the problem. The influx of illegal immigrants who are not doctors and engineers, highly payed, but minimum wage earners, plus their large families to support will add additional expenses to be paid by all of us.

Since the government cannot increase the SS revenue beyond a certain level, the next alternative is to decrease the payouts to retirees.

A means test will be implemented. If you worked hard and saved all your life and have a retirement account of your own, or have assets, savings, investments, or Real Estate investments, your SS pay will be eliminated until you spend your assets. You don't need government assistance, although you paid in the program all your life. Even the people who don't have retirement accounts but have a house with small or no mortgage will receive a reduced SS pay. These unfortunate people will have to get reverse mortgages to survive and there will be no inheritance for their children.

If you fall into this category, you are forced into wealth redistribution without realizing it. Consider yourself "fortunate," like the ant, because you saved and are able to share with the less "fortunate" crickets, people.

Another way to reduce Medicare expenses is by disallowing certain types of medical interventions to the elderly. Population control is easy when the people depend on the State. This sounds cruel and Nazi-style, but it happened all the time in the Marxist-Socialist countries. The choices will be between who gets a heart transplant, a 70 or 50-year-old? The older you get, the more expensive procedures will be disallowed.

Priority 2. Entice the Population to Vote Democrat Socialist.

Universal Healthcare. The Republicans have failed miserably to cancel Obama Care, and here comes the Democrat Socialist Party to the rescue to make it more expensive. Everyone in the US will be eligible for free healthcare. They will institutionalize healthcare; the government will run it to eliminate the profits. I explained the downside of National Health Care earlier, but to many who won't pay will be a positive outcome, and they'll vote democrat.

Pay Off Student Loans. As Bernie Sanders screamed, so will be done. There are 45 million borrowers of student loans, with a debt of $1.6 Trillion. Considering how easy it was to spend $2 trillion to help the economy and the people during the pandemic, $1.6 trillion doesn't look so much anymore. The borrowers would be delirious with joy. The War on Poverty brought the Black voters to the Democrat Party plantation. Now there will be 45 million borrowers who would come on the Democrat Socialist plantation as well, but for a shorter time as it is a one-time bonus, and realities will settle in.

Free Education. Free college education for all. If one is dumb, more education will not make much difference. But brainwashing will help. The problem with free education, like all the other free stuff, is abuse and misuse. We will have a lot of unemployed philosophers and social sciences graduates.

The government's generosity in education will come under duress. The government cannot pay for everyone to get frivolous education, and the economy won't be able to employ those people. There will be free education, but the spots available in any university will be limited, and only the most qualified students will attend by passing a rigorous entrance exam, the way it was under Socialism.

The Green New Deal. Many of the proposals under this resolution would be vote-bait and will receive extensive lip service and promises. It only takes the majority in both houses to pass and a Democrat Socialist President. The Green New Deal already mandates the following:

> Guaranteeing a job with a family-sustaining wage, adequate family and medical leave, paid vacations, and retirement security to all people of the United States.

One of the items left out of the current proposals was a minimum monthly payment to all people not able to work or *unwilling to work*. AOC is all for this. Depending on the political winds, don't be surprised if this won't be one of the returning socialist initiatives.

> Providing all people of the United States with – high-quality health care (covered by Universal Healthcare); affordable, safe, and adequate housing; economic security.

Wonderful, this *Green* New Deal is; providing all that abundance just going *green*. How will that happen? Somehow will happen, "trust" the socialists.

During the Pandemic, financial aid and extended unemployment benefits caused many people in the lower skill levels not to return to work. I see advertisings on billboards "Employees wanted," "Now we hire," or "Competitive salaries and $1,000 bonus." People renting and being excused by the government from paying rents don't have to work either. Why work when you get free housing? Minimum monthly payment to anyone will destroy the work culture, as Socialism did, does, and will do.

Productive labor determines a nation's standard of living. Without that, we will all see our standard of living decrease. We haven't seen the entire economic aftermath of the pandemic, yet.

Black Lives Matter. They will be the heroes, and at first, they'll shower them with awards and prominent positions in the government. The employers will be told to hire more black people equitably, regardless if they can produce or not. And if it ruins a few businesses as the pandemic did, so what?

Priority 3. The Economy.

Provide Jobs. Although the Green New Deal promises jobs galore, *well paid and unionized*, for repairing and rebuilding America, the reality will be different.

What will be true is that jobs will be "concocted" out of thin air, a la Socialist style, with *Livable wages*, I may add. Paying people who don't want to work will upset those who work, so instead, under Socialism, the people "have a *right to a job*" will become law. I said concocted, but instead, the jobs will be mandated from the employers, adding to the cost of living and reducing efficiency. The employers will face a higher tax or hire useless employees. We will all pay for the *economic security* for others.

Nationalization re-imaged. Rule 1 of the Communist Manifesto states: *Abolition of property in land and application of all rents of land and public purposes.*

This is the basis of Marxism. It will not happen unless the Democrat Socialist Party wants to self-destruct. A large middle class depends on a Free-Market economy; they own equities in the corporations in their 401k and retirement funds.

But there is more than one way to skin a cat. All the corporations are under some form of control by the Government/Deep State. But even that will not be enough. The Socialists want the workers to participate in the management of corporations; management by committee.

The Green New Deal is already telling us what will happen:

> (F) ensuring the use of democratic and participatory processes that are inclusive of and led by frontline and vulnerable communities and *workers to plan, implement, and administer* the Green New Deal mobilization at the local level
>
> (3) a Green New Deal must be developed through transparent and inclusive *consultation, collaboration, and partnership with frontline and vulnerable communities, labor unions, worker cooperatives, civil society groups*, academia, and businesses;

Don't be surprised that soon such workers committees will be at first suggested and then mandated by the Federal Laws for larger corporations, and soon after, all publicly traded corporations will have to comply. Expect intensive brainwashing as it is now conducted with the CRT. The Corporate-Bureaucrats won't resist such actions, as long as they keep their jobs and fat salaries why oppose it.

Inflation. After spending all the pandemic relief money, plus for the Green New Deal, National Health Care, and mandatory hiring expect the inflation to be higher than was in the late 70s. Inflation rubs everyone, especially the workers without assets.

Priority 4. Law Enforcement.

Restructure the police. This is necessary because it is not controlled by the federal government and cannot be relied on if there are popular uprisings. All those local enforcement organizations must be weakened, "re-imaged," or defunded under the disguise of *systemic racism* propaganda. They will indoctrinate the police officers in the neo-Marxist/CRT, and the ones found to be "white supremacists" will be kicked out of the force. After the police are re-imaged, they will establish a police organization answerable to the Democrat Socialist Party.

Establish the Secret Police. A totalitarian government cannot survive without the ability to spy and punish the dissenters. Expect to see a new Federal Agency, like the Gestapo, KGB, Stasi, or Securitate in Socialist Romania to prevent any movement towards freedom and against the Democrat Socialist government. At first, it will be disguised as a law enforcement department to combat racism, homophobia (LGBTQ+), misogyny, hate speech, and the worst of all, *White Supremacism.* Pay special attention when *hate speech* becomes punishable by law, after which our First Amendment will disappear, and the Secret Police will become terrorizing us. This may or may not be a new agency, maybe be part of the FBI.

Establish Political Prisons. The people caught by the Secret Police, "the political dissidents" or domestic terrorists, will be incarcerated in the Federal Prisons under the Political Reeducation Department, for reeducation. The Democrat Socialist party will learn from the Chinese and their best practices.

BLM and Antifa. Once in complete control of Germany, Hitler eliminated the Brown Shirts by killing their leaders. After the Democrat Socialist party will be in complete control, and BLM and Antifa have served their purpose, they'll be disbanded. They could go away peacefully, but if they riot, they'll be declared *domestic terrorists* and will be thrown in the political prisons.

LGBTQ+. Just 20 years ago, those people were the perverts. Now they are the outstanding members of our modern society to the point that biological sex is eliminated and replaced by god-knows-what. In California, nurses are fined if they don't address the *gender-confused* by their preferred pronouns. This group served well to cause anarchy in this country. Will they be maintained in high status in the Democrat Socialist government? Only if they'll serve Socialism.

Mutilation of young children on the account that they feel they are of the opposite sex will continue with the help of socialist doctors, educators, and scientists.

Abolishment of Guns.

Guns must go. Totalitarian governments cannot survive with an armed population, no matter how many security forces the government has. This is why the Democrats are enraged over the Second Amendment. Until the Democrat Socialists in Congress can amend the Constitution and socialists pack the courts, there can be many other things to prevent us from owning or using our guns. With a simple majority, they can accomplish the following:

- Tax the gun manufacturers and sales of guns as high as possible, perhaps 100% or more.
- Tax the ammunition the same way.
- Nationalize the Ammunition Industry, and the government will ration or stop altogether selling ammo to private citizens. A gun owner must return the used shells to buy new cartridges.
- Offer a cash-buy-back program to buy the guns from owners.
- Tax every gun owner, high taxes, for the firearms they possess like vehicles, boats, or Real Estate.
- If the citizens don't pay the gun taxes, they'll have their guns confiscated by the police, followed by fines and jail.
- Ultimately, Amendment 2 of the Constitution will be annulled, and there will be outright confiscation of all guns.

Priority 5. Party Loyalists in the Deep State.

The Executive branch appoints their choice of candidates for Head of Departments and other offices. However, the mandate will be that the Heads of the Departments will hire and promote only the Democrat-Socialist party members, strictly enforcing equity. Thus, the more the Deep State belongs to the Democrat-Socialist Party, the more entrenched the Socialists will be.

The same thing will happen in the Military, where they will promote only the Party loyalists. However, unlike Stalin, who executed the officers he deemed disloyal, the Democrat Socialist Party will discharge the so-called “white supremacist” officers, but they will be watched closely.

Priority 6. Indoctrination.

In Schools. The Democrat-Socialist Party came to power because of the rigorous indoctrination of our kids in schools and academia. The indoctrination through schooling will continue with a socialist intensity about neo-Marxism and CRT. Expect the kids to pledge allegiance to the Democrat Socialist Party instead of the United States of America. They’ll sing socialist songs inspired by the “bright future” ahead of us, Equity and Socialist justice for all, warnings of our dark past under the rule of the White men, Capitalism, and religion.

The Critical Race Theory will become Hitler’s "Mein Kampf."

The Media will fly the Socialist flag and promote the Socialist doctrine with impunity. Censorship will apply to all information dissemination channels. Not reporting the Socialist truth will have dire consequences for all. Will there be independent media outlets? Sure. The pretense will be that we live in a democracy and have free speech. After a few courageous journalist rebels write unapproved articles, they will be warned and then jailed if they continue. Shortly after, the Media outlets will auto-censor themselves voluntarily. Most of them do that already.

Employment. Indoctrination at work will be carried out just as they are doing now, making businesses conduct “sensitivity” training—glorifying the Socialist government. *Comrades*, the truth will be told, you’ll stand, applaud, and you’ll cheer loudly, just like in North Korea. Start practicing.

Priority 7. Instill Fear.

Domestic Spying. Everyone will be encouraged to spy on their neighbors, coworkers, and friends, even family members. In Cuba, they have neighborhood watch groups, not against thieves but anti-government agitators or dissidents. They must protect the socialist revolution. The worst will be when our children learn about the anti-Socialism agents, and the enemies lurk everywhere, including at home. The White domestic terrorist must be eradicated. Be vigilant, even against your parents. Hard to believe that one's kid will rat on you? It was expected in the Socialist countries, and parents had been executed on account of what their children reported.

In the USSR, a thirteen-year-old boy, Pavel Morozov, became a national hero when he denounced his father for anti-communist activities. As a result, the communists executed his father. Tragically, the kid's family killed him for what he did, and his family, in turn, was executed as well. After that, Pavel Morozov became a martyr of the USSR. Imagine what any parent would think or do after hearing or seeing in the Media about a kid denouncing their parents and the parents arrested. Parents wouldn't dare to talk ill of the Socialist system in front of their kids. Or anyone else.

Keep America Safe. Not from foreign terrorists, but the domestic ones. The best way to dominate and control a population is through *fear of each other*. The Media will show how the domestic terrorists are arrested just as they showed the arrest of Roger Stone. Political crimes will consider one guilty until proved innocent.

Chapter 2. The Leaders: Wealthy Elites and Statism-Corporatism

Based on what I wrote in this book so far, the responsible entity for our current situation seems to be Academia. In more precise words, the Intellectuals. The intelligent people, professors, mainly from the humanitarian branch of sciences, the ones with vast knowledge of the less and less, but zero practical knowledge. The professors with tenure, guaranteed jobs, and no recourse for what they teach. From their lofty positions, they can examine the little people and society and derive utopian, non-humanistic theories of making people's lives "better." This would be no problem if they could experiment with their theories in a laboratory. Instead, Marxism was and is imposed on people while alive, without "anesthetics." The failure of Marxism caused hundredths of millions of deaths and destroyed generations of the "little people."

The world population in 1918 was 1.8 billion people. The world population in 2020 is 7.8 billion people. That is over four times the increase in the population over a century. Although in the 20th century Marxism failed, the world population, larger now, must be fed and cared for. With modern methods of information, the good life of the West is not a secret, and they want some of it. If they don't get it, they'll emigrate or will revolt.

The Marxists never give up. Although their ideology is mind poison, they would die in oblivion if there wouldn't be the *enablers*.

The wealthy and privileged suffered the most from Socialist Totalitarianism governments. We know them as the Capitalists. The Marxists stole their wealth and killed them. But capitalism has changed over the past century. Most entrepreneurs who built capitalism are gone. (The new Digital entrepreneurs are Socialists already.) We had pure capitalism in the 19th century, but it also evolved into monopolism, threatening the government's legitimacy. The government reacted and banned monopolism. In its place, Corporatism took over, influencing the actions of the government. At the same time, the government grew and promised social reforms to the working classes by one party or the other to win elections. The government enacted laws and regulations for the "public good" to control the corporations and the economy. Today we have *Statism-Corporatism*.

New breed of Corporate Bureaucrats replaced the capitalists, the entrepreneurs of the past. The corporations are managed by Corporate-Bureaucrats —employees with no ownership interests— and ruled by government bureaucrats through regulations. Corporate-Bureaucrats prosper by maximizing the value of their enterprises. For example, take the production and jobs to countries with cheap labor, and the profits and valuations of the corporations will rise. In return, the Corporate-Bureaucrats rip huge salaries and bonuses and became the Wealthy Elites. With Globalization, the corporations have become larger and larger, dominating their sectors of the industry. In a sense they've become quasi-monopolies. New entrants don't stand a chance, and only a radical business strategy (Amazon) or technology (Microsoft) can dislodge the incumbents. The global corporations are juggernauts, and out-competing each other brings slim returns.

Meanwhile, new industries were born, Information Technology, IT. New entrepreneurs rose from the middle class to become billionaires like Jobs, Gates, Bezos, Zuckerberg, and many others. The difference between these new entrepreneurs and the yesteryears ones is their culture, a new breed of entrepreneurs brought up in a Marxist-Socialist culture. A new industry, early startups, and globalism made them billionaires. They have employees educated in the same Marxist universities, and they think alike. For example, Google employees will not work for the US Department of Defense because it is "evil." But they have no problem working with the Communist-Fascist China to develop Artificial Intelligence to control the Chinese people.

The powerful, wealthy elites want to continue living lives of splendor, with many mansions worldwide, yachts, airplanes, private islands, private security, and private chefs. No, they don't want to give up their privileged lives, and they want to stay in the game. They want to give the illusion that they are part of the solution. And there is a powerful ideology out there, Marxism, which makes fanatics out of the adherents. And although it proved disastrous in every country, it can be re-purposed and help them stay in power without losing their "heads," literally.

But there is a big problem when Marxism-Socialism is implemented. Marxism's raison d'être is the destruction of the capitalist system, and along with that, the rich. What are the rich going to do? Pretend they are not rich? No, pretend that they are the champions of the people, the have-nots. Still, Capitalism works, Socialism fails. Luckily, the Marxist professors have a solution. Instead of confiscating the corporations, the workers are empowered to say what an employer can do or not do. In their political correctness zeal, Google employees have demanded the ousting of their executives accused of sexual harassment. Google had no choice and obliged, while the culprits laughed all the way to the bank with their termination checks. What if the employees want to oust the conservative managers? It's bound to happen. What's needed is more proletariat-oriented, more equitable, more socially responsible, and society-friendly corporations. This has already happened and will continue as you see corporations becoming Woke Corporations, like Coca-Cola, Delta, Chase, Nike, Walmart, and others like them.

A new business model is evolving. Capitalism with a heart. Not that it was heartless before, but social benefits take priority over profits. The right to consume takes over the right to produce and profit. No profits, what will the reach do? Suppose the wealthy elites can keep their riches and prosper. In that case, everyone wins, except for the rest of us, the consumers who will pay the higher prices to achieve those socials benefits. The new Elites: Corporate-Bureaucrats, financiers, prefered-employees, government and deep-state bureaucrats, politicians, intellectuals, and community activists will work hand in hand to benefit us all.

It is time to rethink, *re-image* the world. In the past, the wealthy and privileged ended up on the "guillotine," in front of the firing squads or in gulags for a slow death. All these years, the wealthy opposed and fought Socialism until....

... Until the Wealthy Elites became WOKE, with full help from the Marxist Intellectuals.

If you cannot beat them, join them, and stay on top.

Chapter 3. Globalism

The Global Elites have a plan for us. Poverty should be eliminated worldwide, not only in one country. A Global Socialist Totalitarian Government will decide how *we, the people,* should live our lives. The rich will not lose their wealth and keep a seat at the table. The entire world economy will become a cabal, and there will be no need for competition among the enterprises. The corporations continue operating managed by Corporate Bureaucrats with government oversight; their profits will be predetermined, becoming corporate utilities, like the electric, water, and gas utilities. The Corporations will implement all the government's directives, such as who to employ and how many, family-leave for child-rearing, generous vacations, minimum pay, and other social benefits. All people will have free medical care, free education, and no one will starve or sleep in the streets. They will give the people who are not willing to work stipends to live on. The government will take care of all of us. At least that was the plan in the Communist-Socialist countries before they disappeared.

Under this arrangement, either at the country-government level or global level, the "war on world poverty" can be won. At least that's what Mark Malloch-Brown thinks in his book "The Unfinished Global Revolution: The Road to International Cooperation". Mark Malloch-Brown is the president of Open Society Foundations, George Soros' brainchild. He had many other bureaucratic positions: The Minister of State for Africa, Asia, and the United Nations, the development specialist at the World Bank, Administrator of the United Nations Development Program, and United Nations Deputy-Secretary-General. A true global bureaucrat who never managed a business or do real work, like the rest of us. To him, and his mentor George Soros, capitalism doesn't work, because billions of people in the world are "exploited" by the capitalists and the people's fortunes don't improve. Typical Marxist, never occurred to him that even Capitalism cannot provide for an exploding world population.

That fact won't deter them. The Marxist politicians and elites will rule and dedicate their effort to make everyone's life "better." In their supreme education and intelligence, the Elites will guide us to prosperity, equity and justice for all. They'll make sure that Systemic Racism is eliminated. We will all be equal by enforcing equity. They will teach Critical Race Theory in schools and a new American history, and a revised curriculum that every kid will do equally, but poorly. As a result, a new citizen will evolve, the *Global Socialist Citizen.*

The following link shows what our future might be:

https://www.bitchute.com/video/PhAY96MueUTQ/?fbclid=IwAR1ztM5Yv4Jclk6mSwDb_WcEJ0arz1C1aPMGe_Wz2RsDGVXoJtymKYFMaOY

We are prepared for **the Great Reset**. Did you hear about the Great Reset? Klaus Schwab, the self-appointed chairman of the World Economic Forum has plans for us. According to him and others:

- The Pandemic represents a rare but narrow window of opportunity to reflect, reimagine, and reset our world.
- One silver lining of the pandemic is that it has shown how quickly we can make radical changes to our lifestyles. Almost instantly the crisis forced businesses and individuals to abandon practices long claimed to be essential, from frequent travel to working in the office.
- It will change actually us, our own identity, and of course gives life to such policies and developments like smart Traffic, smart government, smart cities
- Everything from economics to our culture needs to change
- Our fragilities exposed
- Our systems need a reset
- Everyone has a role to play
- The Great rest, if we don't, we're headed for disaster
- Capitalism needs to be re-invented
- Western values will be tested to the breaking point
- Fairer outcomes by coordination in tax regulatory, trade, and fiscal policy
- May include "Changes to wealth taxes, the withdrawal of fossil-fuel subsidies, and new rules governing intellectual property, trade, and competition."
- Transitioning from fossil fuels to green energy
- We must build entirely new foundations for our economic and social systems

Instead of talking about overcoming the pandemic, this man and others like him are using it as an opportunity to "reset" the world. Does it look to you that the pandemic was natural and not designed in a lab in Wuhan and released intentionally in the world?

And what's next for each one of us? In the meanwhile, what will happen to the vaccinated people? The vaccines are based on mRNA technology, which might affect our DNA. The planet is over populated, and eradicating poverty might be impossible with the current world population. Will the Elites reduce the world population by releasing an agent that will react with what the vaccine created in our bodies and precipitate mortality in the future? The elderlies are disposable, they add no value to humanity, will they be first to go? Time will tell, and unfortunately, we may live to see that happening.

Humanity is evolving, technology is advancing, and many ideas projected for the future could happen. Some for the better some for the worst. Artificial Intelligence, AI, in the hands of a Socialist government is God-given power, to control us in any way they want. AI and automation will provide for our needs, but will un-employ us. And if a major portion of the population can live without the effort of working, why go to school? What would an ignorant society without the worry of going hungry, and lots of time on their hands do? How will the Global Socialist government manage humanity? Will they implant a chip in each one of us so we can be identified, classified, and tracked? Perhaps that chip will change our behavior, give up eating meat, or population control as I said.

Becoming better than others is bad. Mediocrity will reign. Equity will become the new reality. Ownership of stuff will be eliminated, and everyone will feel "better" without possessions. Global Communism is being built as we speak.

That may be our future if we let them do it.

Chapter 4. The neo-Fascism-Socialism Economy.

The Global Elites: Politicians, Intelligentsia, Corporate Bureaucrats, Billionaires, Media, Hollywood, and UN are our new masters.

However, implementing this Global Socialist plan is too big to do it all at once. The best way is to start with a prosperous nation and then go from there. That nation would be us, the United States of America with one of the largest GDP and income per capita. The United Socialists of America will blaze the trail and everyone will follow with ample economic help from the US. By a well-planned and executed subversive ideology of Marxism and Critical Race Theory, we are closer to socialism than ever.

Marxism-Socialism in its original form has proven disastrous. Even if the Democrat Socialist Party could implement the ten rules of "the Communist Manifesto" to the letter, it will fail within a generation or less. Marxists may convince the people of a poor and ignorant country that prosperity can be achieved through Socialism. They may even convince the people of a *prosperous and oblivious* country that Socialism is the solution, as they do now in the United States of America. But there are no new highs of prosperity to be achieved, only stagnation followed by equal poverty. Capitalism, burdened as it is by the Statism, has produced all it can. Prosperity depends on people's labor-productivity, which is based on freedom and the culture of a country. Even though Thomas Sowell and Adam Smith have described why some countries are prosperous and others are not, because of geography, mineral resources, navigable rivers, climate, and other factors, not all countries have prospered or suffered accordingly. A country like Japan, destroyed by WW II, with hardly any mineral resources or good geography was at one time the second economic power in the world after the US. Why? It is their culture.

Some nations are clear examples of the work-culture such as Japan, China, Germany, USA and a few others and their GDP shows that. But how about the culture of the rest of the world? I'm not saying that people around the world are lazy, they all have to work to survive. I'm saying that they work unproductively. And even capitalism hasn't been able to solve their problems.

Besides all other factors, the main reason a country prospers or not is its Political system. The more freedom a country has, the better the country's prosperity. Socialism implemented in the Third World countries did not bring prosperity, because socialism is anti-freedom, anti-prosperity, which causes lower productivity. Take a look at Socialist Cuba and North Korea.

However, that will not discourage the Elites from implementing Socialism. On the other hand, there are some clear minded Elites who at one time or another listed on a white board the strengths and weaknesses of the different forms of Socialism.

The neo-Marxism-Socialism relies on these principles:

- *Totalitarianism*
- *Elimination of personal freedom*
- *Elimination of private property and profit/wealth.*
- *State Ownership of the economy and social benefits*

However, the "Elimination of private property and profit/wealth," although much desired by the hardcore Marxists, is a big issue. Although the capitalists will be impoverished when nationalization takes place, by default, millions of American citizens who own shares in publicly traded companies, especially in their retirement or IRA accounts, will be impoverished as well. This is the power of the middle class to stop socialism. Impoverishing them will start a civil war. However, there is another socialist ideology.

The neo-Fascism-Socialism relies on these principles:

- *Totalitarianism*
- *Elimination of personal freedom*
- *Maintain some form of private ownership of property*
- *State Control of the economy and social benefits*

The Capitalist economy will continue, but with a Socialist government. That would be a Fascist-Socialist form of government. The neo-Marxists will have no other alternative but take the Fascist route, socialist government with control of the economy, while the corporations are held privately and publicly as they are now. China is a good example of Fascism-Socialism.

China was a basket case of poverty under Mao, but now it rivals the United States since it abandoned Marxism-Socialism and has adopted Fascism —let capitalism do what it does best, but control it politically. In the past, Fascism in Italy and Germany proved successful until they pursued their imperialist tendencies and were defeated. China prospered since it adopted the Fascism form of economy, although it didn't invade any country, it pillaged the United States of America's jobs with our full cooperation. The Fascist-Socialists did not kill many wealthy people as the Marxists-Socialists did, but they controlled the rich and privileged under the Fascism-Socialism ideology.

Why fight the Marxism-Socialism, and create Lenin(s), Stalin(s), or Mao(s) who will kill the wealthy, when the wealthy can become part of the solution? I realize when Fascism is mentioned that most people react as if seeing a snake. The new rulers may not use the word Fascism, but the Global and National Elite will apply its ideology. If they succeed, we will become a Fascist-Socialist country.

Should there be joy?

No. Fascism-Socialism is Socialism, and it is Marxist at its core. This ideology will not destroy the wealthy, but it will have the same economic effects as Marxism-Socialism, except at a slower pace. Politically it will be identical to Marxism-Socialism, with absolutely no freedom. Economically our standard of living will decline, because although the industry is in private hands, the socialist policies and Globalization will make everything more expensive and scarcer.

You may think that this form of Socialism, Fascism-Socialism is what Western Europe is practicing. Not at all. They have a Capitalist-Statism and their social benefits are paid by equally applied high taxes. Under the Fascism-Socialism the Capitalism will operate as utilities, as I mentioned earlier.

Chapter 5. How to Prevent Socialism

Even if the Democrat Socialist Party becomes our totalitarian government, we will have elections, although fake elections, to give the illusion of democracy. Starting in 2022, our next election, and the election in 2024, we may have the following alternatives:

1. The Democrat Socialist Party will consolidate its power in Congress, if they pass a national election law they will win in 2022. If that happens, they will never lose power, and the Presidency and Congress will be theirs for a long time.
2. The elections in 2022 or 2024 will muddy the waters. The Democrat Socialist Party may lose or keep their power in one of the houses, but with a disoriented, turncoats, Remocrats/RINOs and feeble Republican Party, the Socialism, Critical Race Theory, Systemic Racism and Project 1629 will march on. Not uniformly throughout our nation, but it will continue.
3. In 2022, the Democrat Socialist Party will lose both houses badly, and the Republicans will be able to slow down the Socialist's

agenda with Biden/Harris in the White House. If in 2024, the people will elect a Republican President and Congress, we might have a chance of reversing the socialist trend, if they take the actions, I suggest below.

Can we prevent socialism from taking over our country? Yes, however, it will have to be a partisan, and consolidated effort by the patriots in the Republican and Democrat parties. I consider the Republican Party as the only anti-socialist party. If other Democrat members, non-socialists, will join in this effort to keep freedom and democracy in America, it will be better for all of us. The President must be a strong, unwavering leader and take unpopular actions as perceived by the Marxists. America needs *Tough Love.*

There are a lot of things that Freedom loving patriots can do. The suggestions for actions are ample in Dinesh D'Souza's books, "United States of Socialism" and "The Big Lie," or "The Breakdown of Higher Education," by John M. Ellis. However, Mark Levin's book "American Marxism" has a detailed list with references where to go and how to take action as an individual or group.

Unfortunately, we are at the eleventh hour from capitulation to neo-Marxism-Socialism, and I'm afraid that individual action, although helpful, is like blowing against a hurricane to stop it. Short of Civil War we must take draconian actions at government level. I will not propose what Mao Zedong, Joseph Stalin, or Adolph Hitler would do because we are Americans, with freedom, and a Constitution. However, if we don't take the following actions, we'll lose. Socialism will never give up, and the only way to prevent it from reigniting again is the complete *annihilation* of Marxism.

No short measures.

Must-Do Actions

Number 1.

Pass a law to banish the Critical Race Theory and neo-Marxism-Leninism-Communism-Socialism from our educational system. This doesn't mean that the Socialist or Communist Parties must be outlawed. On the contrary, they will be allowed to assemble and indoctrinate people at their own expense and not on the government's pay, infringing on our liberties.

Number 2.

Invoke an Anti-America Activities Commission, similar to the House Un-American Activities Committee in 1938, to investigate subversive indoctrination activities and anti-patriotic sentiments by the Academia, Schools K to 12 and Teachers Unions, Media in print, radio or television, Internet media, Hollywood, and corporations.

I know it sounds like McCarthyism, but we are in *dire times* of having our country and our freedom destroyed and taken over by tyranny.

- Pass a law that our educational system is for learning and prohibit political indoctrination.
- Defund all universities that teach Marxism and anti-Americanism
- All Socialists or politicians with Socialist agendas shall be barred from politics for life.
- All intellectuals and professors found guilty in the schools and academia system should be fired and barred for life from teaching again.
- All people found guilty in the Media should be fired and barred from working in that industry. The Communist Digital Platforms should be stripped of any liability protection and take legal action against those monopolies and dismantle them.
- All people in Hollywood, especially the writers, directors, and producers, should be banned similarly. Actors are not the brains; let them make movies written by non-socialists. Otherwise, go in the unemployment line.
- The Deep-State ideologues should be fired and prevented from government employment.
- Businesses that undertook action in line with the Woke ideologies should be fined and their executives fired. Businesses should be engaged in the economy and not political ideology.
- Create a National List of those people or entities. We need to know who these people are; just like sex offenders, they are liberty offenders.
- We shall institute a tribunal to review, forgive, and rehabilitation programs to reintegrate the guilty back into society

after they prove they corrected their anti-freedom ideology. Except for the Marxists.

- A Republican congress after the 2022 elections should investigate Joe Biden and his family enterprise in obtaining money/bribes from foreign powers, China, Ukraine, and others. If found guilty, he should be impeached in 2023.

Number 3.

- Decentralize the entire educational system, and vouchers must be given to parents to choose the school of their choice for their children. Put the parents in charge of the curriculum.

Number 4.

- We should overhaul all educational material to reflect the Constitution, civics, and patriotic responsibility. History should reflect our national accomplishments. The men and women who made them happened based on their importance to our country. We must eliminate the hatred against the White people or any other race, and we should enhance an agenda of integration and equality without favoritism toward any particular race or sex. Equity is discrimination and must be eliminated. We all have an equal opportunity based on our skills and education, not through special treatment because of the color of our skin. We are all Americans.
- Practical, not theoretical education, in economics and practical trades, must be taught in our schools.

Number 5.

- We shall introduce educational material to show why Socialism is not for the people and why it failed, and it will fail. Students must be made aware of the atrocities committed by all Socialist governments like USSR, the former Communist-European countries, Cambodia, Vietnam, African countries, China and Nazi-Socialist Germany. The crimes committed against humanity by Communism-Socialism is far greater than NAZI-Socialist Germany. We must not forget the 200 million victims killed by this ideology, and those political crimes never allowed to happen again.

Number 6.

- Remedial schools shall be established for all teenagers not attending school but engaged in crimes. This is instead of jails. Once enrolled in these schools, teenagers will stay in them until 18 and graduate from high school. These schools should teach a trade besides theoretical education. The parent(s) should be given the right to enroll their kids in such schools as well if they cannot control their kids.

Number 7.

- The Media that uses national airways should be denied those accesses if they don't correct their behavior toward a Constitutional, Patriotic, American, and Freedom theme.

Number 8.

- We must carry out a national policy throughout our Schools, Media, Hollywood, and places of employment. This would be like the education that was conducted to prevent racial jokes or sexual harassment. The people at large must be made aware of what a disastrous ideology was about to enslave us all.

Number 9.

- All individuals or organizations that conducted acts of intimidation, harassment, property destruction or burning, or lootings, like Antifa and BLM, shall be declared terrorist organizations and be brought to justice for past or present crimes. Any vandalism or toppling, or destruction of our statues and monuments must be punished by minimum mandatory prison if found guilty.

Number 10.

- Dismantle and eliminate any organization, educational or government, that purport to act on behalf of race, women, LGBTQ, etc. Those initiatives created large bureaucracies that, instead of protecting anyone became Inquisitions agencies.

Number 11.

- Mandatory pledge of allegiance in K12 to universities.

Number 12.

- Reintroduce voluntary Christian religious education in schools.

Number 13.

- Fix immigration to *serve* the United States and its people. Complete the wall Donald Trump started. The truth is that no wall will stop the most determined migrants. The Communists didn't stop me from crossing their concentration camp security border. But, the walls will prevent the majority of illegals from crossing, and most importantly, the wall will delay their crossings, and if they make it in, more time to apprehend them.

- Deport all minors, without exception, who were brought here.

Number 14.

- The China problem. We must bring back our manufacturing. If this is not fixed, we're doomed.

Did you know that World War II in Europe was not a continuation of WWI? In order to satisfy the Nazi-Socialism promises, Hitler planned to invade the USSR. He planned to have a pact with the UK not to start a war when he invaded the Soviet Union. The British had a choice between a Hitler leading the Nazi-Socialist Germany, stretching from Hamburg to Vladivostok, with a hardworking, disciplined, and faithful people, and communism destroyed. Or stop Nazi-Socialist Germany and help the backward Soviet Union. We know the outcome now. And Great Britain is not an empire any more.

China's situation today is like that of Nazi-Socialist Germany. The West has industrialized China, it has over a billion and a half population, hardworking, disciplined, and faithful, enforced through fear by obeying the Communist Party. China has a for-life dictator, Xi Jinping, who wants to make China the ultimate super-power in the world. China and Xi Jinping are our modern Nazi Germany and Adolf Hitler.

We are frightened about Russia by the Democrat Socialist Party, through all the lies made about Trump and Russia collusion, cyber-attacks, and other insignificant issues. But Russia is attacking us from outside. China is attacking us from inside with help from our political and business traitors.

The future is the USA versus this formidable growing enemy, China. We can cut it down to size by removing China from WTO or stop importing any goods manufactured in China. The choice is ours. Stay free or teach our children to speak Mandarin.

You may think that those measures sound Draconian, totalitarian, and undemocratic? Would you prefer a Socialist America, without freedom, misery, and poverty? Or a Civil War with thousands of people dead? We allowed the Marxists and reverse discrimination to arise, where we don't know what's normal anymore. The Marxists abused our freedom. Dire times require drastic measures. However, no one found guilty is to be imprisoned or executed, and forgiveness facilitated.

We will not be Socialists.

Chapter 6. What the Future Holds for Us

Is our future a disastrous Socialist Hell, a totalitarian government dictated by elites, or something else? The evilest ideology devised by men has infected our country, our institutions, our economy, our culture. Let's hope that it will not become a reality as Hitler said:

> When an opponent declares, "I will not come over to your side," I calmly say, "Your child belongs to us already. . .. What are you? You will pass on. Your descendants, however, now stand in the new camp. In short time they will know nothing else but this new community." [40: pg 249]

With so many WOKE Zombies within our population, predicting the future is complicated. Humanity, society, and culture are fluid systems. It churns, it flows, it convolutes, it freezes and thaws, it's turbulent or tranquil. We all are participating in it. Our society today is not the same as America of 1776. Or the same as during the Civil War or after WWI, or WWII. Our society differs completely from the 1950s. We are in 2021 when capitalism that brings prosperity is bad, and socialism that destroys is good. We have a Democrat Socialist Party and a socialist President determined to make a "name" for himself by instituting Critical Race Theory and Equity, destroying our energy independence because of the alleged Climate Change, and allowing millions of illegal immigrants to transform our country into a Third World nation.

No one could have predicted that the Internet, the liberalizer of all, could become our enslaver and give rise to Digital Tyranny. No one could have predicted that our society becomes more prosperous and less happy with advances in technology. No one could have predicted that more education would create a dumber and docile society. No one could have predicted the disastrous neo-Marxist ideology combined with the Critical Race Theory would hypnotize so many young minds, who have no experience with daily reality, but only what they are told in schools, CDP, MSN, and Hollywood. No one could have predicted a Man-made Pandemic released in the world to destabilize it, particularly to create a different political outcome through fraudulent elections. No one could have predicted that a large section of our population would be angry and storm the Capitol, the symbol of democracy.

But that's the reality today.

What will be the next fear engulfing the world? Will our society be re-programed or reset on the fear of let's say extra-terrestrials, or UFOs, UAP.

Whatever will happen, our society will transform based on our culture, technology, education, wealth or lack of it, our enemies, and most importantly, the discrepancies between *Realty* and *Propaganda.* What ruined the ex-Communist-Socialist countries was the truth about reality. In those countries, the propaganda painted a picture of heaven and prosperity, superior to the Capitalist countries. But in everyone's life, the reality was misery and shortages, with no chance of changing or improving the situation. As for the Capitalist countries, the reality was exactly the opposite of what they told us. Capitalism was prosperous. Under Socialism we were living a suffocating lie.

Throughout this book, I stressed that reality and propaganda would undo any society's political system if they are not in sync. The younger generation believes that socialism is better than capitalism. But is that the reality? The *Woke Zombies* have not seen socialism at work yet. The race situation is worsening instead of getting better because of Critical Race Theory, a racist ideology. Allegedly, because of *Systemic Racism*, the black society lags economically, even behind new immigrants, legal or illegal. That is true but is it because of Systemic Racism or the failure of the Black Society to improve themselves? Are the rest of the races to be blamed for it? The statistics shown previously, and all the help provided to the black society, clearly shows that Systemic Racism is a fig leaf. However, if statistics are ignored, and we believe in lies, nothing will change. They say the new generations will have a lower standard of living than their parents. Sure, if the new generations will not get educated for future skills. But in my reality, my daughter and her husband, and their friends, are more prosperous than my wife and I used to be. Reality and propaganda will decide our future.

What will happen if the darkest predictions will come to pass? First, the American people are not like the Russians, submissive and malleable. Look at the former Communist-Socialist European countries. Hungary rose against communism first in 1956, but the USSR squelched the revolt. Czechoslovakia used reason to eliminate the shackles of communism, but the "Warsaw Pact friendly forces" stopped their liberation zeal. Poland dissidents used a "novel" idea, Communism-Socialism is for the proletariat, and the proletariat-unions rose against them, asking for a better economic life. The USSR paid Poland to improve Poland's economic situation.

However, other nations like Romania, Bulgaria, and Albania did not rise against the tyranny of Communism-Socialism. Different people, different cultures, and different monsters in charge of those countries. East Germany was an occupied country by USSR troops and could not move a finger without an immediate reprisal by the East German Communists, Stasi.

What would the American people do? Fight or learn to live under socialism? It will depend on the measures the Democrat Socialist Party will take and how fast they'll move. If the economic situation does not deteriorate, the Party will have time to consolidate its control. Many Americans may learn how to live with it until reality becomes unbearable.

Or there will be an *awakening*, and the Americans will either vote out the Socialists or take to arms. If Civil War does not start because of political reasons, the deteriorating economic situation will cause people to revolt.

Margaret Thatcher allegedly said:

Socialism is wonderful, as long as you don't run out of other people's money.

The question is, how fast will the economy deteriorate before the people feel the bite of socialist misery. President Trump has improved the economy and employment unseen in decades. Yet, under the

Democrat Socialist President Joe Biden, in just six months, the gas prices are going up. The labor shortages, despite millions unemployed, persist because people make as much or more money from the government payout than working. This is another fine example of why Welfare will not work. Inflation is rising because of the trillions of dollars Biden is infusing in the economy for socialist causes to buy his next election. And open borders will destroy America, reducing it to a Third World country.

All the initiatives President Biden and the Democrat Socialist Party will undertake, like National Health and free education through college, will increase taxes. The Critical Race Theory and Equity and the Green New Deal will ruin the economy. Equity will provoke great antagonism among the people, seeing that some get preferential treatment based on the color of their skin. If achievement is not rewarded, the achievers will slow down, and the economy will stagnate. It happened in every Socialist country. The Green New Deal will be destructive, as even their propaganda says so. The industrial revolution was positively destructive, but for the betterment of society. It will not be the same with the Green New Deal, which will replace something that is working with things that don't or will be more expensive. Yes, we need to help our environment, but the smart way, not by socialist dictum.

But that's the whole idea of socialism, impoverish everyone and make them dependent on the Socialist Government.

In the end, the main reasons that I escaped from the Communist-Socialist Hell were:

Freedom, or lack of freedom. You cannot express yourself and be critical of the government that is not for the people but their Socialist interests. Portraying Ceausescu on a poster like President Nixon was, sitting on a toilet, would be an act of treason, followed by execution or life in prison. Expressing independent ideas were not allowed. You cannot do what you want; you can only do what's permitted.

Misery: economic misery, and poverty that defies reality. Scarcity of essential goods, and when available, you had to wait in long lines to buy them. You constantly live on the lookout for the next line that forms in the front of a store; something will be on sale there, and whatever it is, buy it.

Fear, or lack of fear. The continuous state of fear that I experienced in that cruel system. The fear from the secret police –Securitate, or Stasi, or KGB– killed the joy of living for everyone. Even when people from Communist-Socialist countries, on rare occasions, could visit a free country in the West, and they intended to defect, half of them didn't do it from fear of the secret police back home. Unimaginable Fear as the Democrat Socialist Party is fostering in each of us now will be the norm.

I read a book by Dean Koontz, "Elsewhere," a fantasy about being able to travel between parallel universes. Some of those universes are worse than ours, others entirely different, but one of them was better than our Earth. Here is what he said:

> Some of the most important [characteristics] were that no one here ever took the work of Karl Marx or Friedrich Nietzsche or Sigmund Freud seriously. So there had been no Lenin, no Soviet Union, no communism or fascism; and two hundred million people who, elsewhere, had been killed by those regimes, had not been killed here. No one ever heard of Hitler or Stalin or Mao. World War II was never fought, nor the Korean War nor any of the wars thereafter. [34, pg 350]

Yes, imagine a world where those people's evil teachings did not poison the minds of some people and start a bloody revolution in Russia, followed by all the bloodshed on all the continents, except Antarctica. And where socialism came to power, the killing followed; 200 million civilians were killed because of the Marxism ideology, which brought only poverty and misery to those countries. Without Marxism or Nazism, there would not have been WW II, Korean or Vietnam wars. Imagine what the world would be without Socialism.

In the old Communist-Socialist country, there was a saying:

I'm doing worst today than yesterday, but better than tomorrow.

Enjoy today because tomorrow, you might experience the Socialist Hell I've experienced, and there will be nowhere to run.

Rise America, and Fight like Hell to prevent Marxism and Critical Race Theory from enslaving us all.

The End

References

1. "The Breakdown of Higher Education-How it happened, the damage it does & What can be done." by John M. Ellis, published by Encounter Books.
2. "Rules for the Radicals, a Primer for Realistic Radicals" by Saul D. Alinsky, published by Vintage Books.
3. Lenin Collected Works, Volume 28 (p. 368-72)
4. Interview in 1984 with Yuri Bezmenov regarding the current situation in the USA, https://www.youtube.com/watch?v=IQPsKvG6WMI
5. Vladimir Lenin Was Part Jewish, Say Declassified KGB Files http://content.time.com/time/world/article/0,8599,2077413,00.html
6. "Left Turn" by Tim Groseclose, published by St. Martin's Griffin.
7. "God's Not Dead " movie by Pure Flix Entertainment
8. "The Communism Manifesto" by Karl Marx and Friedrich Engels, with introduction and notes by Gareth Stedman Jones, published by Penguin Classics.
9. Graduation statistics https://educationdata.org/number-of-college-graduates/
10. "Hitler Was a Socialist" by Dumitru Sandru, published by Chivileri Publishing.
11. "Escape from Communism" by Dumitru Sandru, published by Chivileri Publishing.
12. "The Black Book of Communism" by a variety of writers documenting the crimes against humanity committed by the Communist-Socialists, published by Harvard University Press.
13. "Mein Kampf" by Adolf Hitler, published by Mariner Books.
14. "The Speeches of Adolf Hitler" by Adolf Hitler, Amazon.com.
15. "Hitler" by Joachim C. Fest, translated from German by Richard and Clara Winston, published by A Harvest Book, Harcourt, Inc., A Helen and Kurt Book.
16. "Color, Communism and Common Sense" by Manning Johnson, published by the Stuyvesant Press Corp.

17. "The Pregnant Pope: Satan never sleeps. If he did, we would all be in heaven" by Mit Sandru, published by Chivileri Publishing.

18. "How Socialist was National Socialism" by Alan Brown, Amazon.com.

19. "The Wealth of Nations" by Adam Smith, Skyros Publishing.

20. "Wealth, Poverty and Politics" by Thomas Sowell, Basic Books.

21. "The Big Lie: Exposing the Nazi Roots of the American Left" by Dinesh D'Souza, Regnery Publishing.

22. "Fascism-what it is and how to fight it" by Leon Trotsky, Pathfinder.

23. "Adios America" by Ann Coulter, Regnery Publishing.

24. "Milada" the movie, by Loaded Vision Entertainment.

25. "Bitter Harvest" the movie 2017, Roadside Attractions, B&H Film Distribution Company, D Films Canada

26. "The Death of Stalin" the movie 2017, Entertainment One Films

27. Dr. Simone Gold, https://rumble.com/vd2y2j-banned-from-youtube-dr.-simone-gold-shares-the-truth-about-the-covid-19-vac.html

28. "McMafia: A Journey Through the Global Criminal Underworld" by Misha Glenny, Vintage; Illustrated edition (April 7, 2009)

29. Racial Equality and Civil Rights Prager U https://www.facebook.com/watch/?v=1708042499238599

30. "Antifa: The Antifascist Handbook" by Mark Bray, Melville House Publisher.

31. "1984" by George Orwell, Palgrave McMillan Publisher.

32. "Discrimination and Disparities" by Thomas Sowell, Basic Books.

33. "The Unfinished Global Revolution: The Road to International Cooperation" by Mark Malloch-Brown, Penguin Books.

34. "Elsewhere" by Dean Koontz, Thomas and Mercer.

35. "Atlas Shrugged" by Ayn Rand, Plume Books

36. "Fountainhead" by Ayn Rand, Plume Books

37. "Critical Race Theory: What it is and How to Fight it" by Christopher F. Rufo, published by Hillsdale College.

38. "Shame: How America's Past Sins Have Polarized Our Country" by Shelby Steele, Basic Books

39. "Countdown to Socialism" by Devin Nunes, Encounter Books

40. "The Rise and Fall of the Third Reich" by William L. Shirer, Simon and Schuster

41. "Blitz: Trump Will Smash the Left and Win" by David Horowitz, Humanix Books

42. "Counter-Revolution and Revolt" by Herbert Marcuse, Beacon

43. "Imperialism, the Highest Stage of Capitalism" by Vladimir Ilych Lenin, Rough Draft

44. "The End of Prosperity" by Arthur Laffer, Threshold Editions

45. "Essential Works of Lenin: What is to be done and other works" by Vladimir Lenin

46. "The Program of the Party of Hitler" by Gottfried Feder, Frz. Eher Nachf

47. "White Guilt: How Blacks and Whites Together Destroyed the Promise of the Civil Rights Era" by Shelby Steele

48. "Adolf Hitler" by John Toland, Doubleday

49. "Hitler's Table Talk" by HR Trevor-Roper, Enigma Books

50. "The United States of Socialism: Who's Behind It. Why It's Evil. How to Stop It." By Dinesh D-Souza, All Points Books

51. "How to be a Dictator" by Frank Dikotter, Bloomsbury

52. "Capitalism: the Unknown Deal" by Ayn Rand, Signet

53. "1984" by George Orwell

54. "No Safe Spaces" video by Dennis Prager

55. "Democracy in America" by Alexis de Tocqueville, Create Space

56. "Tipping Points: How to Topple the Left's House of Cards" by Liz Wheeler, Regnery Publishing

57. "The Fallacy of Marx's Theory of Surplus-value" by Henry Seymour, Hard Press

58. "State and Revolution" by Vladimir Lenin

59. "Marxism and the National Question" by Joseph Stalin, Create Space

60. "The Little Red Book: Sayings of Chairman Mao" by Mao Tse Tung, Parvus Magna Press

61. "American Marxism" by Mark Levin, Threshold Editions

62. "Propaganda" by Edward Bernays, ig

63. "The Silencing: How the Left is Killing Free Speech" by Kirsten Powers, Regnery Publishing

64. "The Anti-Capitalistic Mentality" by Ludwig Von Mises

Other Books by Dumitru (Mit, DG) Sandru

Non-Fiction, Political

Escape from Communism, by Dumitru Sandru, a True Story and Commentary.

Life under communism is cruel and inhumane. Commit the smallest political infraction, and the secret police will arrest you. The only ray of hope is the West, but it is a crime to escape by crossing the border illegally, and anyone caught is beaten and imprisoned, sometimes even shot. This is my story of what happened and how I reached freedom.

Hitler Was a Socialist, by Dumitru Sandru, A Comparison of NAZI-Socialism, Communism, Marxism-Socialism, and the United States

THIS BOOK IS PROHIBITED FOR ADVERTISEMENT ON AMAZON

We are socialists, we are enemies of today's capitalistic economic system for the exploitation of the economically weak, with its unfair salaries, with its unseemly evaluation of a human being according to wealth and property instead of responsibility and performance, and we are determined to destroy this system under all conditions.

These are the words of Adolf Hitler. He and the National-Socialist German Worker's Party –the NAZI– was a Socialist Party. Then who told us that Hitler and the NAZI were Fascist? Joseph Stalin, the mass murderer of the USSR said so. And the rest of the world obeyed. It is time to uncover the truth.

Adolf Hitler was a monster, a Socialist monster, just like Mao Zedong, Joseph Stalin, Pol Pot, and many other socialists like them. The facts are out there in plain sight, but the Marxist Academia, Leftist Mainstream Media, and Hollywood will not consider talking about the truth, least it would tarnish the "good" reputation of the Socialism, which killed 200 million people worldwide.

Socialism we must fear, not fascism.

Paranormal, Mystery, Thriller

The Pregnant Pope (Book 1 TIO Series), by Mit Sandru.

The 92-year-old Pope is pregnant. He hasn't undergone any medical procedures, but he carries a fetus in his abdomen. Is this a case of self-cloning, or a mutation? Is this an Immaculate Conception, or Satan's work? Find out how Claire, Travis, and Prescott solve this mystery and the bizarre outcome.

The Devolution of Adam and Eve (Book 2 TIO Series) by Mit Sandru

A pandemic causes billions of people to lose their minds. The world's government health agencies cannot identify the pathogen and develop an antidote. It comes from another realm, and only Claire, Prescott, and Travis can solve this enigma. Will they prevent the end of humanity before it's too late?

Teen, Children Fantasy

Arboregal, the Lorn Tree, by D.G. Sandru. YouTube: **https://bit.ly/2OtDj5c**

Four youngsters, Melissa, Perry, Nathan and Michelle materialize in a desolate world where giant, mile-high trees, support all life. They find shelter in the Lorn Tree among the Lorns. Soon after they discover that an evil spirit, Hellferata, wants them dead. Fearful Lorns

want to expel the youngsters from their tree, which would be a dead sentence since monsters roam the land at night.

Will their ingenuity, cunning, and courage help them escape, or will Hellferata mete out her wrath before they can escape?

Science Fiction

Sferogyls (Timurud Book 1) by Mit Sandru

The Maggotroll Empire invades the Sferogyls' planet. The Sferogyls are unarmed and have no defense against the imperial battleships. The gods resurrect Timurud and send him to help the peaceful Sferogyls fight the invaders. Will the Sferogyls win the war in space and defend their planet, or perish?

Gold Rush Mystery (Terraspantion Chronicles, Bk. 1) by Mit Sandru.

America is back on the Moon, and we intend to stay and establish a self-sustaining permanent base for tourism and mining. The work is challenging, the environment is deadly, but the astronauts Mia, Geo and Roby succeed in building the moon base, even if they landed in a mysterious crater.

Time Hole, (Terraspantion Chronicles, Bk. 2) by Mit Sandru.

Mining on the moon is a hazardous affair. Deedee and Arno, two lunar generalists, find perils beyond what they signed up for when they travel on the lunar surface at night . . . on the dark side of the Moon. Time will not be the same after they fall into the Time Hole.

Folding Reality, by Mit Sandru. Time Travel Adventure

Mike the insurance salesman experiences perilous time travel experiences just by folding a piece of paper. He is crucified on Golgotha, almost gassed at Auschwitz, marooned in a Russian capsule going to the Moon.

Vampires - Thriller & Romance
YouTube: https://bit.ly/2pahMDI

YouTube: https://bit.ly/2lPwAt4

Vampire (Vlad V, Bk 1) by Mit Sandru.

Meeting a vampire isn't something that happens every night, even on the New York City subway. But never in her wildest dreams did Cat Sanders ever expect to meet the vampire Vlad V Draculesti and survive the encounter. Instead, she became his confidant. Why was she so lucky?

R.I.P., The Death of a Vampire (Vlad V, Bk 2) by Mit Sandru.

Vlad V Draculesti is dying because of an incident that happened decades ago. Unfortunately for Vlad V, the US intelligence agencies investigate him to find out his true identity, and centuries old life. Will Cat Sanders and vampire friends be able to help him die in peace, or will Vlad be discovered for being a vampire and die in a US Federal research laboratory?

Vampire Slayers (Vlad V, Bk 3) by Mit Sandru.

Cat Sanders is a billionaire, but not all is well. Her nemesis, Veronica Seyler, allied with a vampire-slayer drug cult, demands extortion money or she will be killed.

Cat's vampire friend, Angelique, comes to her aid. But the cult is more cunning and dangerous than even her vampire friend could handle. Would Cat and Angelique be able to come out of this alive even if Cat pays the ransom?

Vampires of Transylvania (Vlad V, Bk 4) by Mit Sandru

Cat Sanders has a simple task: spread Vlad V's ashes in Transylvania at midnight, during full moon. But in Transylvania Vlad V has centuries old enemies who take her and her friend Tudor hostage, placing them in iron cages among zombies and proto-vampires. Will they be able to escape from the blood sucking proto-vampires and flesh-eating zombies, or become zombies themselves?

The Queen of Vampires: A New Queen Arises (Vlad V, Bk 5) by Mit Sandru

The Vampire Queen, Eleonore von Schwarzenberg, is bloodthirsty and vengeful on Cat Sanders and her friends. She plans the most painful death for them. Cat and her friends find themselves entrapped and helpless to avoid her wrath.

Will Cat and her friends be able to escape and survive the Queen of Vampires' fury?

Coloring Book

Abstract Dreams: Coloring Book 1 (Sandru's Art) by Dumitru Sandru

YouTube: **https://bit.ly/2Ulc9RT**

Reward your soul with the smooth and pleasing lines of Abstract Dreams

https://www.sandru.com/Coloring.html

T-Shirts and other stuff:
https://www.zazzle.com/store/dgsandru/products

Visit my e-Gallery at:
https://www.sandru.com/SferogylsArt.html
https://www.sandru.com/LornTreeArt.html
http://dumitru-sandru.artistwebsites.com/
https://www.pinterest.com/mitsandru/

About Dumitru "Mit" Sandru

Mit Sandru was born in the greater area of Transylvania in the last millennium; make that last century since he's not a vampire. Yet. When he was six years old, a soldier shot him at point blank range with a Kalashnikov. He survived. He outsmarted his German teacher, and survived a tornado in the middle of a wheat field. Not concurrently. When he was 18 years old, he escaped from a country resembling a concentration camp, luckily without being killed. He outran mean border patrol dogs in a foreign country, in the darkness of night, while jumping over six-foot tall stonewalls. Superman he's not. He came to the USA in search of freedom, glory, wealth, and fame. He's still searching for three of those. Lightning grazed him, and he caught a shark by the tail. Once. A monkey attacked him in Japan, but his daughter saved him. He avoided many rattlesnake bites, and built a house. No relation between the snakes and the house. Life eventually tamed him and he became a responsible citizen, with a wife, two daughters, dog and cat. And lately two grandsons. The taming part is questionable. He acquired an engineering and management degree and attempted to acquire other degrees in music, marketing, and IT. A certified student he is. He obtained many professional licenses, which he hardly used, but looked good on his wall. At 59-¾ years old he quit the corporate life and a six-figure salary. Rumor has it that he was given the golden handshake. He was finally free to pursue his dreams of writing, painting and music. During his professional life he painted hundreds of canvases, and composed dozens of tunes, while since his golden handshake he wrote 14 books; although one is a coloring book. And that was in just the first half of his life.

Disclaimer: Everything written here is true, but the bullets were blanks.

I am Mit Sandru and I approve this unabashed bio.

Want to see and read more about the second half of his life?

Visit those sites:

Webpage: http://sandru.com

Twitter: http://bit.ly/1kVzh6Z

Facebook: http://on.fb.me/1OiYOCn

Goodreads: http://bit.ly/1TgVbNa

Amazon: Amzn.to/1UtpTFR

Pinterest: https://www.pinterest.com/mitsandru/

YouTube videos

Arboregal, The Lorn Tree:

https://bit.ly/2OtDj5c

Abstract Dreams: Coloring Book 1:

https://bit.ly/2Ulc9RT

Vlad V Vampire Series:

https://bit.ly/2pahMDI

Lucy the Vampire Dog:

https://bit.ly/2lPwAt4

Printed in Great Britain
by Amazon

28758835R00169